# MOUNTAIN FAMILIES IN TRANSITION

# Mountain
# Families  in

A CASE STUDY OF
APPALACHIAN MIGRATION

# Transition

Harry K. Schwarzweller
James S. Brown
J. J. Mangalam

THE PENNSYLVANIA STATE UNIVERSITY PRESS
University Park and London

Library of Congress Catalogue Card Number: 71-138090

International Standard Book Number: 0-271-01149-1

Copyright © 1971 by The Pennsylvania State University.
All rights reserved.

Printed in the United States of America
The Pennsylvania State University Press
University Park, Pennsylvania 16802
27–29 Whitfield St., London, W. 1
Designed by Larry Krezo

To the people of and from the Beech Creek neighborhoods.

# CONTENTS

# PREFACE

Beech Creek is comprised of three small adjoining neighborhoods located in the relatively isolated, subsistence farming, mountain area of eastern Kentucky. Through shared experiences and interaction over generations, individuals and their families in this locality had formed and still accommodate their lives to a more or less cohesive system of neighborhoods. This book is about the Beech Creek people—their families and their patterns of behavior as they adapted through migration to the increasing pressures of unsatisfactory economic and other circumstances that have been such a dismal and persistent feature of the Southern Appalachian region during the past few decades.

Our focus is on the migrants and the migration process in the context of the sociocultural system whence they were drawn. We describe what happened to those who moved away from the Beech Creek neighborhoods, how they came to make that "big move," and how they fared in the industrial centers to the northwest. We show the ramifications and many intricacies involved in the urban relocation of a mountain people who, for so long, had been isolated from the maincurrent of American society. We believe their story in some ways parallels the ordeals of countless immigrant groups in America at the turn of the century.

One of our aims in documenting the history of the Beech Creek people is to communicate such information to readers who are concerned about the welfare of Appalachian people and, equally, of rural peoples in other underdeveloped regions of the world who have been similarly exposed to those pressures of modernization that foster social and geographic mobility. Understanding the processes of migration from the Beech Creek neighborhoods, which of course was but a trickle in the great stream of migration from Appalachia in recent years, can and does add to our comprehension of the human dimensions of that revolutionizing contemporary exodus, the mass movement of rural peoples to urban industrial centers of the world. If the observations we make and the conclusions we draw about the Beech Creek people helps, even in small measure, in the wise formulation of just programs designed to facilitate the relocation of rural peoples from Appalachia or elsewhere, then some of the larger goals of this book will have been served.

As sociologists, an essential purpose in pursuing the story of migration from Beech Creek is specifically relevant to our professional interests, and we would be less than honest if we did not call attention at the outset to that goal. Our research was designed to be an exploratory study that could make a contribution to the "sociology of migration." Because this cardinal objective dominates our approach to the Beech Creek story, we have found it necessary to attend to the technical and methodological particulars that solidly grounded our observations and guided the evolution of our theoretical perspective. Indeed, these elaborations are a necessary adjunct to any good scientific reporting.

There is a story in, and reflected by, these data. It is a story of people striving to find a place in a larger arena of life. It is a story that is at once as magnificent and sometimes as complex as people are. Though we view their magnificence and complexity through the structured perspectives of a sociologist, and though we seldom grasp more than a partial richness of their whole existence, we urge the reader, by interpolations from his own experiences, to seek out the human meaning symbolized by the events and information reported on the ensuing pages. That is how useful empathy may be fostered, creative insights stimulated, efficient hypotheses advanced, and a sociology of migration nurtured.

The study had its origin in an earlier study of the Beech Creek neighborhoods by James S. Brown. An autobiographical statement by Brown isolates those considerations which at that time led to the selection of this particular research site and study population:

As a native eastern Kentuckian, reared in a mining community, and a graduate of Berea College, I had long been interested in the great changes coming about in the Kentucky Mountain Region. I was concerned especially with the transformation of hill-country neighborhoods dominated by subsistence-farming and strong familial relationships into bustling coal camps with economies tied to the uncertainties of an impersonal industrial society. As a graduate student at Harvard my theoretical interest centered on the interrelationships of various aspects of the social structure and I was greatly impressed by the sociological significance of the few intensive studies of American community life made up to that time. Consequently, in planning research for my thesis, I sought a small, isolated neighborhood that was relatively undisturbed by modern influences.

Beech Creek, as it is called in anonymity, was chosen in January, 1942, for a number of reasons. It was a grouping of thirty-nine families cut off from other neighborhoods by high ridges. The nearest all-weather road was three miles away. The nearest town, a trading and school center with only two hundred people, could be reached by a long hike across a very steep hill. About 17 miles beyond this town was the county seat, with a population of less than 2,000. Lexington, the nearest city, was more than 100 miles away. Beech Creek people in those days had no automobiles, electric lights, or telephones, and few of them had radios or subscribed to a daily newspaper. Furthermore, no missionaries had ever lived there. Finally, a means for legitimate entree into the local social system was available to me through friendship ties with a classmate who had married into a Beech Creek family.

Brown's work was predominantly an anthropological account. It evolved into an intensive investigation of families residing in three adjacent neighborhoods which, collectively, we now refer to as "the Beech Creek neighborhoods" or, more simply, "Beech Creek." Information was gathered by participant observation and informal interviews during approximately six months of intermittent residence in the area between February 1942 and April 1943. Brown recalls his field work routines and strategies, saying:

> In the field situation I openly assumed the role of a "researcher" or "student" doing "school work." After an initial period of suspicion, most Beech Creekers eventually accepted the notion that I was writing a "sort of history" of this area. And they soon discovered that I knew the country, was accustomed to the local speech and mannerisms, and had an intuitive understanding of the mountain way of life. Though it required time, patience and planning, an atmosphere of trust was achieved.
>
> I would stay on the Creek for two or three weeks, then go to a nearby town where I typed and reviewed my field notes and made plans for the next field trip. Some time was spent in the neighborhoods during each calendar month so that the year's round of social and economic activities could be observed.
>
> I lived at various times with families belonging to different kinship and social class groupings. Three or four families were visited each day. I also attended weekend activities and special events in the

neighborhoods, and much valuable information was collected by simply observing who visited whom in the area. Supplementary data were obtained from official county records, including land documents and marriage records, and from the original census schedules on population in the National Archives and the Bureau of the Census for as far back as 1810. Schedules were used to collect data on genealogies, family budgets, family property, family visiting patterns, and for a general census of the neighborhoods which included data on migration. For the most part, however, the information at the core of this study was non-quantitative, and it was gathered during intensive field work and participant observation over a long period of time. The raw data are recorded in journals and extensive field notes which include verbatim interviews, descriptions of the situations in which the interviews took place, and descriptions of the behavior of Beech Creek people in many situations.

The goal of Brown's ethnography was to provide a description and analysis of the social organization of an isolated rural neighborhood in the Kentucky mountains. Prior to entering the field it was clear that one of the more important focal points would be the family-kinship structure. It also became apparent, not long after he became acquainted with Beech Creek, that the neighborhood had a class structure and that, in order to understand the life style of the neighborhoods, it was important to see the interrelationships of class with many other aspects of the social structure including, of course, the kinship structure. Furthermore, in order to understand the system of stratification it was necessary to attempt to understand the set of standards or values by which individuals and families were ranked.

In general the work focused on the family-kinship structure, the class system, and the value system, and their place within the total cultural configuration of this "miniature society," Beech Creek.

After its completion, Brown kept in touch with the neighborhoods and with many of the people who moved away. Changes were observed as they occurred, and at least once a year a "census" of the neighborhoods and of the original 1942 population was made, noting such vital statistics as births, deaths, marriages, and migrations. Emergence of the re-study idea, a natural consequence of this continued interest in and rapport with the Beech Creek people, is explained by Brown in the following way:

As a student of migration and the social problems peculiar to eastern Kentucky and the Southern Appalachians, I found that I could use my knowledge of Beech Creek as case material to illustrate and explain regional demographic trends. For Beech Creek represents, in many ways, the small-sale commercial and subsistence agricultural areas of the Southern Appalachians; changes occurring in the social structure of these neighborhoods, I felt quite sure, indicated social changes coming about in the region.

Over the years, many of the original Beech Creek families moved to nearby towns "closer to the road," or to Ohio, or elsewhere. In the absence of in-migration to counter the outward stream, was the social structure of Beech Creek threatened with extinction? People still living there were having to make major adjustments; migrants from Beech Creek who were resettling in modern, industrial, metropolitan communities of the Ohio Valley had to do a great deal of adjusting as well. The situation invited study.

Because of the evident practical need for reliable information about the impact of heavy out-migration on the rural communities of Appalachia, and about the processes by which migrants adjust to the new situation in the areas of destination, I became convinced that restudying the Beech Creekers was an idea that merited serious consideration. The sociological significance of such a longitudinal study, i.e., which follows a specific group of individuals through time and through the process of migration, was not difficult to comprehend; it offered exciting possibilities.

Research support was sought in a request to the National Institutes of Health which was approved and funded (as project M3912).

The tasks we envisioned for this extension of the Beech Creek study entailed a set of new departures that would give shape to our collective interests. Our aim was to follow up *all* those persons still living in 1961 who had been residents of the Beech Creek neighborhoods at the time of the initial study. We knew that many had moved away from eastern Kentucky and were living elsewhere; their adjustments to the circumstances associated with migration became our central concern.

In order to pursue our research goals, we partitioned the project into four separate, but interrelated phases of activity: first, there was an exploration of the problem, a comprehensive survey of the literature on migration, and the development of a theoretical frame of reference; second, we undertook a social survey of the entire study population; third, and later, there was an intensive case study, by quasi-participant observation techniques, of three selected *family groups;* and fourth, a focused interview study of the male migrants' adjustment to the industrial work situation. The present volume draws mainly upon results of the survey research, though materials are incorporated, where appropriate, from all other phases of activity. (See Appendix A for further details on the research program, survey organization and field work procedures.)

This new inquiry rapidly came to demand a reconceptualization of the entire Beech Creek experience. An over-all guiding hypothesis, which is a concise way of indicating our theoretical orientation, can be stated as follows: The greater the functional adequacy of the stem-family (and its associated branch-family network) of the Beech Creek sociocultural system in responding to the changing needs of the Beech Creekers, the more adjusted the migrants will be, both as individuals and as families, under specified conditions. The derivation and development of this hypothesis, which emerged from our exploratory work with the contemporary literature on migration as well as our consideration of various unexplained facts about the Appalachian migration stream, will be made clear in a subsequent chapter. Indeed, one purpose of this book is to demonstrate the utility of such a sociological approach for the study of migration phenomena.

Our theoretical perspectives and our position vis-a-vis previous research and theory-building efforts on the problem of rural-to-urban migration have been made public earlier. (See J. J. Mangalam, *Human Migration: A Guide to Migration Literature in English 1955–1962,* University Press of Kentucky, Lexington, Kentucky, 1968.) There is no need to repeat those statements here; the reader should be aware, however, that we are attempting to develop and exploit the theoretical guidelines suggested in that earlier volume. Here it must be noted especially that we conceive of migration as a social process linking two systems of social organization. Consequently this conceptualization requires that knowledge about both systems (whether empirically delineated or historically reconstructed) is essential for an adequate understanding of the intricate social dimensions bound up in the phenomenon. To take into account only the *recipient system,* at the place of destination, or only the *donor system,* at the place of origin, represents an inadequate sociological approach and yields incomplete knowledge about this social process. In 1942, for example, Beech Creekers were only beginning to respond to, and be affected by, the swirl of modernization seeping into the neighborhoods from the outside world. The most impressive and significant response, which is the central concern of our study, was the great migration out of Appalachia that followed in the wake of World War II. But one cannot fully comprehend or appreciate the meanings of the patterned responses and changes, particularly as they relate to the relocation of Beech Creekers in the urban industrial centers to the northwest, without some understanding of the way of life of Beech

Creekers in the mountains. Hence, in Part I of this book we describe the general social organization of Beech Creek as it was in 1942–43, emphasizing the tone as well as the structure of life in the neighborhoods.

The major foci of the present inquiry are as follows: (1) to describe and document in a systematic manner the patterns of migration of people and families from Beech Creek neighborhoods to communities in southern Ohio and elsewhere; (2) to explore the utility of viewing this type of rural-to-urban migration as a sociological phenomenon, i.e., as a migration system in a sociological sense; (3) to acquire an understanding of the problems and processes of adjustment encountered by people who move from a low-income, rural area to an affluent, urban industrial one; (4) to ascertain the part played by family and kinship in the migration process and in the social adjustment of migrants during the transitional period.

# ACKNOWLEDGMENTS

We are indebted in many ways to many people and organizations for help, advice, and encouragement during the various phases of this research project. It is difficult, indeed, to acknowledge all persons who were involved and all sources of support of one kind or another without committing some errors of omission.

Unquestionably the most important element in facilitating this research endeavor has been and continues to be the patient and sincere cooperation of the Beech Creek people. While their anonymity must be preserved, it is with great warmth that we, the research staff, acknowledge their kindnesses to us, our families, and our field interviewers, and their faith in the ultimate utility of information they were asked to volunteer (the kind of information we were seeking must at times have appeared strange indeed). Their trust is our inspiration.

We are also greatly indebted to the agencies which supported this research. Most of the funds to carry out field work and preliminary analyses came from a research grant from the National Institutes of Health, U.S. Department of Health, Education, and Welfare. Additional financial as well as administrative support came from the Agricultural Experiment Station at the University of Kentucky; we especially recognize and respect the calm and uncomplaining endurance of both Dr. William A. Seay, Dean of the University of Kentucky College of Agriculture, and Dr. Charles C. Barnhart, Director of the Kentucky Agricultural Experiment Station. We further acknowledge the services of the Kentucky Research Foundation in administering the research grant, and the University of Kentucky Computing Center in providing the equipment, facilities, and technical assistance necessary to analyze the survey data.

Many people were involved in and contributed to this project during the exploratory phase and during the early stages of formulating a theoretical framework and research design. In particular, the work of Dr. Joy M. Query, a member of the research staff (from Sept. 1960 to Sept. 1961) should be noted. Dr. Query's professional interest in problems of mental health and her acquaintance with the literature in this area made her a valuable member of our planning team.

A professional Advisory Committee was organized to help in the processes of exploring the problem and planning a study design with an eye toward building a measure of interdisciplinary depth into the research venture. The members of this committee were:*

Richard L. Blanton, Ph.D., Associate Professor of Psychology, University of Kentucky;

A. Lee Coleman, Ph.D., Professor of Sociology and Rural Sociology, University of Kentucky;

Milton Coughenour, Ph.D., Associate Professor of Rural Sociology, University of Kentucky;

Martin Jay Crowe, Ph.D. candidate, Sociology and Rural Sociology, University of Kentucky;

Gordon DeJong, Ph.D. candidate, Sociology and Rural Sociology, University of Kentucky;

Thomas R. Ford, Ph.D., Professor of Sociology and Rural Sociology, University of Kentucky;

Richard Griffith, Ph.D., Director of Psychological Research, Veterans Administration Hospital, Lexington, Kentucky;

George A. Hillery, Ph.D., Assistant Professor of Sociology and Rural Sociology, University of Kentucky;

Donald L. Hochstrasser, Ph.D. candidate at the University of Oregon; Research Fellow in Anthropology, National Science Foundation, University of Kentucky;

John L. Mabry, Ph.D., Associate Professor of Behavioral Sciences and Sociology, University of Kentucky;

Earl Mayhew, B.S., Associate Rural Sociologist, University of Kentucky;

Shirley Newsome, Ph.D., Associate Professor of Home Economics, University of Kentucky;

Marion Pearsall, Ph.D., Associate Professor of Behavioral Sciences and Sociology, University of Kentucky;

---

* Professional titles and institutional affiliations are listed as of the period when the committee met actively as a seminar group. Since then a number of individuals have changed titles and affiliations.

Eldon Smith, Ph.D., Associate Professor of Agricultural Economics, University of Kentucky;

E. Grant Youmans, Ph.D., Social Science Analyst, Economic Research Service, U.S. Department of Agriculture.

The contributions of these persons, both individually and collectively, are gratefully acknowledged.

A Sponsoring Committee was formed to help with the problems of establishing effective rapport, maintaining good public relations in the field, and providing us, the research staff, with a sounding board of persons who, in one capacity or another, had been directly acquainted with the Beech Creek study population. This committee included:

Howard W. Beers, Ph.D., Professor of Sociology, University of Kentucky;

Mrs. Birdena Bishop, Instructor in Sociology, Warren Wilson College, North Carolina;

Miss Helen H. Dingman, former Executive Secretary of the Conference of Southern Mountain Workers;

David Greeley, Ph.D., Director of Clinical Services, Harlan Memorial Hospital, Harlan, Kentucky;

Burton Rogers, Director, Pine Mountain Settlement School, Pine Mountain, Kentucky;

Frank Thompson, Assistant Personnel Manager, The Champion Paper Company, Hamilton, Ohio;

Mr. and Mrs. "X," an original Beech Creek family now living in one of the migrant communities in southern Ohio;

Mr. and Mrs. "Y," an original Beech Creek family still living in the Beech Creek neighborhood.

These persons, including the two Beech Creek families, helped in various ways to implement our research plans.

We are especially cognizant of the fine job performed by our interviewers in the survey phase of the project. They not only obtained the information we sought in a systematic manner under the often trying circumstances of a difficult field situation, but they created a favorable image that permitted us to do additional field work the following year. We appreciate the efforts of:

Mr. Martin Jay Crowe (field director and trouble-shooter);

Mr. and Mrs. Donald C. Mavis;

Mr. and Mrs. Thomas E. Dunn;

Mr. and Mrs. Jim Castle and their daughter, Tammy.

We also wish to acknowledge the field assistance of Sylvia Mangalam and Elizabeth Schwarzweller during the case study phase of the project. They, along with our children—Harry-Joe, Paul, Kunyi, and Tom—helped directly in the process of establishing rapport and collecting information. Sylvia Mangalam also read the whole manuscript and made a number of useful suggestions.

For the long, tedious chore of reducing the survey information into a form for data processing, it was our good fortune to have employed a patient, conscientious team of coders. The team included Miss Ann Hamilton, Mrs. Cornelia B. Morgan, Mrs. Evamay Ritter, Mrs. Charles Snow, and Miss Marie Soulis.

A number of graduate students were involved at one stage or another of the study. Martin Jay Crowe (Ph.D. candidate) was responsible for initiating and developing one entire phase of the larger project dealing with the occupational adjustment of male migrants. John Seggar (M.A. candidate) took on the task of analyzing a portion of the survey data dealing with various "adjustment" indicators. Miss Kathleen Moran (M.A. candidate) assisted in the analysis of survey data at a later stage.

The first phase of the Beech Creek Study as reported here was carried out by James S. Brown as part of his doctoral work. (See James S. Brown, The *Social Organization of an Isolated Kentucky Mountain Neighborhood,* Ph.D. dissertation, Harvard University, 1950.) That part of the study greatly benefited from the counsel and encouragement of Professors Carle C. Zimmerman, Clyde Kluckhohn, Lawrence J. Henderson, Pitirim Sorokin, and Talcott Parsons.

We are indebted to the various journals which have granted permission to reprint portions of our published papers which were derived from this study and to the Audio-Visual Department of the University of Guelph for preparing the map of the three neighborhoods.

Finally, and with deep gratitude, we call special attention to and acknowledge the careful and thorough work of Mrs. Cornelia B. Morgan in her role as research assistant in the processing of data and in the preparation of bibliographical materials.

H. K. S.
J. S. B.
J. J. M.

West Virginia University
University of Kentucky
University of Guelph

October, 1970

# PART ONE
# ORIGINS

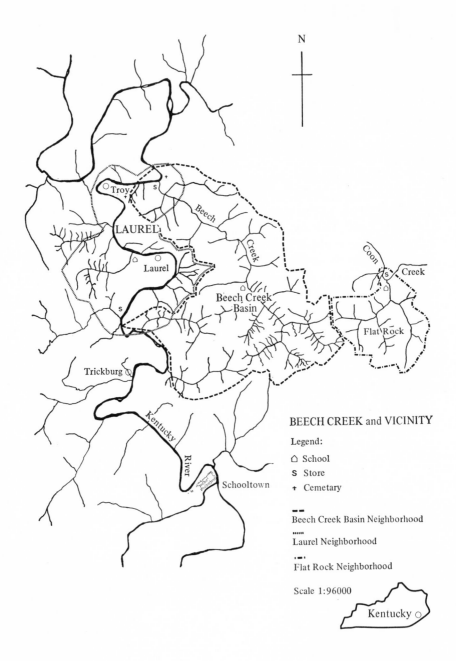

N

BEECH CREEK and VICINITY

Legend:

⌂ School
S Store
+ Cemetary

▬ ▬
Beech Creek Basin Neighborhood

▪▪▪▪▪
Laurel Neighborhood

▪▬▪
Flat Rock Neighborhood

Scale 1:96000

Kentucky ○

# 1 BEECH CREEK:
## An Appalachian Mountain Locality and Way of Life

Beech Creek, a mountain locality in eastern Kentucky, was settled about the year 1800. Almost all of the early pioneers were native-born Americans from North Carolina, Virginia, and Tennessee. They brought with them a culture that was predominantly of English origin and a belief system that was for the most part derived from Protestant fundamentalism.[1]

The earliest families settled along the river and at the mouth of the creek where land was fertile and level. Since by the nineteenth century the Indian menace was past, a pattern of dispersed settlement was possible. A family's nearest neighbors in those early days were often two or three miles away, and the settlements soon evolved into "stringtowns" or "line-villages" stretching for miles along the river and its tributary creeks and branches. Travel followed the streams, and the river was the main artery of communication with the outside world.

A few men initially secured rather large tracts of land, much of which was steep hillsides, and this land, subdivided into parcels, was handed down from one generation to another. Though some new families moved into the area from time to time, the scarce bottom land remained under the control of a relatively few families and, consequently, the present population of Beech Creek is composed in the main of descendants of those first settlers.

By the time grandchildren of the original landowners were grown, the area was so thickly populated relative to the agricultural potential of the land that many families had moved up hollows and coves until the entire length of Beech Creek and its tributary valleys was inhabited. Indeed, some people were compelled to move elsewhere. As the population increased, clusters of families residing in geographic proximity and bound together by ties of kinship, friendship, mutual aid, and common concerns came into being, forming approximately the present neighborhoods of Beech Creek, that is, the original Beech Creek basin settlement plus the two adjoining neighborhoods of Flat Rock and Laurel. In 1942 the Beech Creek neighborhoods consisted of 79 households with a total population of 399 persons.

## GEOGRAPHIC SETTING

Beech Creek lies near the head of a fork of the Kentucky River. Like most of eastern Kentucky, the area was once part of a great peneplain, the Cumberland Plateau, which through a process of uplifting and subsequent stream dissection became a maze of V-shaped valleys and steep slopes culminating in long, narrow ridges. This land of streams is socially one of creek-bottom settlements.[2]

The Kentucky River, Buck Creek, and Coon Creek form a rough triangle enclosing much smaller Beech Creek. The Kentucky River meanders in a northerly direction from Schooltown to the mouth of Coon Creek to form one side of the triangle, and Buck Creek, flowing from east to west and emptying almost at right angles into the river at Schooltown, is the base. Coon Creek, the headwaters of which are intertwined with those of Buck Creek, forms the hypotenuse of the triangle as it flows from southeast to northwest and joins the river eight or ten miles north of Schooltown. Within this triangle, Beech Creek parallels the course of Coon Creek and flows nearly five miles before it empties into the river a mile and a half above the mouth of Coon Creek.

From the air the Beech Creek basin looks like a great gulley with many subsidiary ditches branching off in vine-like fashion. Most of the land lies in steep slopes with only narrow strips of level land along the creek and its branches. Indeed, valley lands probably account for less than ten percent of the entire area.[3] The Beech Creek basin is bounded on three sides by ridges which rise five to seven hundred feet above the valley floor. On the fourth side, the creek empties into the river which itself is bounded by high ridges.

Across the steep ridge which separates the basins of Beech Creek and Coon Creek is Flat Rock Fork. Unlike Beech Creek, a relatively long stream, Flat Rock Fork runs only a short distance from Coon Creek before it begins branching. The Flat Rock basin is a system of big ditches with steep slopes, V-shaped valleys, rock valley bottoms, and scarcely any level land.

Across the ridge which runs along the southwest side of the Beech Creek basin is the river. From a point not far above the mouth of Beech Creek, the river has cut a great meandering U-shaped trough, the sides of which are long, steep ridges. In this stretch the river makes two big bends in which lie wide expanses of level and gently sloping land. This area is Laurel.

# NATURAL RESOURCES AND CLIMATE

The great natural resources of eastern Kentucky have been timber and coal. But, as in the rest of the Cumberland Plateau region, virtually all valuable timber in and around the Beech Creek area was cut over—slashed—prior to, and especially during, World War I.[4] Though most of the area is still wooded, the trees are second or third growth and often not of any commercial value.

Extensive coal beds underlie much of the area.[5] These beds, however, are relatively inaccessible—difficult and costly to mine on a commercial scale—and the coal is of lower quality than that found in other parts of the Appalachian region. A few marginal "truck" mines have been and are in operation nearby, but these have never employed many men. The only mining that has been done in the Beech Creek area is that of local farmers "raising coal" for their own home use.

The climate of eastern Kentucky and the Beech Creek area is of the warm, humid type with marked contrast between winter and summer. The frost-free season averages about 180 days, and the average annual precipitation is from 51 to 53 inches.[6] A high proportion of the rainfall comes during the winter and spring months, and then the creeks and rivers are often so swollen that travel is very difficult; the not infrequent floods are a special danger to those living along the river. At other seasons of the year, paradoxically, the smaller streams and wells "go dry."

# ECONOMY AND STANDARD OF LIVING: 1942

From its very beginnings, Beech Creek has been an area of small, self-sufficient, subsistence-type family farms. To acquaint the reader with this aspect of the situation, we should summarize some of the observations made from an intensive study of thirty families living in the Beech Creek basin neighborhood in 1942.[7]

Every family in the Beech Creek basin at that time lived on a farm, according to the 1940 U.S. Census classification. The land owned or rented by a family usually consisted of a single tract of land which was farmed almost exclusively by the labor of family members. Home and economic enterprise were combined into an interrelated whole with occupational and family roles inextricably combined, except from an analytical standpoint. The family was the main unit of production as well as of consumption, and about 89 percent of the total farm production was consumed at home.

Gardens and truck patches occupied only small proportions of the land under cultivation, but they were very important, for most of the food produced and used by the family came from these little tracts. The main field crop was corn. Hardly any corn, however, was sold; most of it—as ears and fodder—was fed to hogs, cattle, and chickens for meat and eggs to be consumed at home or, if there was a surplus, to be traded or sold. About a third of the farms in 1942 had small tobacco acreages as well. Burley tobacco was the only major cash crop and, though no farmer grew more than one and a half acres, it accounted for about 35 percent of the total cash income from farm products. Egg and livestock sales accounted for most of the remainder.

In 1942, then, the farm was still a major source of sustenance for the Beech Creek family. Nevertheless, the self-sufficiency of this frontier economy had already been exposed to disturbing influences from the "outside," and these influences were destined to become ever stronger and more erosive to that traditional subsistence economy. This trend was reflected by the fact that nonfarm income had become an integral supportive part of the Beech Creek standard of living.

It is estimated that, of the total income of all families living in the Beech Creek basin in 1942 (which amounted to about $24,000 inclusive of the fair value assigned to farm products produced and consumed by the farm households), nearly two-thirds was cash income.[8] The reader should recall here that our data refer to thirty families collectively; money was quite scarce in Beech Creek in those days. Of the total cash income, about one-fourth came from the sale of farm products and three-fourths from nonfarm sources (about $11,500). Nonfarm income was an important supplement to the main source of income, farming.

Many men, for example, worked in the forest on a part-time or seasonal basis for local lumber companies, cutting what little timber remained. The Works Projects Administration and the Civilian Conservation Corps provided other opportunities for nonfarm employment on road and bridge construction jobs nearby. Direct governmental aid, in the form of old age pensions, military pensions, and unemployment insurance benefits, altogether constituted about a fifth of this total income. Indeed, all told—including WPA, CCC, and other federally financed employment—more than a third of Beech Creek's nonfarm cash income came from the U.S. Government; that the Beech Creek economy in 1942 was no longer self-sufficient is clear.

Beech Creekers were poor relative to other Americans in 1942;[9] their average cash expenditures for that year were estimated as $425 per family and $84 per capita. The largest cash expenditure, nearly a third, was designated for farming needs such as seeds, tools, fertilizer, stock, and so forth. More than a quarter of the cash income went for food staples such as flour, lard, sugar, and coffee, and nearly a fifth for clothing, either "ready made" or "yard goods." What little remained was used for medical expenses, taxes, various household supplies, and sundry personal needs.

Property owned by the average Beech Creek family in 1942 was valued, roughly, at about $1800 (ranging from $100 to about $6000). Value of house and land made up nearly half of that total; houses, for example, averaged $580 in estimated value (ranging from $100 to $1200). Barns, farm equipment, livestock, household furnishings, and clothing accounted for most of the remainder; only a few families had been able to accumulate any cash savings. Beech Creekers were poor indeed.

The 1942 Beech Creek economy, then, was for the most part anchored in the past and only beginning to seek out interrelationships with the present. It was an economy of rural poverty. Economic self-sufficiency through farming was no longer practicable nor practiced; farms were too small, too hilly, too economically inefficient to provide Beech Creek families with the means for satisfying their basic needs and acquired wants.

# RELATIVE ISOLATION

Because of the poor transportation linkages with the outside world, largely the result of the rugged topography of the area, and because of the subsistence nature of its economic enterprises, the Beech Creek settlement, like much of eastern Kentucky, was both geographically and culturally isolated from other parts of the State and from the main currents of change in American Society.[10] Perhaps Beech Creek in some ways had been even more isolated than the typical mountain locality of Southern Appalachia. Much of Beech Creek's recent history can be interpreted as a breakdown of this isolation and an increasing integration into the mainstream of modern life.

During the early 1900's and before, there was no large town within seventy-five miles of the Beech Creek neighborhoods. Schooltown, a little trading and high school center with a population of two hundred or so in 1942, was about three to five miles distant over a steep hill from the basin neighborhood, usually traversed by foot, or on a horse or mule. The seat of the county in which Beech Creek lay, a town with a population of less than two thousand in 1942, was about seventeen miles beyond Schooltown. The closest city was Lexington, more than a hundred miles away.

There were no improved roads touching the neighborhoods until 1938, when a gravel road was finally built along the river connecting Schooltown with the Laurel neighborhood. Only crude wagon trails, which often followed and crisscrossed the creek bed, provided access to that road from other parts of the locality. Furthermore, the river, shallow throughout much of the year and swollen at other times, was never an easy and convenient connection with the outside. Journeys outside the immediate environs were infrequent and difficult. Prior to the late 1930's, many people who were born in this area had never set foot out of the mountain region throughout their entire lives.

In those early times the neighborhood schools, which met in homes only two or three months a year, were taught by local people, many of them just beyond the illiterate stage themselves. Church groups likewise were led by self-taught local preachers whose main occupation was farming and who preached "on the side;" church groups usually met in the preachers' homes.[11]

The self-sufficient social organization which Beech Creekers had developed was not unlike that of the pioneers in frontier communities in many other parts of America; it was a response to the geographic isolation of life in the mountains. But it persisted for years after other sections of the country had become more closely associated with national trends. Beech Creekers continued to be isolated, and sociocultural developments within Beech Creek consisted mainly of families getting larger, more homes being built, and more and more hill land being cleared to accommodate the expanding population. But Beech Creekers and their sons and daughters clung to those patterns of living passed on to them by their elders.

Various forces of change were nevertheless gradually bringing the outside world closer to the neighborhoods. The 1942 survey showed that Beech Creek families still had no automobiles, electric lights, or telephones, and few of them had radios or subscribed to magazines or a daily newspaper. But it was also observed that the dirt roads within the locality were being improved to accommodate motor vehicles, and post offices had been established in homes in two of the neighborhoods. One-room schools had been built only a few years before in each of the three neighborhoods. More significantly, control of the school system had shifted from locally elected trustees, as so long had been the custom, to the county and the state levels, and the county and the state had assumed considerable authority for setting standards for teachers and for financing the local schools. On the other hand, because the roads were all but impassable during the wet winter months, few children could live at home and attend high school; they either had to board in Schooltown or terminate their education after the eighth grade, and most, because of contingent circumstances, chose the latter alternative.

The most effective of the numerous and sundry forces which were beginning to break down the geographic and cultural isolation of the Beech Creek neighborhoods were generally initiated by the outside world and especially as a direct consequence of America's mobilization of manpower for the war and defense industries. The outside world, in effect, moved into the Beech Creek neighborhoods and moved the underemployed manpower out and into more "essential" jobs or the military. Because Beech Creek migrants continued to maintain communication with their families and kinsfolk in the home neighborhoods, this communication network became—and was in 1942—an important link with the outside and a persuasive stimulator of change. The changes that were introduced are now seen to have affected the whole social structure of Beech Creek. Beech Creek was becoming and had become a pocket of mountain isolation and rural poverty which people were leaving.

# FAMILY HOMESTEADS

Life in Beech Creek was patterned around farming activities, and central to those activities and the farm was the house itself. A family's house and lands were usually referred to as their "place," and most of a Beech Creeker's life was spent with his family on the place with which he became identified both in his own and his neighbors' eyes.

Most homes in Beech Creek were constructed from sawed lumber, though several families in 1942 still lived in log houses.[12] Some of the houses were built of rough, unpainted lumber with planks set on end and strips nailed across the cracks; others were weatherboarded and painted. Some had hand-rived shingle roofs; others had tarpaper or tin roofs. Some were two stories, but most only one. All of the houses were small; in the basin neighborhood 70 percent had three rooms or fewer.

Each bedroom usually contained two double beds, for families were large and sleeping room was at a premium. Husband and wife shared one bed; sometimes the baby also slept with them. The remaining beds were divided among the other members of the family, the boys sleeping together and the girls together. One of the rooms was commonly used as a "living room," and here was the best furniture the family possessed: a dresser, a couple of rocking chairs, and beds carefully made with matching spreads and embroidered pillows. There were always plain, cane-bottomed chairs made by some local craftsman. Usually each bedroom had a fireplace, but fire was regularly kept only in the room used as a sitting room. Most of the families burned coal in grates, though it was acknowledged that heating stoves were more efficient. In the mountain neighborhoods, the hearth was not obsolete but a symbol of home life; in cold weather it became the center for family activities.

The kitchen served both as a room for preparing food and for eating, and it contained the essential furnishings for fulfilling these functions. Always there was a stove; in some of the houses the stove was a shining, enamelled, modern kitchen range; in most of them it was a battered, cast-iron, flat-topped range. But in all cases, the stove was one of the most important pieces of furniture the family owned. The kitchen also invariably contained a long narrow table covered with oilcloth around which the family gathered for meals. Usually a cupboard holding a few plain dishes, inexpensive cutlery, a few cooking utensils, cans or bins for flour, meal, and sugar, a water bucket and a dipper, a dishpan or two, and a few other things completed the furnishings of a typical kitchen.

Every house had a front porch and most houses also had a back porch. The back porch was used as an integral part of the kitchen for storing food, tools, and clothes, for washing in the summer time, and in warm weather as a place to eat. The front porch was less utilitarian; it was more of a social center, and during the summer much of the family's leisure time was spent there. It afforded a good view of people going up or down the creek.

Surrounding the house was a yard enclosed by a paling fence and frequently divided into areas called the "back" and the "front yards."

The back yard, which was nearer the kitchen, was an adjunct of that room. The smokehouse where meat, lard, and soap were stored, the warm house where canned food, potatoes, and fruit were kept, the wood pile, the well, and the wash kettle were in this section of the yard. The front yard, in the more public position beside the road, was more likely to be a decorative area with flowers and grass or at least well-swept bare ground. Frequently what fruit trees the family had were in the yard.

Always close to the house and frequently adjoining the house yard itself was the garden. Invariably surrounded by close-set palings to keep out stock and chickens, the garden occupied the best and most level ground the family owned. Also near the house, but outside the yard itself, were the chicken house and privy, if the family had either.

Not far away, often up a little branch at the back of the house, was the small barn where the stock was housed and the feed was stored; a loft was often used for curing tobacco. Somewhere near the barn, sometimes a part of it, were the pig pens and the corn crib.

Around these inner features of the homestead were the fields, pastures, and woods, most of which lay on the steep slopes of little V-shaped valleys. Pastures and corn fields were apt to be some distance away, for the land closest to the house had often long since been worn out. Few farmers had good fences, and makeshifts of all sorts were common; finding the cows at night, even with the help of cowbells, was not an easy task for the younger children when the cattle roamed far.

Family homesteads like these on farms of varying shapes and sizes were scattered up and down along the streams and branches of Beech Creek. Some houses were a half mile or more from their nearest neighbors; most, however, had at least one and many had several neighbors close by. Within the limits of this place, that is, the family homestead, and the immediate neighborhood most of the family's activities were carried on. The family homestead was the focal point in Beech Creek's social organization and an important reference point and stabilizing concept in the migrant's adjustment to socioeconomic circumstances which he encountered in the urban industrial situation.

# RHYTHM OF LIFE

Beech Creek families, of course, differed in their daily activities, and the activities of every family varied with the seasons. But to convey some notion of the tone of life in the neighborhoods in 1942 it may be useful to describe the round of activities of a more or less representative family on a single day.

September always was a busy time for Beech Creek people. For the Combs family the day began early: around five o'clock Tom Combs got up and built a fire in the cook stove, and then his wife arose, dressed, and started getting breakfast. Preparation for the meal had begun the night before when kindling and wood were brought in and stacked by the stove and butter was churned. Martha Combs automatically began the accustomed routine of measuring and mixing the ingredients for hot biscuits to go with the fried sweet potatoes, fat meat served in deep fat, jam, boiled coffee, and milk. While his wife bustled around the warm kitchen cooking, Tom tended the fire; they talked and together planned the day's work. About 5:45 the four children still at home (two older children were married and living elsewhere and one older son was in the Army) got up and came to the table, sat in their usual places, and ate. Conversation at breakfast was, as usual, not very lively.

After the meal the members of the family scattered to do their early morning chores. Tom and his wife went to the barn, and while she milked he took care of the new calves. The older son, who was nineteen, also went to the barn to feed the mule and the horse, and his younger brother, who was fourteen, vacillated between going to school or staying home to work with the family. Meanwhile the two girls, who were twenty-three and seventeen, washed dishes, cleaned up the kitchen, and made the first of many trips during the day to the well in the yard, this time to get water to fill the reservoir of the stove. Martha or her daughters fed the chickens scraps left from the meal, supplemented by some corn which they shelled off by hand. By the time all of these chores were finished and the family had sat around talking for a while, it was seven o'clock or later, and the main work of the day was about to begin. The younger son finally decided to stay home from school (not an unusual decision), and the father, two sons and two daughters started up the branch to the cornfield to pull fodder, leaving only the mother behind to do the housework. In younger families, at this time the children would go down the creek to school, leaving their mother alone at the house with the smallest of her children.

Like most Beech Creek cornfields, the family's fields lay on steep hillsides, and it was a long hard climb to the highest part, just below the crest of the ridge. Because the fields were so steep and it was all but impossible to place the whole cornstalks into shocks or haul them out of the field, they pulled the blades off, leaving the stalk with the ears of corn still standing. The blades were then tied into bundles and stacked, to be hauled to the barn later. A division of labor was worked out, with some pulling the blades, others tying and stacking the bundles.

At the house Martha Combs was too busy to be lonely, and she sang and occasionally talked to herself as she went about her housework. There were only three rooms in the house, the kitchen and the two bedrooms. In each of the bedrooms there were two double beds; in one of the rooms the husband and wife shared one bed, the two daughters the other; the two boys slept in one of the beds in the other room, leaving an extra bed for guests. Martha first made up the three beds, carefully stripping them of bedclothes, fluffing up the big featherbeds, and then putting the quilts back on, smoothing the wrinkles out of each, and finally covering the beds with white sheets. Then she swept the two bedrooms, drew water, and scrubbed the porch, after she had chased the chickens off it. She went out into the garden, which lay just back of the house, and worked a little while, and then returned to the house to get ready for the noon meal. Earlier she had strung some green beans and put them on the stove in a big pot with a generous piece of salt pork. Now she shucked roasting ears, cut the corn off the cob (for both she and her husband had false teeth and could eat it easier that way), and fried it in a big iron skillet. Sweet potatoes—long, stringy, light yellow ones—were put in the oven to bake, and for this meal, like most Beech Creek wives, she made cornbread of meal ground from their own corn at the mill down the creek. Dinner was ready to put on the table when the family returned from the cornfield at noon and, after washing hands and faces, they sat down at the table again and ate.

It was a very hot day, and there was no great rush back to the field after dinner. In fact, the girls decided they wouldn't go back at all. After sitting on the porch for awhile, the men went back to foddering. The girls washed the dishes and swept the kitchen and then rested awhile; then they went out on the porch and began to string beans for drying. The mother fed the chickens again, and then joined her daughters on the porch. Later, the girls walked the mile or so to the "office" (post office) in the hope of getting a letter from their brother, a soldier stationed in Iceland. They returned without the letter but with news which they had gathered of the neighborhood on visits along the way.

The men had worked hard in the field and by five o'clock were glad to leave the heat, dust, "pack-saddles," and cutting blades. It was nearly 5:30 by the time they had climbed down the hill and walked home. Again, barn-chores occupied the family. The younger son went up the branch to drive the cows home; Tom and his wife then went to the barn, Tom to look after the calves, Martha to milk. The sons fed the horse and mule and threw some corn into the hog pen near the barn. Then they all went back to the house, and while Martha strained the milk and got part of it ready to hang down the well to keep cool, the boys and their father drew water and washed on the porch. The girls were busy in the hot kitchen getting supper on the table. There were sweet potatoes, green beans, and cornbread left from dinner; and to these they had added fried corn, fried Irish potatoes, sliced tomatoes, coffee, milk, butter, and as a special treat, a cake—for a cousin from Flat Rock had come over to help them the next day and something extra was called for. Tonight the men and Martha sat down at the table together and the girls stood around and served. Conversation was free and lively at this meal as news about Flat Rock and the Beech Creek basin neighborhood was exchanged. Somehow attention was turned to the exploits of a woman in the neighborhood, and the adults rivalled each other in telling funny stories about her; by the time the meal was finished everyone was roaring with laughter. Martha and the men went out to sit on the porch; the older son went up and saddled his horse and rode down the creek while the younger son brought in kindling and wood to the kitchen and then went up the branch to listen to the radio at his brother's house. The girls ate and again washed dishes, and then they too brought chairs out to the porch and talked. The boys soon came back, and about 8:30 everybody went to bed.

A major cluster of activities that is missing from the daily cycle of the Combs family described here, but which characterized the lives of other Beech Creek families, dealt with the presence and care of young children. For example, another typical family at this time had nine children still living at home: a daughter twenty years old, a son of sixteen and another fourteen, who had either finished the eighth grade or had quit school; four children in school, ranging from twelve to six years old; and two who were not yet old enough to go to school. The twelve-year-old daughter usually was the first to rise; she built a fire in the cookstove and began breakfast; as soon as the stove was hot her mother joined her and completed the meal. Then the whole family arose and attention turned to getting the younger children to eat, and to washing and dressing those who went to school. The oldest daughter took the lead in this while the mother fed the baby. The father and two older boys started for the cornfield about 7:30, and the school children left soon after, as school began at eight o'clock. The oldest daughter seldom worked in the field; her mother needed her to help with the household duties and to do the cooking and other work in the kitchen for the rest of the day, helping also, as her mother needed her, in caring for the children, washing and ironing, making up the beds, cleaning the house, and doing all the other endless tasks of a big family. Since the school-house was not far away, the children usually came home for dinner, and this meal was served promptly so that they could get back to school on time. This kept the women left at home busy, and if anything special was to be done, arrangements had to be made. For example, one day in August the family had some apples which would spoil unless prepared for sulphuring—but it was a wash day. The twelve year old daughter stayed home from school to look after the baby and a young brother; the oldest daughter prepared the apples for sulphuring and got dinner, while the mother did the washing. Everybody came home for dinner. The father and all the sons ate at the table first, and then the mother and two daughters ate. By this time, the mother had the washing well in hand; so the younger daughter went to school in the afternoon, and the oldest daughter took over the care of the baby and straightened up the house in the afternoon while her mother finished the washing and sulphured the apples.

There were differences, then, among Beech Creek families in their patterns of daily activity and, to be sure, household routines varied from day to day during the week. Nevertheless, those activities described above may be considered as fairly representative and provide some indication of the tone and tempo of life in the mountain neighborhoods. A greater variation—in the content as well as tempo of activity—resulted from the seasonal nature of farm work.

For most of December, January, and February, when the weather was usually cold and raw, farm work was irregular. There were things for men to do around the house and barnyard: feeding and caring for the stock, killing a hog, repair work on the house and barn, fixing fences, and cutting wood. But these activities were not pressing, and people did them or not as the mood struck them. Many men in 1942 were away working in defense plants at this time, leaving their wives and older children to do the daily tasks and keep things going on the farm while they earned some cash. They returned every three or four weeks for a weekend at home. Other men and boys stayed at home and worked during the winter months in the logwoods, walking two, three, and four miles over the ridge to parts of Coon Creek before daylight and returning home after dark. Others had WPA jobs on the road being built nearby.

In March the weather "began to break," and warm days turned people's minds to their traditional ways of farming. Already those who raised tobacco had cut brush, burned their plant beds to rid them of weeds, and sowed them. Those heads of households who had been working elsewhere started drifting back to the neighborhood to put in a crop. In late March, men and older boys were occupied with clearing new land and with grubbing locust and sassafras sprouts out of corn land which had been lying idle. Once the land was free of brush, the plowing—with one-horse double shovel and turning plows—began and the land was readied for planting. Around the first of April corn was planted. Also in late March and early April palings around the garden were replaced, the ground was manured and plowed, and planting began. Chicks were hatched or were bought from hatcheries by many people at this time, and the housewives carefully watched over the little broods. In early April potatoes had been planted and tobacco beds, which had been canvassed to protect them from the cold, were being weeded; sweet potato beds were prepared.

In May, June, and much of July cultivating and hoeing corn occupied most of the families' time, with all of the children over seven or eight years old, girls and boys alike, joining their parents in this common task. Because most of the corn land lay on steep hillsides, corn cultivation was almost entirely a hand operation. As a rule, they went over the corn with a hoe three times; then it was considered "laid by." With the completion of this job the work peak of the farm year was over for most of the families; the heads of households and their older sons often then went off to outside industry or got local jobs in the forests or on the road. At this time too, when corn had been laid by, children who were six years old or over turned their attention from farming to school, which began about the first of July.

Most farmers had small hay fields, a few had several acres, and all of them had haying to do—in July, in late August, and especially in September. In 1942 one of the men had bought an old mowing machine which, because of the shortage of manpower, was in great demand all over the neighborhood. The few farmers who raised tobacco tended their little patches—chopping weeds, hoeing, worming, and topping—off and on through the latter part of July and August; and then about the middle of August they cut the tobacco plants, split the stalks, and hung them on sticks in the barns. Tobacco cutting was about over by the beginning of the second week in September, and foddering had begun—a long, hot job in which almost all the family members were involved through most of September.

During the off times in September and October men and boys snaked logs out of the woods to be used for winter fuel and spent several days "raising coal." Farmers put up the hogs they intended to kill and began to fatten them on corn. During October, Irish and sweet potatoes were dug and stored, Irish potatoes in great holes in the garden with high mounds of dirt piled over them to protect them from freezing, and sweet potatoes in closets in the house or in the warm house. In late October and in November, the men and boys gathered corn and hauled it to the cribs. By this time the weather was changeable, and they had to "pick their days" for this activity. Tobacco, which had been curing in the barn since August or September, now was ready for stripping. Every day when the tobacco was in "case" (that is, had the proper moisture content to make it easy to handle without damaging the leaves) the leaves were stripped from the stalk, graded, and tied into little bundles called "hands." Some Beech Creek farmers were busy off and on through most of November in caring for their tobacco. In early December the tobacco was marketed: some people hired trucks to take their tobacco to Lexington; others sold their tobacco to a neighbor, at considerably below the market price, and he then took the tobacco to market himself. When cold weather came, usually in late November and early December, hogs were killed, and most of the meat was salted down or canned to last the family until the following year. Sausage was made and most of it canned. Lard was rendered out for use in cooking, and grease for soap was saved. By Christmas the farm year was over and activity was at its lowest ebb.

This, then, gives some idea of the yearly round of farm and off-farm work by the Beech Creek families. The shifts from farm to nonfarm work took place in an informal, irregular sort of pattern. Some men needed to take only a day or two now and then to carry out their farming activities, for they may have had several grown boys or enough women at home to carry on the farm operations. On the other hand, some men not so fortunately supplied with family labor had either to spend most of their time during the farming season at home, or to hire outside labor at crucial times to work the crop out. Managers of timber projects in the area, often local men with farm duties of their own, expected this fluctuating labor schedule, and it was understood that workers would be free to stop when farming had to be done.

Women's work varied less with the seasons than men's work, but the descriptions of family activity above do not indicate adequately what variation there was. In the spring, for instance, women were busy caring for young chickens and in supervising and cultivating the garden. During the summer great amounts of food were canned and preserved for winter use, and this kept women and girls busy when they were not helping with corn-hoeing, or foddering, or other outside activities in which the whole family was involved. In late fall and early winter, when hogs were killed, women had to work hard making sausage, helping in cutting up and curing the meat, and preparing it for storage. When the husband was away at nonfarm work, the wife took additional responsibilities in directing the farm work. During the winter, too, housewives whose children were in school had some extra time to sew and to quilt. But this was no time of leisure; the regular chores of preparing three meals a day, washing, cleaning, mending, and caring for the children all continued. And in this locality, where modern conveniences were few, carrying water, keeping up fires, cleaning up the winter mud, and many other household tasks demanded a tremendous amount of time.

Though there was some seasonal variation in women's work, in one respect it was nearly always the same: women and girls worked in and around the house. Even when women worked in the fields, and this was not uncommon during rush seasons, they were not off the place but were with other family members. The men's work had much more variety and was much less centered around the homestead, especially as more and more they turned to nonfarm jobs to supplement the family's farm income. The war year of 1942, when industries outside eastern Kentucky were offering good wages for unskilled labor, and the armed forces recruited many young men out of the mountain neighborhoods, saw an increase in the variety of jobs that Beech Creek men were gaining familiarity with and could do. Thereafter they were less tied to their own farms and less dependent upon farming than ever before. In fact, in the three neighborhoods that comprise the Beech Creek locality, probably not over ten percent of the household heads in 1942 could have been called, strictly speaking, full time farmers.

# DIVISION OF LABOR BY SEX AND AGE

The economic activities of the Beech Creek households in 1942 were so intricately intertwined with all other activities of the family that it would be exceedingly difficult to discuss them separately except perhaps in an analytical, abstract sense. The farm work was done by family members who were united into a cohesive group by bonds of kinship; familial obligations and work duties were inseparable. Within each conjugal family a division of labor was understood; and this, organized in terms of sex and age, was the product of a lengthy process of socialization.

Children were subordinate to their parents' direction; boys and girls alike in their earliest years were supervised by their mothers on tasks around the homestead. Training for the male and female sex roles began at a fairly early age, and even by the time children started school—when they were only six years old—they had begun to assume sex differentiated roles in their work. Boys tended to spend more of their working days with their father and brothers, and the girls with their mother and sisters. By the time they were fifteen or sixteen years old most children were ready to assume full adult status. At that age boys and girls were often doing as much work as an adult; a boy might be doing all the plowing and a girl might have full charge of cooking for the family.

Within larger families, specialization in work tasks was a common pattern. For example, one of the girls may have been assigned to care for the younger children, another to do the cooking, and perhaps another to do the cleaning and washing.[13] At the same time, one of the boys may have had the responsibility of doing barn chores, and another of tending the fences and doing repair work. In such families, marriage of a daughter or migration of a son necessitated considerable readjustment of the family routine.[14]

The husband-father was generally expected to direct the farm work and take the initiative in actually doing the work. Obviously this was related to the traditional view of the father being head of the household (a patriarchal pattern). Upon him and his sons fell the heaviest work of the farm—clearing land, fencing, grubbing, plowing, planting, taking care of the stock, raising coal, and cutting wood. Men did the repair work on the house and other farm buildings. They did the necessary hauling as well as cutting fodder, gathering corn, and cutting and housing tobacco. If work off the farm was necessary to supplement the family's income, then it was the duty of the head of the household to get such work. The sale of tobacco, livestock, corn, or hay was in the husband's province, and the money received from such sales was allocated by him, but seldom without consultation with his wife or without conforming to the expectation that the money must be used to meet the family's needs. Purchases of farm equipment or work stock were also made by the husband.

While the husband was regarded as the director of all activities of the farm family, the housewife was in charge of the house with her daughters as helpers under her direction. The familiar household duties of cleaning, cooking, washing, canning, and taking care of children made up the principal tasks of the Beech Creek housewife. In addition to these duties at the house, the garden and the chickens were under her supervision, and she was primarily responsible for the success or failure of these enterprises. If garden produce or chickens or eggs were sold, the proceeds were considered the wife's to spend; though she, like her husband, was expected to use such income for family needs.

Most of the economic activities of the Beech Creek family, then, were organized in terms of the family homestead and oriented toward the well-being of the group. Family members all had their assigned roles in the work on the farm, and these economic roles were interwoven with their roles as family members. The description of a family's farming activities is therefore essentially a description of intrafamilial relationships; Beech Creek was a "familistic society."[15]

In the next chapter we shall examine more directly the organization of family and kinship relationships in Beech Creek, for one aim of this book is to explore, if not delineate, the full significance of this familistic form of social organization in the process of rural to urban migration. At this point, however, it is relevant to consider the extra-familial social life and inter-family relationships of Beech Creekers as these patterns were manifest in 1942.

# NEIGHBORHOODS AND NEIGHBORING

Neighborhoods develop among people who have frequent and regular contacts with each other, and in this region the topography has been a definite factor in determining the social relationships of the inhabitants and the formation of neighborhood groupings.[16] Most of the families residing in the Beech Creek basin neighborhood were territorially—or by ease of communication—nearer to each other than to families in other neighborhoods; likewise, families in the Flat Rock neighborhood and in the Laurel neighborhood were nearer to each other and, at the same time, relatively closer to families in the Beech Creek basin neighborhood than to other families in the general area. Travel routes, fixed in part by topography, to some extent determined the neighborhood to which a family belonged and also significantly influenced relationships within and between the neighborhoods.

Social interaction of a formal kind was not an important unifying factor within these neighborhoods. One-room schools, as we have mentioned, were located in or near each of the three neighborhoods but, except for church meetings which were usually held once a month in the school houses or in the preachers' homes, there were no extracurricular neighborhood activities centering around the school. By regularly bringing together the children from a specific area, however, the schools did serve to establish some neighborhood cohesion among those families. This identification was supported further by the fact that two of the neighborhoods had their own post offices—in private homes—and that some local trading was done in the few small stores in and around the neighborhoods, also in private homes. Yet these neighborhood focal points were more important as gathering places for informal interaction than for any symbolic representation they accorded the neighborhood.

Indeed, there were no regular gatherings, either formal or informal, where a majority of the adult men or women of a neighborhood came together. Except among families belonging to the same kin group, the visiting of a whole family as a unit with another was uncommon, and there was rarely an occasion when several whole families visited together, except perhaps at a memorial service or burial. But there was considerable visiting by adults on an individual basis, and these visits served as an effective network of communication within the neighborhoods which in turn contributed to neighborhood integration.

Young people from the age of twelve to about twenty in general had more and wider contacts than their elders. They too tended to visit each other on an individual basis (i.e., dyadic visiting pattern). Nevertheless, friendships made in school often developed into strong peer groups that included youngsters from various family groups. And because the schools were small, their solidarity was often manifested in activities outside the school. For example, on summer Sundays the neighborhood youngsters would get together, both boys and girls of different ages, for an informal baseball game. On Saturday nights some would gather at a home to talk or to listen to the radio barn-dance program (a few parents disapproved of these meetings, insisting they were "vice-dens"). Other than such small, informal gatherings and those that were managed after church meetings, however, there were no parties, bees, dances, or regular events for young people in Beech Creek.

Beech Creekers, then, were not organized into strongly integrated neighborhood groups to which they were "loyal" or about which they felt great pride or a sense of belonging. Strong ties of mutual interdependence among the different kin groups were all but lacking, and there was little cooperation in common tasks for the good of the whole neighborhood. Few interfamilial economic relationships, such as borrowing farm implements or exchanging labor, existed; occupational specialization was not important. In short, the Beech Creek neighborhoods were by no means socially cohesive entities.

On the other hand, the people residing in the Beech Creek area were remarkably homogeneous in many cultural respects. They shared the same language, similar religious beliefs, common values, and occupational interests. They wore the same kind of clothes, used the same expressions of speech, liked much the same sort of music, and had had very similar experiences in formal schooling, and there was a real sense of being "mountain people." Furthermore, the families in a neighborhood were bound together by what might be called their "general living, experiencing, and acting together."[17] Most Beech Creekers had been born in these neighborhoods (81 percent), or in adjacent neighborhoods; there were virtually no "outsiders" in the area.

Beech Creekers shared a common history of crises, happenings, and events which demarcated them as a particular "neighborhood"—a real social entity. They all knew whose grandparents had been good friends or bitter enemies; they recalled when somebody had been "burned out" and what folks in the neighborhood had done to help. They remembered the day somebody was shot and the resultant confusion and fear that had gripped the neighborhood; they remembered when typhoid struck and carried off three of the young Barnett boys at one time; they could recall when the fine preacher had "fooled" them all and had walked off with most of their ready cash and a lot of their clothing; they remembered the time a Holiness meeting was panicked by the calm, though untrue, announcement that a couple of sticks of dynamite were about to explode under the floor. They all knew the story about an old reprobate who agreed to be baptized but finally refused at the last moment because he wouldn't enter the water after some people he considered to be "trash" had been baptized in it. There were hundreds of such experiences which Beech Creek had shared and which therefore provided them with a common historical perspective.

One of the more important factors, however, in binding together the families within and between neighborhoods was kinship. Because of the early settlement patterns, the families comprising an extended family group were, in general, located near each other, and the neighborhoods had become intricate matrices of kin relationships.[18] Since Beech Creekers were highly particularistic in their orientations toward others, the lines of "socializing" and "neighboring" for the most part coincided with the kin network; bonds of kinship were considered more important than neighborhood ties and social life outside the immediate family and the family homestead was essentially provided for by activities within the larger family group.

# 2 FAMILY AND KIN
## in Beech Creek

The kinship structure of Beech Creek in many ways resembled that of American society at large.[1] It was a conjugal system in that it was constituted "exclusively of interlocking conjugal families." Typically, an individual in this mountain locality, as in the greater American society, was during his life a member not of one, but of two conjugal families; the family into which he was born or in which his original socialization occurred (the family of orientation) and the family formed by his marriage, in which he was a spouse (the family of procreation). Concerning the American kinship system, Parsons writes, "In most kinship systems many persons retain throughout the life cycle a fundamentally stable—though changing—status in one or more extended kinship units. In our system this is not the case for anyone."[2] Therefore the kinship structure of Beech Creek was a variant from the general, contemporary American pattern described by Parsons in that there *were* extended kinship groupings which were exceedingly significant in the lives of the Beech Creek people.[3] Nevertheless, the more important social group within the Beech Creek neighborhoods was the conjugal family.

Beech Creek households were large.[4] In 1942 the median size of seventy-seven households in the three neighborhoods was 5.4 persons; about 44.2 percent of these households (compared with 14.1 percent and 28.5 percent in the 1940 total United States and U.S. farm populations, respectively) had six or more members.[5] Most of the Beech Creek households were made up of husbands, wives, and their children, and occasionally other persons as well. Some contained husbands and wives without children, some were broken families, and a few were households headed by persons with neither spouse nor children present (see Table 2.1). In short, the most usual type of household consisted primarily of a single conjugal family, with very few extended households.

**Table 2.1.** Distribution of households by family composition, Beech Creek Neighborhoods, 1942.

| Type of household[a] | Beech Creek | |
|---|---|---|
| | Number[b] | Percent |
| Total households | 77 | 100.0 |
| Husband-wife households | 12 | 15.6 |
| Husband-wife-children households | 56 | 72.7 |
| Broken-family households | 7 | 9.1 |
| Other | 2 | 2.6 |

[a] The composition types of households used here are as follows:

A husband-wife household consists of a husband and a wife who have no children present, though other persons may be living in the household.

A husband-wife-children household consists of a husband, a wife, one child or more, and perhaps others present.

A broken-family household is headed by either a father or a mother with one child or more, and perhaps others present.

A household designated as "other" is one headed by a person with neither a spouse nor children present.

[b] There is no reliable information available on two households.

# THE FAMILY CYCLE

In Beech Creek, as in every society, the family moves through a number of stages from its formation to its final dissolution.[6]

Regardless of birth order or sex, every youngster in these mountain neighborhoods was "pointed" toward marriage, receiving in the family (of orientation) in which he or she was born the necessary training for many of the adult roles in the family (of procreation) to be established at marriage. Virtually everyone in the Beech Creek area married, and the few who remained single were looked on as odd and unusual. There were no such patterns of marriage by contract and with dowries as, for instance, in the Irish[7] or the French-Canadian[8] communities, but choice of a spouse was not as free and undirected as it often is in present-day American urban life. Although Beech Creek households were normally conjugal units, the interaction pattern within the neighborhood was characterized by extended family relations. And since the intimate, daily relationships of many more than the young couple were involved, the choice of a marriage partner usually reflected the common judgment of those affected. The pressure to make a choice acceptable to this wider group was not formal or even obvious to a casual observer, but it was there nevertheless, and it was powerful. And, because young people were limited in their contacts with other young people outside the immediate area, marriages tended to be with a local person.[9]

This was not a society of ceremony or religious pomp and rites, and nowhere was this more evident than in the rites connected with marriage. Marriage was the most important step in the whole cycle from birth to death, and yet there was remarkably little ceremony connected with it. Most marriage ceremonies were conducted by such civil authorities as magistrates or justices of the peace, and less frequently by local ministers. Church weddings with all the formality of decorations, wedding gowns, best men and maids of honor, wedding breakfasts and luncheons, printed invitations, receptions, and so on, were unknown. Not infrequently even the parents of the bride and groom were not present when the ceremony was performed. In fact, many couples "slipped off" to get married, sometimes asking a few friends, or perhaps only some convenient bystanders, to serve as witnesses. Afterward it was common for the young couple to have an "infare supper" at the home of the groom, which emphasized the change in the status of the son and signalized the entrance, for a time at least, of his wife into the household.

At the age of marriage the groom was usually about twenty-three, and the bride was generally little more than eighteen years old.[10] Often the young couple spent a year or so with one of the parental families (usually the husband's), having a room by themselves if the house was large enough. This was looked on as a temporary arrangement, and immediately plans were begun by the young couple to secure a house of their own. (At this stage of the family cycle, as we shall see later, many couples contemplated migration.) Not infrequently, before they had founded a separate household, their first child had been born; but rarely was the second child born while the couple was still living with the parental family.

Within eight to ten years after marriage, the average couple had three or four children nearly all younger than school age (six years old). This was a time when all of the children were at home and when they demanded a great amount of parental attention and energy. The families were normally in separate households, but few owned their own places and many were to some extent dependent upon their parental families. Relationships with the parental families on both sides were usually close, but often, for various reasons, somewhat closer to one or the other of the families. There was much visiting, some exchange of labor, and frequent sharing of crises, with siblings and parents of both partners of the marriage.

By the time the wives were in their thirties, the families had grown so that most had four, five, or six children, ranging in age from less than one to fourteen years. Some of the children—always at least one, more commonly two or even three—were in school, but probably most of them were not of school age. The family was still growing, and the older children were sufficiently mature and skilled to take important roles in the family's work. Often the oldest girls took charge of the youngest children, or did most of the cooking or housekeeping. The oldest boys did most of the plowing, woodchopping, and corn cultivating. By this time the families had probably developed much closer relationships with the siblings of one partner or the other, though relationships with the other side would still be frequent. A few lived on places which the parents of the husband or wife owned, but usually they owned farms themselves, having secured possession sometimes through purchase, but most often through inheritance. (Their parents had died and the estate was divided, or else their parents, though still living, had decided to deed to them their shares of the estate).

By the time wives were from thirty-seven to forty-five years of age, the number of family members resident at home had reached its maximum. Almost all families had more than four children still at home; most had six or more. The children ranged from infancy to nineteen or twenty years old, but most were of school age. Virtually all of the families had at least one child, and some two, who had grown up and left the parental home.

At this stage in the family cycle, the family had more adult or young adult labor available for chores around the homestead than at any other time. Often a rather intricate but informal division of labor, by age and sex, had been routinized among family members. The oldest boys worked off their father's farm in the log-woods or as hired hands for other farmers; they were beginning to break away from parental control, and usually went through a more or less expected period of drinking, fighting, and running around over the country with gangs of fellows their age. The oldest girls, however, were not so obviously intent upon showing their growing awareness of, or need for, independence. They seldom worked away from home, though many of them were doing the work of adults at home—caring for children, cooking and canning, working in the garden, taking care of chickens, sewing, and so on. Nor did they seem to indulge in such flamboyant adolescent behavior as their brothers, though this was the courting age and the time when dress and grooming had their greatest emphasis. Parents were at the prime of their working lives; they were not thinking of retiring. For that reason, when the oldest children left the homestead, usually at or shortly after marriage, the parental farm was seldom divided. The parents were concerned about consolidating their own gains and in raising the rest of their large families to maturity. Oldest children usually had to shift for themselves. The parents of both husbands and wives in a number of cases had died, but the family's closest social relationships at this stage were still with those remaining among the husband's and wife's brothers and sisters.

Middle-aged families, in which wives were from forty-five to fifty years old, still included children of varying ages (from seven to twenty-six years old); but the child-bearing period was past, and the children at home were the youngest and last. The oldest children had grown up and left the homestead; indeed many families had more children away than at home. Usually two or three married children lived nearby, and there was great interest taken in their affairs and especially in the births of their children. Sometimes a young married couple resided with one or the other parental family, and they became closely tied into the routine of life on the homestead. Even when not living in parental homes, there was much visiting back and forth, and sharing of help in times of sickness or in peak work periods, between married children and their middle-aged parents. A stronger tie in terms of mutual aid began to develop between the newly-formed family and either the maternal or paternal family, and for the middle-aged couple familial ties tended to shift from the families of their parents and siblings to the families of their own children. By this time their own parents and some of their oldest siblings had died. It was not uncommon, therefore, to find the mother or father of either the husband or wife in a middle-aged family residing in the household, and occasionally both old parents—especially when they were in poor health—might be living with the family at this stage. The heads of these households were usually still active in directing and doing the farm work and many of them did off-farm work at certain seasons of the year. But they were beginning to "slow down" and their oldest sons at home carried a good part of the heavy work.

Finally, in the family's cycle from formation through dissolution, there is the period of old age. Among Beech Creek families, a number of patterns were discernible, each an adaptive response to unique situational circumstances. Some older couples still had a few unmarried children, anywhere from eleven to forty years of age, living at home. In several families young grandchildren had joined the household, usually because something had happened to the children's parents—death, separation, or migration—which made it necessary for them to be cared for by the grandparents. Some older couples lived with a married son or daughter's family, as a joint family household but generally in the parental family house. Others lived alone, as a couple, or in some cases in which the spouse had died, as single-person households.

As long as elderly couples were physically able to maintain their separate homes, they were inclined to do so; and even when one partner died, there was an effort on the part of the survivor to preserve his own home. As long as a man was able to work, he continued to participate in and direct farming operations on the family homestead. With increasing age, of course, older people became increasingly dependent upon their children to do more and more of the farm work and homestead chores. Sometimes, at this stage, parents began to distribute their land among the children, though more typically ownership was retained to the last.

In this familistically-oriented rural society, socially differentiated mainly in terms of sex and age, old people performed very important integrative roles, both symbolically, and as focal points for intricately balanced networks of kin interaction. Older persons were the nuclei, so to speak, of family groups consisting of their grown children's families and often including other kin. We shall discuss that phenomenon at greater length in a later section.

Having explored the various stages through which the Beech Creek family's mode of life progressed, we turn our attention toward relationships among members of a single family, various roles within the conjugal family, and the interdependence of these intra-family roles.

# RELATIONSHIPS WITHIN THE CONJUGAL FAMILY[11]

The Beech Creek family tended to be of a patriarchal type. According to prevailing normative standards the husband was regarded as head of the household; he was expected to be dominant and to assume a leadership role in all matters pertaining to the well-being of the family and the maintenance and operation of the family homestead. This dominance was not confined to economic concerns alone but, at least in principle, was applied to all social relationships within the family. As head of the household, he was expected to speak for the family in public, and to negotiate any extra-familial affairs; in short, he was supposed to be the family decision-maker.

Though the ideal pattern prescribed dominance in the family by the husband, there were many deviations from that norm. In some cases the wife was the main decision-maker.[12] This did not necessarily make for an unhappy situation. For example, in one family, though the wife was universally recognized as the "boss" around the homestead, she had been able by skillful management to get the farm work done without antagonizing her husband. The husband himself even thought he was the actual head of the house. "Some of 'em might say I wasn't the boss, but I am. My wife never tries to boss me," he would explain. However, in other cases dominance by the wife had less happy results; the husband felt inferior, neighbors gossiped, and strain was manifested in the family setting. Neighbors generally approved and advocated the husband's dominance. But where it was evident that a wife had greater managerial ability and that her husband could not completely perform his expected roles, neighbors relaxed their sanctions and indeed encouraged the wife's "take-over." There was then, an approved alternative to the traditional patriarchal pattern.

Husband-wife relationships, according to normative standards, were assumed to have affective content, but public manifestation of affection such as kisses and embraces were not approved. Indeed, such demonstrations obviously embarrassed Beech Creek people and generally called forth censure of some kind—gossip, ridicule, or laughter. Kindness between husband and wife, on the other hand, was expected and looked upon with great admiration; one of the most complimentary things which could be said about a Beech Creek man was that he was "good" to his wife and family. Though a double standard of sexual morality was evidenced, any extramarital sexual relationship by either partner was strongly disapproved by the neighborhood and considered a serious violation of norms.[13] Husband and wife were expected to be completely loyal and to stand by each other through every fortune or misfortune. Marital fidelity, along with complete devotion to the welfare of their children, was regarded as the main obligation in life; loyalty to others outside the conjugal family (such as to the parents of either the husband or wife) was definitely secondary.

Within the conjugal family, parents were in superordinate and children in subordinate positions. Parents were expected to direct their children; children were expected to obey their parents. Parental control was established over a long period of time, through the process of socialization, so that it was mostly not repressive from a child's standpoint, but anticipated and natural, backed by the beliefs of the children as much as by those of the parents. In addition to this internalized reinforcement of parental authority, there were also external reinforcements. Physical punishment, for example, such as whipping or spanking, was considered an appropriate means to use in building good behavior and obedience. Failure of the children to meet expected standards of conduct in Beech Creek brought neighborhood disapproval upon the parents. Since parents were held responsible for their children's behavior, they were compelled to exert their culturally sanctioned authority over them. Indeed, with the possible exception of the school teachers and the older children in a family, no one other than the parents had the vested right to punish children physically and, hence, to establish and enforce the standards of conduct for children.

Affective bonds between parents and children were manifested in many ways. To be sure, emotive feelings were not often expressed openly, and any obvious expression of affection in public was not considered in good taste. Even so, parents were expected to be affectionate and kind toward their children, and vice versa. In two families, for example, people in the neighborhood felt that the fathers were not sufficiently affectionate. In both of these cases the children left home as soon as they were grown. In one of the families the daughters married when they were seventeen or eighteen, and left at once. Two sons left home, against their father's will, to go to school when they were fourteen or fifteen. His other two sons would not live with their parents but lived for several years with friends and relatives on the creek. The father was ill and fractious. He beat his children a great deal, made them go to bed at dark and get up before daylight; he worked them unreasonably long hours and would not buy proper clothing for them. Only one of the children (married) lived nearby and relationships between the two families were not cordial. Such deviations as these were the subject of much neighborhood discussion.

Every infant or young child was almost entirely in his mother's care and the care of his mother's helpers, his sisters. As an infant he was entirely her responsibility; she fed him (breast-feeding was the common practice), kept him clean, rocked him to sleep, and tended to his every need. All this was done in a very affectionate manner. After a child learned to walk and began to do chores and to sense his position in the family, his life was still centered around the house, and he was therefore principally under the supervision of his mother. Even when children were old enough to assume roles which tended to divide them on the basis of sex, there were still close relationships with the mother. Girls, of course, did most of their work in and around the house and were under the direct supervision of their mothers. Boys, after reaching school age, assumed more and more man's work, usually with brothers under the direction of their father. But it was the mother who was the center of the family's affection. She was always at home—to go to or come back to. Children, boys and girls alike, confided their troubles and secrets to her, and in later as in earlier years the surest source of sympathy and understanding was apt to be the mother.

The father, on the other hand, had less close affectional relationships with the young child than the mother. Though he was usually not away at work to such an extent as the urban middle-class father, his work, nevertheless, was outside and away from the house. Fathers, and especially young fathers, were almost always very affectionate and proud of their children, "nursing" them and fondling them, but they were seldom so abandoned and so free in their caresses, and they did not have such constant, continuous contact with the young children as the mothers. Undoubtedly it was during these important early years that the ties of affection to mothers were so strongly knit that they significantly influenced the sentiments of children all the rest of their lives.

Perhaps the best way of stating the difference in the attitudes of children towards fathers and mothers is to say that the dominant feeling for mothers was love, for fathers respect. Boys and their fathers were not likely to be "pals," for there was a certain constraint in boys' behavior around their fathers that impeded the development of such a relationship.

One important observation must be made about the parent-child relationship: the kinship terminology in Beech Creek did not and does not distinguish children by birth order, but only by sex.[14] This reflects an important aspect of the actual parent-child relationship—parents were expected to treat their children equally. Any deviation, such as favoring one child more than another, might well have evoked protests from the others which would have been approved by the neighborhood. The fact of equality among all children was illustrated by the patterns of land inheritance which set up the ideal of equal inheritance among children, regardless of sex and age. Deviation from this pattern aroused much antagonism among the children.

But there was one pattern of favoritism sufficiently widespread to note: the "baby," the youngest in the family, often seemed to have a special status. Around him or her there developed special bonds of affection, and even when the child was grown he might be referred to by a parent, usually facetiously, as "my baby." Not infrequently older siblings also had this special affection for the "baby one of the family." An informant who knew a great deal about the patterns of inheritance in this part of the country suggested that while the ideal pattern of property inheritance called for equal division among all the children, there was some evidence that often the youngest child had been deeded the farm, especially the homestead. This practice might well have been connected with the "baby" pattern, although, as the older children grew up and moved into their own homes, the youngest was more likely to be with the old parents at the time when they would be ready to retire.

With the arrival of a new baby the youngest child lost his position as the center of the family's affection. This undoubtedly was a potential point of strain among siblings but difficulties arising from this situation were mitigated by the fact that usually a child occupied the affectional spotlight for only a short time. Also, the effect on the youngest of the arrival of a younger brother or sister was carefully—though largely unconsciously—softened by the comments of the other members of the family which oriented him to the new child and stimulated in him a great interest in the baby. In homes where there was a newborn child, there was always such comment on the attitude of the ex-youngest as, "Mildred Ann's as jealous as she can be of the new baby. She's not the baby anymore. But she loves it more than any of us, and even wakes it up so that she can play with it."

On the whole, brothers were treated as equals within the family. They worked together under their parents', especially their father's, supervision. They saw much more of each other, as a rule, than of other boys, and in the years of work and play together usually developed a solidarity and loyalty which lasted all their lives. In the same way, sisters, possibly even more than boys, developed very strong friendships in their long period of close association.

The brother-sister relationship was close, too. Brothers and sisters were expected to be affectionate, kind, and loyal to each other and the family. There often was, as Arensberg and Kimball say of brothers and sisters in the Irish family,[15] much the reaction a boy had to his mother in his attitudes toward his sister; and the girl looked on her brother much as she looked on her father.

In many cases, especially within the larger families in which an older sister had to take charge of the younger children, a younger child might have developed feelings toward his older sister much like those toward his mother, and the older sister, in turn, sometimes had developed maternal feelings toward the younger brother or sister. Another facet of the same situation was that frequently among brothers and sisters of nearly the same age there was greater loyalty, solidarity, and affection than with siblings who were much older or much younger; older siblings were often married and independent of their parental family by the time the younger children were born. Within the same conjugal family, then, there were often smaller clusterings of siblings that evolved as a natural consequence of child-rearing practices and birth order.

To an observer from an urban society outside the mountains, the self-sufficiency of the Beech Creek family in both economic and social relationships was striking. We have indicated how the greater part of a Beech Creek family's time was spent performing the activities necessary to earn a living and maintain the family economy, and that each family constituted a separate unit, the members of which did their work together with little assistance from outsiders. Apart from this, however, one is struck by how much time members of a family spent together and how little time different members of a family spent in other groups. There were few, if any, formal organizations in the neighborhoods, and informal recreational groups outside the family did not exist to the extent common among urban people. Except for school and play with close kin or near neighbors, most children in Beech Creek had as playmates only their brothers and sisters. It is not surprising, under these circumstances, that siblings developed very close friendships, and that brothers and sisters seemed to "think more" of each other than is general in the urban situation.

# EXTENDED KINSHIP RELATIONS

We must again emphasize that the family of procreation had primacy in the social organization of Beech Creek. It was expected to be in many respects independent of the families of orientation of both husband and wife. Indeed the conjugal relationship was the most important single relationship in the Beech Creek kinship system. This meant that in the formation of the new family—and in making secure its primary importance—social ties with both parents and siblings of the marriage partners had to be, and were in effect, modified and weakened. Here, then, was a possible point of strain in the social organization of these mountain neighborhoods.

Around this point of strain clustered a number of patterns having as their functions the buttressing of the new conjugal family's independence against too great an interference from parental and other kin families, and the stabilization and maintenance of the neighborhood system as a viable social entity. Thus there was a strong belief in a separate residence for the new family; the consequent isolation of the new family had the effect of withdrawing it from many influences which might have threatened its independence. Usually when a Beech Creek couple married, they went to the husband's parental home to live *temporarily*. But they did not expect, and were not expected, to stay there very long, usually not more than a year. In that time the young couple had probably accumulated enough household goods to set up housekeeping and had arranged to move into a house by themselves. Even if the couple planned to live on the husband's father's farm, a separate house was considered necessary so that the households could be independent. It was seldom deemed satisfactory to have two families living in the same house, and almost every time such an arrangement was attempted, trouble—quarrels, bickering, and sometimes actual physical conflict—resulted.

After long years of association in the intimate atmosphere of family life, it was difficult for both parents and children to orient themselves to the new situation created by the departure of children for their new families. Again and again mothers said they did not want their children to marry, or that they did not want to think about their children leaving. The ideal patterns centering around this situation demanded on the one hand that parents not interfere with the new family, and on the other that the spouse accept responsibility in the new home as the primary interest. If parents interfered in their children's families of procreation, the community disapproved.

Like the relationships between parents and their married children, the relationships between married siblings also tended to be weakened as the conjugal relationships were strengthened. That this was a point of strain in the social organization of Beech Creek was evident from numerous instances (observed in the field) of jealousies, bickerings, quarrels, and serious difficulties between the families of siblings.[16] Analysis of these instances suggests that: (1) the antagonisms practically always arose after the siblings were grown and had families of their own; (2) many of the controversies centered around the spouse of one or the other, or perhaps both, of the siblings—that is, the old relationship of siblings was changed by the new relationships formed with spouses at marriage; (3) very often the antagonisms centered around "class differences."

# THE KIN NETWORK

The kinship system of Beech Creek was an open system; that is, there was no preferential mating on a kinship basis. Ideally, because of the incest tabu, marriage partners in this mountain society were not to be related by blood.[17] Also, the kinship system was multilineal—kinship was traced through both mother and father, maternal grandfather and maternal grandmother, paternal grandfather and paternal grandmother, and so on. Every conjugal family at the time of marriage theoretically brought together two otherwise unrelated kin groups. We shall consider later the problem of whether there tended to be an emphasis on greater solidarity with the kin of the husband or of the wife. It is sufficient to note here that in this relatively stable Appalachian Mountain locality, where people had married and intermarried for over a hundred years, kin relationships were very extensive.[18]

Beech Creek people often said, "Everybody around here is kin," and systematic observation (in 1942) proved that statement almost literally true. For instance, it is theoretically possible for each of the thirty-eight families in the Beech Creek basin neighborhood for whom data were available to have been related by blood to each of the other thirty-seven families. If one considers each household as a unit for analysis and counts only the closest relationship of the head or his spouse to each of the other families in that neighborhood, then one would have some idea of the nature and extent of kin relationships among these families. This was done for the Beech Creek basin and Laurel neighborhoods, and partially also for the Flat Rock neighborhood (see Table 2.2).

It was found that of the total number of possible single, closest relationships among the thirty-eight Beech Creek families, nearly three-fourths were kin relationships in some degree. Many of these relationships were those of third or fourth cousins, but 18.7 percent of the total possible relationships were "close kin" (parents and children, siblings, aunts or uncles and nieces or nephews, grandparents and grandchildren, or first cousins). An additional 24 percent were relationships of first cousins once removed or second cousins.[19] Comparable data for the Laurel neighborhood revealed that there, too, nearly three-fourths of the total possible relationships were kin relationships in some degree; nearly half of the total relationships, however, were those with close kin; and an additional 13.3 percent were relationships of first cousins once removed or second cousins. In the Flat Rock neighborhood also, nearly half of the total relationships were those of parents and children, siblings, aunts or uncles and nieces or nephews, grandparents and grand-

**Table 2.2.** Closest kin relationships among families within the specified neighborhoods, Beech Creek Basin, Laurel, and Flat Rock neighborhoods,[a] July 1, 1942.

| Relationship | Number of Specified Kin Relationships | | | Percent of Total Possible Relationships | | |
|---|---|---|---|---|---|---|
| | Beech Creek Basin | Laurel | Flat Rock[b] | Beech Creek Basin | Laurel | Flat Rock[b] |
| Total number possible | 703 | 136 | 66 | 100.0 | 100.0 | 100.0 |
| Parent-child | 20 | 8 | 3 | 2.8 | 5.9 | 4.6 |
| Sibling | 35 | 22 | 5 | 5.0 | 16.2 | 7.6 |
| Aunt, uncle-niece, nephew | 33 | 21 | 8 | 4.7 | 15.4 | 12.1 |
| Grandparents-grandchildren | 1 | 1 | 0 | 0.1 | 0.7 | 0 |
| Great aunt, great uncle, great niece, great nephew | 2 | 1 | 0 | 0.3 | 0.7 | 0 |
| First cousins | 43 | 12 | 15 | 6.1 | 8.8 | 22.7 |
| First cousins, once removed | 79 | 10 | 0 | 11.2 | 7.4 | 0 |
| First cousins, twice removed | 4 | 1 | 0 | 0.6 | 0.7 | 0 |
| Second cousins | 90 | 8 | 0 | 12.8 | 5.9 | 0 |
| Second cousins, once removed | 87 | 8 | 0 | 12.4 | 5.9 | 0 |
| Second cousins, twice removed | 8 | 1 | 0 | 1.1 | 0.8 | 0 |
| Third cousins | 55 | 0 | 0 | 7.8 | 0 | 0 |
| Third cousins, once removed | 38 | 4 | 0 | 5.4 | 3.0 | 0 |
| Fourth cousins | 13 | 4 | 0 | 1.9 | 3.0 | 0 |
| None | 184 | 35 | 35[b] | 26.2 | 25.7 | 53.0[b] |
| Unknown | 11 | 0 | 0 | 1.6 | 0 | 0 |

[a] The closest kin relationship between the husband or wife in each family and the husband or wife in every other family in the neighborhood was determined for thirty-eight Beech Creek Basin, seventeen Laurel, and twelve Flat Rock families. Among Beech Creek basin families there were then 703 possible relationships, if only the single closest kin or non-kin relationship was counted, and in Laurel and Flat Rock there were 136 and 66 possible kin or non-kin relationships respectively.

The kinship data were incomplete, largely because complete data were not available for ten Laurel families. If data for them had been obtained, the proportion of Laurel people who were close kin would have been smaller, though it would still have been appreciably greater than in either of the other neighborhoods.

[b] Kin relationships other than those of parent-child, siblings, aunt, uncle-niece, nephew, grandparent-grandchild, and first cousins were not worked out for the Flat Rock families. The only figures in the table above, therefore, which are directly comparable to those of the other neighborhoods are those in these categories. But the percentage of non-kin relationships in Flat Rock is comparable to the percentage of non-kin in the other neighborhoods *plus* all the kinship categories not listed above.

children, or first cousins. It is obvious that, according to this index, kin relationships were extensive in all the neighborhoods, and that many of these were close blood relationships. It is also clear that Laurel and Flat Rock families were more closely related by blood than those of the Beech Creek basin neighborhood.[20]

The intricacy of kin relationships in Beech Creek may perhaps be best suggested by listing the closest relationships of one family, the Gamble family, with other families in the basin neighborhood.

| Families living on Beech Creek[21] | Closest kin relationship of any member of specified family with either Mr. or Mrs. Gamble |
|---|---|
| 1 | Third cousin, once removed |
| 2 | Second cousin, once removed |
| 3 | Third cousin |
| 4 | First cousin, once removed |
| 5 | Second cousin, once removed |
| 6 | First cousin, once removed |
| 7 | Niece |
| 8 | Second cousin |
| 9 | First cousin |
| 10 | First cousin, once removed |
| 11 | First cousin, once removed |
| 12 | Son |
| 13 | Third cousin, once removed |
| 14 | Third cousin, once removed |
| 15 | Third cousin |
| 16 | None |
| 17 | First cousin, once removed |
| 18 | First cousin |
| 19 | First cousin |
| 20 | First cousin, once removed |
| 21 | First cousin |
| 22 | First cousin, once removed |
| 23 | Nephew |
| 24 | Third cousin, twice removed |
| 25 | None |
| 26 | Second cousin, once removed |
| 27 | First cousin, once removed |
| 28 | None |
| 29 | None |
| 30 | First cousin |
| 31 | First cousin |

Both this instance of the closest blood relationships of one Beech Creek family with other families in the neighborhood and the figures cited earlier to show the extent of kinship within the neighborhoods tend to simplify the complexity of the kinship ties among Beech Creek people by considering the households, rather than their separate members, as units and by disregarding all but the closest relationships between households. In reality, of course, the network of kin relationships within *and between* these neighborhoods was far more complex and entangled than can be shown by simple tabular analysis.

There were important differences in the patterns of social interaction between Beech Creek people who were of different degrees of kinship. Parental family and sibling ties, of course, were very strong and tended to supersede all other social obligations and relationships. First cousins were usually closer friends and more likely to come to each other's aid in crises than second cousins. And relationships among third cousins were not likely to be close, at least not because of kinship bonds; they might well have been considered a part of a large, vaguely defined group known as one's "people" or "relatives," toward whom one had little direct responsibility.

A quantitative indication of differences in patterns of social interaction with kin of various degrees can be found in the visiting relationships among a selected group of families in the Beech Creek basin neighborhood (Table 2.3). Old parents and their adult children's families visited each other far more often than did families having any other, more distant, blood relationship; and as the degree of kinship decreased, the number of visits also tended to decrease. Thus, nearly three-fourths of the families of parents and of their adult children had visited their children's or their parents' families, as the case might be, more than a hundred times during the year, and more than a third had visited them an average of nearly once a day for the entire year. Only 19 percent of the siblings studied, however, visited each other a hundred or more times during the year; 27 percent of them visited from twenty to ninety-nine times, 32 percent from five to twenty times, and 22 percent less than five times. Visiting among aunts or uncles and their nieces or nephews was much less common than among siblings, for only a fifth had called on each other more than five times in the year; 31 percent had made one to four visits, and exactly half had made no visits at all. Among first cousins, 28 percent had made from one to four visits, and 57 percent had not visited at all. Nearly two-thirds of the second cousins had not visited, and a fifth had visited only one to four times.

In short, there was a great deal of "visiting" back and forth among Beech Creek families, and their social interactional network by and large followed kinship lines.

Table 2.3. Estimated number of visits made by head and/or spouse of twenty-four families upon thirty-one families of various degrees of kinship, Beech Creek Basin neighborhood, 1942[a].

| Number of Visits During 1942 | Parents and Children | Siblings | Grandparents, Grandchildren | Aunts, Uncles, Nephews, Nieces | First Cousins | Second Cousins | Great Aunts, Uncles, Great Nieces, Nephews |
|---|---|---|---|---|---|---|---|
| | Number of Visits Between Families with the Specified Kin Relationship | | | | | | |
| 0 | 0 | 4 | 0 | 18 | 30 | 54 | 2 |
| 1–4 | 0 | 4 | 1 | 11 | 15 | 16 | 0 |
| 5–9 | 3 | 4 | 1 | 1 | 4 | 6 | 2 |
| 10–19 | 2 | 8 | 0 | 3 | 2 | 1 | 0 |
| 20–99 | 4 | 10 | 0 | 2 | 2 | 3 | 0 |
| 100–299 | 11 | 6 | 0 | 1 | 0 | 1 | 0 |
| 300 and over | 11 | 1 | 0 | 0 | 0 | 1 | 0 |
| Number of cases studied with indicated relationship | 31 | 37 | 2 | 36 | 53 | 82 | 4 |
| Range of number of visits by families by specified relationship | 5–720 | 0–720 | 2–8 | 0–150 | 0–24 | 0–372 | 0–7 |

[a] Data on visiting were obtained by asking twenty-four informants how many times the head of the household and his spouse, if any, in their families had visited each of the other families in the Beech Creek Basin Neighborhood. "A visit" was not carefully defined, though an attempt was made to eliminate "business calls" (such as trips to stores, to the post office and to the mill). Since no one kept records on family visits, these figures should be looked on simply as rough estimates. It is likely that the smaller figures are more accurate, for it was easier for informants to remember the number of times a family had been visited if they had made only one or two visits than if they had made a great many visits. Two checks of the accuracy of informants' estimates were used: (1) the twenty-four informants were asked not only what families they visited, but what families had visited them. It was therefore possible to make cross-checks; (2) because the interviewer lived in the Beech Creek Basin neighborhood during this period, he had some idea of the frequency of visits among the families.

## FAMILY GROUPS

It became apparent, early in the initial field work, that there were distinctive social groups in the Beech Creek neighborhoods, each composed of two, three, or more family-households that were particularly solidary and bonded together by strong ties of mutual aid, friendship, and frequent visiting exchanges, as well as by ties of kinship. These were primarily groups of siblings' families or of siblings and their parental families; that is, in the main they were extended families or socially cohesive segments of larger extended families. To emphasize the familistic aspects of this bonding, yet not to violate generally accepted definitions of the term "extended family," the term "family group" was devised.

Twelve such family groups were delineated in the Beech Creek basin neighborhood; five of the thirty-eight family-households in the neighborhood could not be assigned to any particular family group because of insufficient data available about their social relationships with the other families. Similarly, four family groups in the Laurel neighborhood and two family groups in the Flat Rock neighborhood were delineated as complete social groups on the basis of observations made in the field.

These groupings of families were not arrived at merely by discovering the nature of kinship ties between families. Rather, the delineation was based upon a variety of social data—indicants of meaningful social intercourse and social-psychological identification—collected by quasi-participant observation of the social relationships of the families with each other over a period of one year (1942–43). There were, in fact, several instances in which the families of siblings were assigned to different family groups. Thus, for example, the family of Sam Andrews, whose wife was the daughter of Ed Barnett, was included in the Barnett group rather than in the Andrew Johnson group with the family of his sister, because the strongest social relationships of the Sam Andrews family were with the other families in the Barnett group. Factors other than blood relationship determined, therefore, the closer social relationship of the Sam Andrews family with the Barnett family group rather than with the Andrew Johnson group. In this particular case it was relatively easy to ascertain to which group the family belonged, but in other cases it was more difficult. Many families designated by the researcher as belonging to one family group had significant, even close, relationships with the people of another family group; thus these were natural groups with indistinct, and in some respects arbitrary, boundaries.

Another point which must be made clear is that family groups were in a process of continuous change. During an individual's lifetime he passed through several stages in his social relationships with kin. As a child he usually had his closest contacts, outside of his own family of orientation, with the families of his grandparents and his parents' siblings. Often close bonds of affection and solidarity very like those among brothers and sisters developed at this stage among first cousins. Aunts and uncles too were highly regarded, and even after children had reached adulthood and had families of their own, they maintained close relations with their aunts and uncles, some of whom were looked on as "almost fathers and mothers." Nevertheless, as a young adult with his own family of procreation, an individual's closest relationships were with the families of his own and his wife's parents and siblings. And as an older parent, an individual's closest contacts tended to be with his own children's families.

An individual's shift from one family group to another in this cycle was not sudden, but rather came about gradually over a period of years. At any specific time, an observer would find family groups at different stages in the cycle.

The Andrew Johnsons, for instance, were a relatively young family group; Andrew Johnson's oldest children had not been married and away from home long. In his youth Andrew had been associated with several other family groups: his father, Charles Johnson, as a young married man had apparently been part of the Joshua Johnson family group—original settlers in the Beech Creek basin—which consisted of the families of Joshua and his adult sons, Julius, Tom, Charlie, and Preston. Therefore, Andrew presumably had had close social relationships with his uncles and their children, his first cousins, in that family group. (Actually when Andrew was a child his father had moved to another county, and so Andrew had not had as close contacts with his father's brothers' families as might have been expected.) There was still some feeling of solidarity among the people who had been associated in the Joshua Johnson family group (that is, among the Andrew Johnsons and the Preston Johnsons—Andrew's uncle and first cousins; the Gambles—Mrs. Gamble was a daughter of Julius Johnson; the Carters—Tom Carter's first wife, mother of Lewis Carter and Mrs. Edward Carter, was a daughter of Tom Johnson; and the Carters and Johnsons—the mother of Randolph Johnson, who married a sister of Edward Carter, was a daughter of Julius Johnson). But the former members of the Joshua Johnson family group had passed the stage in which that larger group absorbed their interests, served their needs, and commanded their loyalty, and had reached the stage when interests had been redirected and new family groups constituted to serve those changed needs.

Every conjugal family, as noted earlier, represented the bringing together of two separate groups of kin, that of the husband and that of the wife. Since there were no institutionalized preferences, a Beech Creek family was not expected to become more closely tied to one side or the other. Actually, however, this often happened, and in the large majority of those cases identification tended to be with the husband's kin. One reason was that sons were more likely than their sisters to remain on the family's land, though according to the ideal pattern each child regardless of sex was supposed to receive a share of the parental family's land. Since the parental families of spouses seldom lived side by side, it was almost inevitable if they settled on the land of one family or the other that they would live geographically closer to one parental family than to the other.

Another factor, important both in determining the sons' greater likelihood of remaining on the family's land and in determining closer association with the husband's parental family, was the structure of the family: the husband was expected to be the head of the family, to be dominant. When a man took his bride to his parental home, he was still in many ways subordinate to his parents. But this was a subordination to which he had become accustomed and which he had accepted for many years. This subordination, too, was from the standpoint of the husband's parents much more easily retained than if the head of the new family were, so to speak, a complete stranger. A husband who went to his wife's home to live was inevitably, to some extent, subordinated to his wife's parents, but this was a *new* subordination and one which, because of the solidarity of his wife and her parents, might well threaten his status as head of the family. Such a situation was apt to result in disagreement or at least in a warped relationship of the new husband and his family.[22]

Some families of course were associated with the kin of only one spouse because only one had kinsfolk in the neighborhood. The land resources of the spouses' parental families as well as the class status (about which we shall say more later) were also important in determining the residential location and hence the social interactional patterns of a family. And, to be sure, there were many other individual reasons why a family became socially bound to one family group rather than another to which it had equally strong blood ties. In general, however, family groups tended to be groups of a husband's kin.

Family groups, in a very informal but nevertheless persuasive manner, had a leadership structure. Often the old father, or occasionally the old mother, was the accepted leader, the arbitrator of family disputes, the focal point in the group's activities, and the symbol of the group's existence as a cohesive, valid social entity. In some groups one of the patriarch's sons may have been designated, informally, as the main advisor or, indeed, responsible leader. Generally, however, leadership roles were delegated in terms of age, and one of the more important functions performed by the elderly in this rural familistic society was to "hold together" the family groups and to represent symbolically the family homestead.

But what did it mean for an individual to be associated with a family group? How did relationships among its members differ from those with other people in the neighborhood? How did the family group contribute to the solidarity and survival of the Beech Creek social oragnization and to the well-being of individuals who resided in these mountain neighborhoods?

Family groups were typically not only collectivities of close kin but also territorial groups; that is, they consisted of families who lived close to each other, usually because they had inherited parts of the same estate. This ordinarily meant that visiting among them was very frequent; wives, for example, would be at each other's houses and children of the families would play together almost every day. There was constant social intercourse among the families within a group.

It was primarily within the family group that members of different conjugal families—and especially the children—ate with each other. On Sundays, particularly, members of a family group gathered at one family's house to share dinner.

Most co-operative farming activities were carried on within the family group. It wasn't unusual for various members to develop skill in particular crafts which they shared within the group. Thus, one man became a good blacksmith: he would shoe the mules of his brother-in-law, and the brother-in-law, who was a good carpenter, would in turn help him fix his barn. At hog-killing time, the men worked together. There were frequent exchanges of food among the families—the old mother would send her daughter's family a "mess" of beans; the daughter might reciprocate by sending her mother a chicken or some fresh butter.

Through their daily, intimate contacts the members of a family group built up a strong feeling of group solidarity. They thought of themselves as a group, and the neighborhood thought of them as a group. Such a cluster of families were often referred to as "the Smiths" or "the Joneses," or perhaps by a nickname.

In crises the group stood together. When a member of one family was sick, persons from the other families would take turns "setting up" with him at night. It was expected that members of a group help each other in times of sickness, and not to do so was to risk severe censure. When a baby was born, the other children in that family were taken care of by the other families for a few days, and the other wives and other girls in the group usually took turns in doing the family's housework and cooking, especially if there were no older girls in that family to take the responsibility. If the father of a family was sick and couldn't take care of his crop, the other members of the family group took over and did the necessary farm work. When somebody died, men from the family group usually made the simple coffin, and members of all the families came to sit with the bereaved family and helped to take the body to the graveyard. If a mother or father died and left young children, and it became necessary for somebody else to care for them, members of the family group took the responsibility. If one of the families had trouble with an outsider in the neighborhood, the other families could be counted on to rally to its support.

It was among the members of a family group that neighborhood happenings were discussed and opinions formed. Since members of the family group had such frequent contacts, information spread through the neighborhood primarily by contacts within these groups. Something said to one person in the morning was usually known to everybody within his group by night. These groups were exceedingly important in controlling the actions of an individual, for hardly any decision was made without all the other members of the group knowing about it, discussing it, and reaching a common decision on it. An individual who had deviated from some accepted norm could usually count on family support against outsiders, but he could also count on intragroup criticism and ridicule.

In this mountain society, help on a wider basis than the conjugal family often had to be called upon. Crises such as sickness, death, and fire, for example, in many cases could not be met by the members of a single conjugal family. There were no governmental or private agencies such as city and town people could call on, so there was a need for a larger group which could share responsibilities, and upon which one could depend, whatever the circumstances. Because marriage often took place at such early ages in this society, young couples often required the help of their parents and siblings in getting started. Also, the care of the old and the infirm was a function which a single family would have had difficulty performing in this society but which a family group could meet much more adequately. Linton says of bands that "there is the need for companionship and for the reassurance and emotional security which comes from belonging to a social unit whose members share the same ideas and patterns of behavior."[23] Unquestionably one of the most important contributions the family group made to the individual in the Beech Creek society was the feeling of belonging to a wider group with which he shared common values and ideals, within which he found affection and security, and on which he could count for help in time of crisis.

# 3 BEECH CREEK:
## Social Classes, Cultural Themes, and Changing Needs

We have described how the Beech Creeker was socialized in and bound by three main groups: the conjugal family and its homestead, the family group, and the neighborhood. In this chapter, which concludes our discussion of the socio-cultural origins of the Beech Creek migrants, we explore the system of social stratification and the cultural themes or value bases that undergirded the form of social organization in Beech Creek. (These organizing principles, of course, also supplied the *raison d'etre* of, and legitimating foundation for, the system of social stratification.[1]) As an introduction to the next phase of the Beech Creek story, that is, as a transition from the past to the present, we suggest how a breakdown in the relative isolation of this Appalachian mountain locality came about and how, as a consequence, the needs and wants of Beech Creekers changed, disturbing the very forms of social organization and setting the stage for subsequent waves of migration to areas of greater economic opportunity.

## DELINEATION OF SOCIAL CLASSES

A class structure, readily discernible to a trained observer, was woven into the fabric of life in Beech Creek. Indications of a social hierarchy appeared, for example, in the comments of local people about each other.

"I never go around such people as that; so I don't know anything about them."

"If you're going over there on Flat Rock you'd better leave all your money here if you want to keep it."

"They're as good a people as you'll find anywhere."

"Sam married beneath himself."

"Them Barnetts think they're something. But they're no better than anybody else. In fact they're not as good because they keep the whole creek in an uproar."

"The Carter name went a long way with people. Just because they's a Carter, a good class of people wouldn't mix with them. They've had their records for years and years, and I never found anything good about them."

"They's a more classy type doing a hell of a lot worse than the Carters or as bad. I can show you people trying to make light of the Carters that's just as bad as the Carters. Martha Combs would laugh at people having illegitimate children, saying things belittling and now she's got one in her own family. You can take as general source all the way around, everywhere I've been, that classy people'll not be no better."

"All the Johnsons were dry, quare-turned. You know they're good, honest people, but don't know enough to know that swearing lies is a sin."

"I wouldn't want a Harmon in my family, girl or boy. No, sir, they're bad on every corner."

Clearly, statements such as these suggest that an understanding of the class structure of Beech Creek was essential to an adequate understanding of many of the social relationships of Beech Creek people.[2]

According to Parsons, a social class consists of "the group of persons who are members of effective kinship units which, as units, are approximately equally valued."[3] In American society the kinship unit of the class structure is the conjugal family; this was also, in a somewhat more limited sense, the case in Beech Creek. But moreover, in Beech Creek it was found that all the conjugal families bonded together in a family group generally shared (that is, were assigned by their neighbors) the same class status. Hence, because of the organization and functioning of the family group, it is perhaps more valid to assert that the family group was the "effective kinship unit" of the Beech Creek class structure. In researching the phenomenon, however, the focus was on the conjugal family or family-household.

To determine which families were equally valued, the techniques used in the earlier works of Warner and his associates were, in general, followed.[4] Visiting patterns among families, for example, as well as marriage (whether these marriages were approved or disapproved) could be and were studied. But much of the final delineation was based upon the "verbal expressions of individuals," not only about their willingness to associate with others in marriage and social groups, but also about their more or less direct evaluations of each other.[5]

No two families could be ranked exactly equal.[6] However, it was evident from the evaluative remarks of many informants that some families were considered "top" families, others were ranked at the bottom, and still others belonged somewhere between the two extremes. Though these were not, it must be emphasized, sharply defined groups, it seemed as satisfactory (that is, useful) a division as any. Consequently, Beech Creek families were eventually grouped into three classes: high, intermediate, and low.

Of the seventy-nine family-households in the three neighborhoods, seventeen were designated as "high-class," twenty-five as "intermediate-class," twenty-five as "low-class," and twelve, for one reason or another were unclassifiable. The "unclassified" families, generally speaking, were either newcomers in the neighborhoods, or more or less temporary residents, or, because of their extreme social and geographic isolation, not well known by the investigator. Only if there was sufficient evidence to warrant a reliable composited evaluation were families included in the over-all ranking.

If these classes represented valid hierarchical groupings of families, it seemed reasonable to suppose that data on marriages and patterns of visiting would indicate, for instance, that members of each class tended to marry members of the same class and that a family's strongest visiting relationships were with families of the same class. This actually was the case.

It was found that there had been no marriages of high-class with low-class persons among the young adults (the "recent" marriages, that is) in Beech Creek.[7] Young adults from intermediate-class families, if they married outside their class, tended to marry downward; only a few marriages were with high-class persons. The intermediate-class, it appeared, was more closely bound to the low-class than to the high-class segment; high-class families manifested a pattern of aloofness. Complete visiting data for a period of one year obtained from one representative high-class family, thirteen intermediate-class families, and ten low-class families showed much the same kind of interactional pattern. The high-class family almost never visited with any low-class family. The low-class families rarely visited with any high-class family and only occasionally with any intermediate-class family. The intermediate-class families seldom visited with families outside their own class. These data then, crude though they were, helped to corroborate the impression that social interaction was channeled along class lines;[8] the validity of the class delineation was supported.

Furthermore, detailed analyses were made of various economic, educational, familial, and other relevant attributes of the three classes, and these findings also tended to substantiate the validity of the class delineation.[9] The educational attainment of young people in Beech Creek, for example, was markedly correlated with their families' social class position. Data were obtained on one hundred seventy-five of the younger generation of adults (eighteen years of age and older, who were neither heads of households nor principal homemakers). It was found that those in high-class families had completed on the average 9.8 grades of school work, compared with 6.5 grades for the intermediate-class and 4.6 for the low-class. Of the high-class groups, 93.4 percent had finished at least the eighth grade, compared with 38.0 percent of the intermediate-class and 8.6 percent of the low-class. Explanations of important differences such as these were inextricably interwoven with the style of life, attitudinal Gestalt, and sociocultural configuration characteristic of the various class groupings.

# ATTRIBUTES OF THE CLASSES[10]

### High-Class Families

High-class families generally were descendants of the original Beech Creek settlers. Either the husband or the wife in every one of these could trace his ancestry back through three generations of Beech Creekers. Such continuity of residence was of course linked with the fact that those ancestors had been rather large landowners who had settled on the best bottom land.

Families of this class were far more economically secure and successful on the whole than other Beech Creek families. They owned their houses and lands; their income and the value of their properties were higher, and they usually had better and larger houses, and more and better furniture, clothing, and equipment than other families. Furthermore, the houses and farm buildings of every high-class family were in good repair; their yards were well taken care of; their fences were mended. Women in these families spent a great deal of time scrubbing, cleaning, and washing. Spotlessness of floors and cleanliness of clothing—in this area of mud and many children—were important symbols of the housewife's industry and pride in her family.

High-class people were inclined toward "keeping busy all the time" and as a rule their daily routines—indeed their very lives—centered around the work to be done. They stressed the "economic virtues": industry, frugality, self-denial, steadfastness, prudence, honesty, and punctuality. And they clung to a strong belief that the practice of these virtues brought economic success and security. A good income, ownership of property, and economic well-being were considered to be prima-facie evidence of an individual's adherence to those virtues.

At the same time, high-class families were what Beech Creek people called "good livers." That is, they maintained a higher level of living relative to other families in the area. They ate better and had more balanced menus as their expenditures were greater; they spent much more for food per capita (and they also raised much more per capita themselves); they spent more for clothing and for such things as doctors' care, magazines and books, permanent waves, postage, stationery, and the like. Yet, they were conscious of the future and were capable of the self-denial of present desires.

Like the middle-class Americans which Davis and the Gardners described, the Beech Creek high-class considered it important to "improve one's self." The idea that a person "ought to amount to something" was constantly emphasized. As a result, they were much better educated than other people in these mountain neighborhoods. Almost all of their children had finished the eighth grade, some had gone on to high school, and a few had made it to and through a college or university.

In general the high-class families conformed much more closely to the mores of this mountain society than did the families of either of the other two classes. Indeed, they tended to be what Perry has called "moral athletes."[11] Drinking, dancing, gambling, card playing, and sexual promiscuity were strongly disapproved; moreover, according to the evidence available, high-class people for the most part actually adhered to these ideals and did not indulge in these "vices," or at least indulged to a lesser extent than persons from other classes. To be sure, most of the men had "drank some" during their younger, unmarried days. But it was obvious that among the younger married men those from high-class families had "settled-down" quickest and had given up drinking and other irresponsible conduct associated with the youth culture in the mountains. None of the high-class families had ever been accused of moonshining. Disturbance of the peace, theft, fighting, and shooting were almost unheard of as involving persons from these families.

Formal organizations and associations, as mentioned earlier, had little social significance in this mountain society. But, in what organizational activities there were, high-class people participated more than either intermediate- or low-class people. A greater proportion of them were church members and attended church meetings regularly. As a group, they were more concerned about the schools and more interested, for example, in who would be the teacher and in how the school facilities could be improved. In political affairs and neighborhood-benefiting projects they were more likely to be the leaders.

The high-class families, partly because of greater literacy gained through education, were less isolated from the "outside world" than other families in the neighborhoods. They kept in closer touch with kin who had migrated to Ohio and elsewhere. They generally received and read more magazines, newspapers, and books, and they listened more to the radio.

These families seemed to be among the first to accept many of the new ideas from the "outside." They followed somewhat more efficient farming practices and favored "modern conveniences" such as pumps and sinks in the kitchen, kerosene refrigerators, sewing machines, lawn mowers, sanitary privies, toilet paper, and so forth. They used wallpaper bought at the store rather than newspapers and magazines for papering their walls. Women in these families were inclined toward stylish clothing (rather than the old-fashioned, long dresses), permanent waves, and cosmetics. In short, compared with other Beech Creek families, high-class families were anxious to keep in step with the outside world; they wanted more things and were eager to enhance their material style of life; they were the pace-setters of modernization in this Appalachian mountain locality.

### Low-Class Families

Low-class families, on the other hand, were likely to have been relative newcomers in the area. Less than half of the low-class families represented the fourth generation of Beech Creekers, compared with two-thirds of the intermediate-class and all of the high-class families. In general, the ancestors of these families had been poorer, had owned less land, and had been less succcessful economically than the ancestors of families in the other two classes.

Families of this class were in a relatively insecure economic stratum; poverty and extreme material deprivation were prevalent. Only about half of the low-class families were landowners; what land they owned was poor and hilly. They had poorer houses, smaller farms, less and cheaper quality furniture, clothing, and equipment than other families, and savings were almost nonexistent. They were seldom able to raise enough meat to last the entire year, and they could not and did not raise nearly as much food of any kind per family or per capita as did high-class families. While high-class families spent much more per capita for food, it was clear that low-class families had to purchase a higher proportion of the total amount of food they consumed. It is not surprising then that low-class families spent very little on such things as doctors (they rarely sought out professional care when they were sick), or on newspapers, magazines, books, and radios, or on clothing and other personal frills.

These families, furthermore, did not take very good care of their property. In the Beech Creek basin neighborhood, for example, only one of the eleven houses in which low-class families lived could be considered by the investigator as being in "good" condition. Even a casual observer would have noticed the general difference between high-class and low-class families in their emphasis upon cleanliness. Bedding of the low-class families was apt to be filthy; cookstoves were more often than not grimy and unpolished; plates and silver were frequently greasy; dogs and cats invariably ran in and out and all through the houses; chickens used the porches; clothing was often dirty and in need of mending.

Low-class people seemed to care little for the "economic virtues" which were held in such high esteem by the high-class. The latter often said of low-class people, "They're lazy, loafing folks that just won't work"; "They lay around on the riverbank fishing while everybody else hoes corn," and "They don't work unless they have to." Many such statements of course were gross exaggerations; indeed several low-class families were recognized by their neighbors as being notably industrious. But in general, low-class people were less industrious, less thrifty, and less steadfast in their resolve to acquire the amenities of life than their more economically secure neighbors, the high-class people. They preferred, it seemed, to be "around the house doing nothing."

Ostensibly, they were also happier and more contented with their lot than other families; they were certainly more relaxed and less restrained. They appeared to live more for the present and less for the future; a pattern of indifference prevailed. It was often said that "they don't know where the next meal is coming from and they don't care"; this assertion by the high-class people carried an element of truth.

In contrast with the "moral athleticism" of the high-class was the "moral laxity" of the low-class people. Sexual deviation was not uncommon; illegitimate children were not unusual. Several of the adult men in these families were notoriously heavy drinkers, and, according to neighborhood gossip, a few of their women also imbibed. The biggest moonshiner in the area, and indeed the only one about whom there was absolutely clear-cut evidence (acquired by the researcher) was the head of a low-class family on Beech Creek. Most of the "shooting and scraping" in the neighborhoods involved low-class people. It is fair to conclude that, in general, low-class families were less conforming to the mores of this mountain society than high- or intermediate-class families.

Except for a few families on Flat Rock Branch who were very active in the neighborhood Holiness Church, low-class people were not inclined to participate in church organizations. Moreover, they had little interest in school affairs and were not likely to encourage their children in school work or compel them to attend regularly.

On the whole, the low-class families were the "most backward" in the area—the least-educated, the least modern, and in many ways the most "conservative" and "traditionalistic." They had few contacts with, and little knowledge about, the main currents of life in American society. Some of the adults were functional illiterates; most had great difficulty with reading and rarely saw a newspaper or magazine. They maintained only tenuous ties with kinsfolk and friends who had migrated elsewhere; letter-writing was for them an enormous chore. As a result, this class, by circumstances and "choice," was not openly exposed to new ideas and socially-disturbing influences from the "outside"; their old-fashioned, self-sufficient, pioneer style of living was sheltered from, and sheltered them from, the forces of modernization.

**Intermediate-Class Families**

The sociocultural configuration characteristic of the intermediate-class way of life in this mountain locality was not so much a distinct, unique pattern as a combination of the high- and low-class patterns. Some of the intermediate-class families were descendants of the original Beech Creek settlers; many were relative newcomers. For the most part, their ancestors had not been large landowners, and for that reason residential mobility over the years—even intra-locality movement—had been quite common.

Sixteen of the twenty-five intermediate-class families owned their houses and land—a higher proportion than among the low-class but a lower proportion than among the high-class. Economically, in terms of size of farm, property value, income, and expenditures, they ranked on the average between the upper and lower classes.

Most of these families took very good care of and great pride in their property, though houses were rarely painted. Few were "free spenders," as was often the case among low-class families. High standards of cleanliness were maintained. Moreover, the economic virtues, such an integral part of the belief system in these mountain neighborhoods, were regarded as self-evident truths; industry, honesty, thrift, and concern for the future were emphasized. In these respects, intermediate-class families were somewhat more in accord with the high-class than with the low-class configuration of attributes.

On the other hand, standards of "morality" were neither as strictly adhered to nor moral reputations as stringently guarded by the intermediate-class as among the high-class.[12] For example, a number of intermediate-class adults were reputed to be "drinkers"; two of the families were said to have been involved in moonshining operations; one family was said to "bootleg" liquor. Though cases of adultery were rare—intermediate-class families were notably stable—incidents of sexual promiscuity among older adolescents were not unusual. In general, it seemed that intermediate-class people were less conformant to, and less likely to sanction conformance to, the social mores of this mountain society than high-class people; but neither were they as inclined to ignore or abandon those mores as were low-class people.

Finally, intermediate-class families were not likely to encourage their children in the pursuit of schooling beyond the eighth grade. Of course they could perhaps have ill-afforded to do so, for going to high school often meant that a youngster had to "board-out" during the week in Schooltown, and such an arrangement often was beyond an intermediate-family's financial means. Hence, with respect to the pattern of school attainment, intermediate-class families tended to be more like the low- than the high-class. Coupled with a general apathy toward self-education, this attribute left its stamp upon many other aspects of life characteristic of intermediate-class families in Beech Creek.

# ACHIEVEMENT AND CLASS STANDING

Certainly the two fundamental elements in the Beech Creek system of stratification—as, broadly speaking, in American society at large—were achievement within the occupational sector and the emphasis on ties of kinship, especially those developed within the conjugal family. But in both respects there existed in Beech Creek important differences in the degree of emphasis, particularly when compared with modern, urban America. In this section, by way of summary, we shall discuss the nature of the "achievement" factor in the Beech Creek case, and we shall focus in the next section specifically on the kinship factor in social mobility.

High-class people in Beech Creek regarded the class position of individuals and families as the deserved result of their own accomplishments, that is, as achieved rather than ascribed status.[13] Low-class people, on the other hand, accounted for the position of high-class people as an accident of birth (ascribed status), and they contended, implicitly of course, that it was wrong to rank a person on the basis of who he was; he should be judged rather by what he had accomplished. Their own low status—reflected by the low esteem accorded to them in the neighborhood—was, they felt, due to chance, bad luck, and especially to not having had an equal opportunity. Both interpretations of this social reality had some bases in fact.

It was in general true that in the Beech Creek locale economic achievement was a significant criterion of class status. But most Beech Creekers were engaged in more or less subsistence-type farming. To be sure, some were owners and some were tenants, some had large farms and some had small farms, and some were better farmers than others. Yet, there was not a great "spread" between the more successful and less successful farmers; there were, for instance, no commercial, or even semi-commercial farm operations in the area. Indeed Beech Creekers, as a whole, would have been relegated to the lower end of the social class hierarchy in American society, but not at *the* lowest end for the obvious reasons that all of them were of "old American stock," most of them were landowners, and some of them had gone beyond the eighth grade in school.

Nevertheless, in spite of the fact that there was no recognizable hierarchical structuring of occupations which was differentiated from the family structure in this mountain neighborhood-society, differences in the level of economic achievement attained *within* the dominant enterprise did exist. Some of the outward, or symbolic manifestations were mentioned earlier, for example, size and condition of house and lands, quality of furniture and clothing, and the like. These things—the material amenities of life and the means to acquire them—were valued highly by Beech Creekers. Those who possessed them were considered to have achieved culturally defined goals through economic enterprise, and they became, thereby, the objects of social deference and respect; that is, they gained status in the eyes of their neighbors. The groundwork for a man's "economic achievements" may have been laid by an ancestor, who happened to have been an original settler; or perhaps by a man's forebearers: but the important thing to note is that these economic achievements were regarded as valid achievements of *the family*—and the man and his household became the recipients, or custodians as it were, of that social heritage.

Economic achievement per se, and as reflected by a family's material style of life, though a major determinant in the sense indicated above, was of course not the sole criterion of social class status in the Beech Creek neighborhoods. Achievements of non-economic kinds also mattered. One might mention educational attainment here, except that this was far less meaningful than other criteria within the social context of Beech Creek and much more associated with "economic achievements." The degree to which individuals and families observed the religious and moral precepts of their culture, however, was of considerable importance as a basis for stratification.[14] Indeed a man, through "immoral" behavior or "brushes with the law," could squander his social heritage—that is, the bases for status inherited from his ancestors—and thereby bequeath to his children a social legacy of ill repute. In other words, the extent to which individuals within a family, and the family as a collectivity, adhered to the moral standards of this mountain neighborhood-society determined in large measure the level of social respect accorded that family by its neighbors; economic achievement alone was not sufficient to assure a family's position of prestige among other Beech Creek families.

# FAMILY GROUPS AND CLASS MOBILITY[15]

In Beech Creek, as in American society at large, an individual at birth was, and is, ascribed his initial class status from his family of orientation. Thereafter, however, that accident of birth assumed far greater social consequence vis-a-vis future social mobility within the Beech Creek context. Indeed, the class structure of Beech Creek had certain caste-like qualities; compared with urban American society, there was an institutionalized tendency for an adult's class status in Beech Creek to have been an ascribed designation rather than an achieved "reward." Many sociocultural factors must be taken into account in explaining this phenomenon: subsistence agriculture was the dominant enterprise in this mountain locality; the social organization of Beech Creek was characterized by "stability of culture and fixity of residence"[16] to a far greater extent than in American society; a much higher proportion of the socialization of Beech Creek children took place within the family.

Still another and more pertinent factor in explaining the tendency toward ascription is that the class structure of Beech Creek had its setting in a familistic society in which the family group performed almost all of the vitally important functions for the society and for the individual. The class system of this society had therefore developed in such a way as to protect the stability and solidarity of the wider kinship group. Great class mobility among members of a family group tended to be disruptive; conversely the prevention of too great mobility tended to preserve the solidarity of the group.

Beech Creekers, as we noted earlier, were inclined to lump the members of a wider kinship group into one class and to rank equally the members of such a group even though some conjugal families within that group might, on the basis of their own achievements alone, seem to have deserved higher or lower ranking. Contributing to this tendency was the fact that the history and background of all the families were well known in the community. It was in many respects true that the sins of the fathers were visited upon their sons; thus some Beech Creek people inherited the stigma of their parents' past. One man, for example, was hampered in his attempt to rise in the class structure by the fact that his father was an illegitimate child. Some of the low-class families had made considerable achievements, in wealth for example, and were held in some esteem by the upper classes; they nevertheless were still considered low-class people by the latter. High-class people strongly disapproved of intermarriage with these people simply because they belonged to certain families. On the other hand some high-class members had seriously deviated from approved patterns, but family ties had been so strong that the class status of the deviant persons apparently had not been lowered in the eyes of the high-class, though their prestige had decreased.

There were a number of patterns that tended to restrict the rise of one member of a kinship group above the other members and which tended therefore to preserve the solidarity of this wider group. For example, there was much criticism of a low-class person who began to establish contacts with people of the upper classes and who was therefore inclined to neglect relationships with his own kin. The patterns of loyalty and friendship expected among the kin group were in themselves brakes on the mobility of people "on the rise"; for, in addition to the control by criticism if they failed to meet such expectations, upwardly mobile people themselves had feelings of loyalty and affection toward their own kin and these were difficult to give up.

There was much jealousy of people who were succeeding to such an extent that they were exceeding their kin; this was especially noticeable, perhaps because it was most patently observable, in the economic sphere. For instance, in discussing why one of the local ministers was not paid, the minister's brother commented that the people he preached to were mainly his own kin, that he had a good farm and made as much from it as any of the others, and that his brothers and sisters didn't see why they should put his children through school by draining their own resources to pay him a salary. Another aspect of this tendency to keep an individual from rising above his kin was the general practice of awarding jobs with money incomes (teaching, political and road jobs, and so forth) on the basis of need, rather than on the basis of competence in the particular position. One schoolteacher remarked that he did not dare fix his house the way he and his wife really wanted it—even though they could afford to do so—because he knew the people in the neighborhood would be jealous of him, would think he was getting too far ahead of them, and would as a result vote not to re-hire him.[17]

Several further points should be made explicit. Family groups were continually changing.[18] This meant that while families within a family group tended to have similar class status, the individual conjugal families may have been developing, or "maturing," quite differently so far as economic ambitions and style of life were concerned. In such cases, some interpersonal strains were inevitable. Moreover, as noted earlier, a conjugal family might have become part of a family group centering around either the husband's or the wife's family. Consequently siblings were, in a number of cases, in different family groups. And again these different family groups sometimes developed in such ways that the families of siblings were in different classes or, as was more common, were differently evaluated and esteemed within the same class. Often the development of status differences was so gradual that it produced relatively little strain among the siblings' families. In other instances siblings' families belonged to different class groups because one sibling had married into a family whose status was so low that his brothers and sisters more or less excluded him from their family group. In cases of this sort the excluded sibling's family of procreation probably became part of the family group consisting largely of his spouse's siblings. Even in such cases as these the development was usually not rapid.

Membership of family members in different classes seemed to weaken kinship solidarity. As a result, when people from different classes married, as a conjugal family they tended to develop closer relationships with the kin of one spouse and to weaken relationships with the kin of the other, and thus to assume the class status of one spouse or the other. Many factors entered into the determination of whether it would be with the side which had the higher or the lower status.

Being in different family groups often meant that siblings lived considerable distances apart so that it was "natural" not to have everyday contacts with each other. There is little doubt that this territorial separateness and the resultant lessening of daily contacts helped to prevent conflicts which might easily have arisen because of the different class positions of the siblings' families.

The very vagueness of the class lines served a useful function in preserving the positive relationships formed among siblings (and indeed among other kinsfolk) who eventually occupied different class statuses. Kin with different class positions may not have maintained intimate social relationships, but occasionally they did come together, and thus reaffirmed the presence of what might be called "latent" kin relationships. Crises such as sickness or death brought forth affirmations of solidarity among kin who occupied different levels in the class structure.[19] And, as we shall make clear later, kin relationships played a key role in the process of migration from this isolated mountain locality.

# CULTURAL THEMES:
## The Value-Orientations of Beech Creekers

We shall now suggest some of the more important cultural themes that characterized the Beech Creek way of life. These foci of social organization, which have been abstracted from the concrete, overt patterns of behavior of Beech Creekers,[20] represent the legitimating foundation for the form of social stratification in the mountain neighborhoods. Moreover, because they likewise indicate the value standards and perspectives employed by Beech Creekers in making decisions and in managing their normal, day-to-day affairs, our discussion of them provides a useful summary of the sociocultural origins of the migrants.[21]

### Familism: A Dominant Orientation

Beech Creek was a "familistic society" in the sense that all social relationships and institutions were "permeated by and stamped with the characteristics of the family";[22] a traditionalistic, family-centered social organization was the prevailing pattern. Kinship units tended to be culturally insular groups, kin relationships the most meaningful interactional bonds, and familistic norms the most important mechanisms of social control. In short, in the sociocultural system of Beech Creek, familism appeared to be a dominant theme.

The values of family life, for example, were constantly emphasized and reinforced by the social norms. Almost every Beech Creeker eventually married, usually at a very early age, and much of the socialization of children was directed toward that end. Indeed, this mountain neighborhood-society was so exclusively organized on the pattern of family life that it was very difficult for single persons to exist socially by themselves, and such an existence was looked on as undesirable or, as Beech Creekers would say, "quare."

Great emphasis was also put upon the maintenance of family unity and stability, and numerous social patterns served to buttress the sanctity of the conjugal family and the inviolability of the family group. Divorce was so strongly disapproved and resulted in such harsh criticism that there had been remarkably few divorces. There was widespread recognition of the prime importance to the individual of a happy family life and spontaneous expressions of solidarity among its members, and likewise a recognition that "family trouble" was the worst kind of trouble.

In many ways, the family was the main functional entity or unit of control in Beech Creek. Beech Creekers were quick to hold a person's family responsible for his actions; his actions reflected honor or shame, as the case might be, on all members of his immediate family and, generally too, on members of his extended family. On the other hand, individuals felt a deep sense of responsibility toward their family and kinsfolk so that, as all Beech Creekers were acutely aware, "if you step on one's toes, you step on everybody's."

The family, moreover, had almost exclusive control—a cultural mandate, so to speak—over the socialization of its young; hence, the family held "effective" reign over the mechanisms of social mobility. For example, an individual's initial class status, as we have noted, was determined by the class status of his family of orientation. Because so much of his training and development were exclusive functions of his family, the possibility of changing the course of his life, and hence changing the eventual class status he would enjoy, was rather limited. Nearly every family had a long moral and economic history well-known to everybody else, and its members were expected to possess certain attributes and to behave in certain traditional ways; norms peculiar to a family, then, were perpetuated via the manner of a "self-fulfilling prophecy," and the individual personality, as a consequence, became inextricably bound with the cultural vagaries of his family.

Earlier it was pointed out that the Beech Creek family was the unit of both production and consumption and that it was impossible, except perhaps analytically, to separate the economic roles of family members from their familial roles.

Little has been said, however, about the political life of the Beech Creek people; here too it was virtually impossible to distinguish these roles from familial roles. To say that one had always voted the "straight

Republican ticket" and that one was a Republican because his father and grandfather were Republicans did not label a Beech Creeker as a die-hard reactionary who was unable and unwilling to think for himself. Rather, such a person was approved and applauded. One bragged about one's consistency and integrity in upholding the principles of one's ancestors. Members of Republican families could understand why members of Democratic families voted the straight Democratic ticket, even though they almost certainly did make caustic remarks about them. They "had been raised that way," and it was right that a person in a Democratic family be a Democrat. A person who shifted from one party to another was looked on as fickle and untrue to his "raising." Similarly, family connections often influenced local and even county-wide elections, and during a campaign candidates took great pains to make their genealogies known and to cultivate their kin.[23] It was often said that the candidate with the most numerous kinship relations won, and there was some truth in this assertion. Relationships between elected officials and the people were expected to be personalistic and friendly, like relationships within the family, rather than impersonal, objective, and specific to an issue. Favoritism of a governmental employee in an official capacity toward his own family at the expense of others was understood as a loyalty more or less to be expected and, hence, tolerated as a fact of life in the mountains.

The religious sector of life in Beech Creek was also "marked to a greater or lesser degree by the cult of the family and its ancestors." Like a family, a church group was apt to keep records only in the "heads" of its members; there was little set routine to a church service, and formal organization was at a minimum. Members of church groups, in fact, often referred to each other as "Brother" and "Sister"; and the "brotherhood of man" was a favorite phrase used in conversation. The same sort of informal, personal relationships that one finds in the family were carried over into church meetings. Actually, of course, many of the church members were kinsfolk; so it was both literally and figuratively true that church gatherings were "one big family."

There was, then, in the Beech Creek neighborhood-society a tendency for all social relationships to take on some of the characteristics of family relationships. Interaction between merchant and customer, for example, was not patterned merely as an impersonal business deal. A visit to a local store, or to the post office, was a real social event (not at all specific to the manifest goal) involving much time, exchange of information about each other's families, and discussion of neighborhood events; indeed the journey to and from the store itself could best be described as a series of neighborhood visits.

Relationships among neighbors, especially if they had lived near each other for a long time, also tended to take on familial tones. The friendship ties of neighboring children, for example, often assumed the quality of sibling relationships; in some instances, a boy and a girl might say "they wouldn't think of marrying each other" because they felt too "close." Another indication of the familistic-type informality in neighborhood relationships was the custom of addressing everybody by his first name, old and young alike. To be called "Mr." or "Mrs." was a clear sign that one was considered an outsider. As a mark of respect for age, older people were often called "Aunt" or "Uncle," even though of no kin whatever to the addresser. Neighboring of course was largely a family affair, and the informal relationships, the mutual aid and resulting network of reciprocal obligations, and the leadership structure which evolved within the locality were subjected to the careful scrutiny, biased appraisal, and constant vigilance of the family group.

This mountain society so emphasized the informal, intimate relationships of the familial type that any kind of secondary, formal organization—the proliferation of which is such a characteristic trait of urban American society—was virtually non-existent. The few secondary organizations that did exist, such as the church, invariably lent support towards maintaining the solidarity of the kinship structure and preserving a belief in the sanctity of the family. Special interest groups did not fit into the familistic type social organization of Beech Creek.

In short, the individual Beech Creeker experienced very little active engagement with the greater society other than through his family group. As an integral part of a close-knit family network, he had a place in the scheme of things—a haven of safety. Yet, viewed from another perspective it might be said that the individual was caught in a web of familism. To the extent that his family group was isolated from the mainstream of American society and from the changing thoughtways of the modern world, the individual, too, was cut off from the outside and restricted in his world view.

**Puritanism: A Frontier Faith**

From its earliest settlement Beech Creek had been a stronghold of Protestant fundamentalism. The first settlers were probably Baptists. Around 1890, the Christian Church (a denomination which had split from the Presbyterian Church) was established in the area, and by 1942 most Beech Creekers who were church members belonged to the Christian Church. A Holiness group was active in the Flat Rock neighborhood, but only a few low-class families were involved, and not only did they not regard themselves as a separate denomination from the Christian Church, but they actually maintained affiliations with it.[24]

That the Christian Church was so predominant in Beech Creek was rather unusual, for the eastern Kentucky mountain region as a whole was primarily aligned with the Baptists. However, the two sects were similar in many respects even though there were distinguishing differences in doctrine and ritual considered important by their adherents. Both were derived from the same religious tradition; both shared the same basic philosophical and theological beliefs, and in both the system of ideals called "puritanism" was central.

While the puritanism of Beech Creek people was not exactly the same as the puritanism of the early Calvinists, of the early settlers in New England, or of Jonathan Edwards and his followers in the American colonies, it was nevertheless a form of puritanism,[25] though a modified, diluted, and softened variety. This system of beliefs was woven into one of the fundamental value complexes in the Beech Creek culture.

Even casual observation of Beech Creek people revealed their tendency to interpret events in moral terms and to see everything as "right" or "wrong." The familiar puritan dualism with its distinct and precise "blacks" and "whites" and without tolerance for any intermediate "gray" areas of behavior was an obvious characteristic of the Beech Creeker's mode of thought. Indeed there was such a preoccupation with the threat of evil that an observer sometimes felt that "good" was a neglected, perhaps even an embarrassing, concept in the culture.

All aspects of Beech Creek life were marked by an absence of elaborate ritual and trappings; what people in other societies, such as urban America, might look upon as aesthetically pleasing would have met with active disapproval in Beech Creek. The lack of interest in the cultural arts, like the fear of ritual and ceremony, was based in part on the puritanic belief that the pursuit of lesser "goods" would in some way negate the attainment of higher "goods"; as a consequence, for example, even the architectural beautification of a homestead was disparaged.

Among the more obvious evidences of puritanism were the attitudes of Beech Creekers toward the so-called "physical appetites" and their frequent reference to the dangers of "things of the flesh." Of course they never explicitly verbalized the connection between the basic theological tenets of puritanism and their own negative attitudes or feelings of guilt about physical pleasures. But their patterns of behavior suggested an implicit acceptance of the puritan creed which so stressed the supreme good, namely, personal salvation, that it tended to obscure the value of lesser ends. Physical pleasures, for example, were feared because they jeopardized one's attainment of ultimate personal salvation.

To overcome evil and achieve spiritual strength "the puritan engaged in exercises and went into training, much as a youth now sets out to excel in sports."[26] He became, in a word, a moral athlete. As Perry points out, the particular indulgences which the puritan of the seventeenth century battled against were those of his time—"drunkenness, sexual looseness and perversion, the brutality of sport, licentiousness at carnivals and feasts, dancing, cardplaying"—and were therefore "in some degree a historical accident."[27] But these were still the evils attacked by Beech Creek preachers in 1942, and a large proportion of their sermons dealt with these very evils. The concern with evil at the expense of good, and the consequent fear of satisfying the "physical appetites," gave Beech Creek, as well as other puritan societies, a somewhat cold, bleak, and austere character. Beech Creek people, like other puritans, "neglected the fact that lower goods will often pave the way to higher; and that the most effective method of dealing with lower evils is not to aggravate them by a sense of guilt, but to meet them on their own ground."[28] From the point of view of an outsider, for instance, there appeared to be an entirely unnecessary fear of showing familial affection through kissing, caressing, and so on, and an equally unnecessary feeling of guilt and shame in connection with sexual behavior which led, it seemed, not so much to a reduction of sexual desire to its proper place in the whole pattern of life as to a morbid preoccupation with it.

The omnipresent dissatisfaction of Beech Creek people with their present lot, their inability to be satisfied with the present situation, in a word their emphasis upon "becoming" rather than upon "being," was also a manifestation of their puritan philosophy. An urge toward self-improvement, notably in the moral sector of life, and a great desire "to amount to something," particularly in economic terms, were at least partially to blame for the fact that Beech Creekers, especially those from high- and intermediate-class families, rarely exhibited outward signs of happiness—a *joie de vivre*—even when it seemed they had the materials of happiness at hand.

Mention was made earlier of the value placed by Beech Creekers upon the "economic virtues." Like puritans in general, they tended to believe that when "an individual possesses the qualities of austerity, reliability, energy, industry, self-control, marital fidelity, frugality, sobriety, thrift, self-reliance, and foresight, the effect is wealth."[29] Wealth, then, tended to be regarded as evidence of having lived a virtuous life. The general sentiment (often expressed in rather dogmatic statements) that in the economic world "one got about what he deserved" was one of the consequences of this high valuation put upon the economic virtues, and so, too, were the deprecating attitudes of

Beech Creekers toward some of their own extremely poverty-stricken neighbors; on the other hand, "the self-made man" was viewed with great admiration.

Beech Creekers accepted the capitalistic system "as God's plan for administering the affairs of this world in the interest of human society as a whole."[30] The general opposition, especially of high- and intermediate-class families, to the Work Projects Administration (WPA) and relief programs of the federal government during the depression years stemmed in part from the fact that the relatively high wages offered participants in these programs made it difficult for upper-class farmers to hire cheap local labor and that in some cases these programs gave lower-class people more cash income than their higher-class neighbors who were ineligible for WPA jobs. But this opposition was also buttressed by the strong prevailing belief, which was partly derived from puritanism, that every man should be economically independent and that poverty was due to individual failings. (It might be added that, in the context of Beech Creek's self-sufficient, subsistence-farming economy, where an individual had somewhat greater control over the means of production than did a factory worker in urban America, such an interpretation was perhaps justifiable on rational grounds.) The tenacity of the Beech Creeker's conservatism in politics and in economic matters was certainly fostered by this basic orientation.

Our tendency to dwell upon the negative character of Beech Creek's puritanistic code of conduct—its concern with evil, its slighting of the physical appetites, and its chronic discontent with things of the here and now—should not obscure the fact that there were many positive guidelines for behavior emanating from this puritanistic code. For instance, the belief system not only legitimized but sanctioned an individual's drive toward economic success, his concern for the future and repression of immediate desires, his hard work, and his conviction that he had within himself the power to "become."

### Individualism: An Unsettling, But Driving Strength

Individualism, an obvious characteristic of the Appalachian mountaineer, appeared in the Beech Creek case to have been derived from the basic tenets of a puritan creed coupled with a firm belief in the ultimate "rightness" of democracy. Beech Creekers regarded every individual as "a child of God." As a child of God, every individual had the right and responsibility of reaching his own conclusions about matters affecting the course of his life. Moreover, the individual was wholly and solely responsible for his relationship with God, and while this dignified and exalted a person's worth, it also put a tremendous pressure upon him, often leading to a great deal of insecurity and uncertainty. The Beech Creekers' God was stern, just, and all-powerful, the God of the Old Testament rather than the loving, gentle God of the New Testament. Furthermore, by its emphasis upon the right of each individual to interpret God's word and thereafter to act with deference to it, the puritan creed with its Calvinistic overtones furnished the bases for innumerable quarrels, bickerings, family feuds, and neighborhood divisions resulting from different interpretations of the Bible. This phenomenon of sanctified individualism within a familistic subculture, and its divisive effect, functioned to an even greater extent than in the Beech Creek neighborhoods to impede social and economic progress in the Appalachian mountain region as a whole, where the lack of an educated leadership and the resultant isolation from the well-springs of progress left the human and natural resources of the region open and exposed to the ignorant arrogance of men who were relatively untouched by the restraints of reason.[31]

The individualism of Beech Creekers was also firmly rooted in that system of ideals called "democracy" which, according to Perry, "in the most fundamental sense, affirms that the 'good life' consists in the enjoyment or successful pursuit by John Doe and Richard Roe of what they themselves consciously desire and will."[32] An important aspect of the democratic creed, as espoused by Beech Creekers, is its emphasis upon equality, particularly equality of opportunity. The land tenure pattern, for example, which stressed the right of every child, regardless of sex and age, to an equal part in his parents' estate, was derived from this democratic code. On the other hand, it should be noted, the Beech Creek culture tended to resist the elevation of women to a position of political equality; there was still some strong sentiment in 1942, especially among older people, that women should not vote. Obviously, a cultural emphasis upon individualism within a familistic social organization would set the stage for role conflicts in those areas of social life most exposed to disturbing influences introduced from the outside.

In the social organization of Beech Creek this cardinal tenet of individualism, namely a belief in equality, was often obscured by behavior (e.g., class deference) which seemed to indicate that inequality was accepted not only as a fact of life but also ideologically. However, in view of the pattern of evidence, both covert and overt, that conclusion can be quickly rejected as false. For example, the hesitation of Beech Creek people to say flatly and openly that there was a social hierarchy of families in the neighborhoods, and that some people were intrinsically better—and some worse—than others, was one indication of a discontinuity between social fact and valued ideal. It did not seem "right" or "moral" to Beech Creekers to admit the existence of such inequality. And this was not simply "lip service" to an ideal; Beech Creekers manifested feelings of guilt in making evaluations of that kind, even when the purpose of inquiry was disguised. Moreover, in normal day-to-day social intercourse within the neighborhoods there was, built up around "class differences" and called to the fore in conversation about such matters, an array of "defensive beliefs," or rationalizations, which were in many ways like those found by Dollard surrounding the caste system of the Deep South.[33] These defensive beliefs served much the same purpose in Beech Creek as in Dollard's Southern Town: they legitimized actions that were unethical, or not in accord with the valued means of the society by making such actions appear to be expedient and in line with its valued ends or culturally defined goals. As a result, to use a familiar example, high-class families in Beech Creek might have said, as Southern whites said of Negroes, that low-class families deserved the status which they occupied since "the present-day social situation represents the outcome of an honest competition with a fair start all around."[34] (We, of course, have heard analogous "defensive beliefs" applied to the contemporary tragedy of Appalachia as a whole by spokesmen for more affluent regions of America.)

People who were "uppity" and "overbearing" were strongly criticized. Open assertion of superiority brought a response of righteous indignation from the offended, which was looked on by many if not most Beech Creek people as a reasonable and proper reaction. The Carters, for instance, were so embittered by the Barnetts' openly declaring their feeling of superiority in opposing the marriage of their daughter to a Carter that physical violence broke out between the two families; neighborhood opinion legitimized the Carters' action.

Another important dimension of the value complex of individualism was the emphasis upon individual achievement. On the one hand, as mentioned earlier, there was great admiration for people who had "amounted to something" through their own efforts and, on the other hand, a tendency to belittle people who had inherited "everything they had." Though this distinction did not affect, to any marked degree, the class status of an individual and his family within the familistic social organization of the neighborhoods, nevertheless the self-made man was held in high esteem—a model to be emulated by Beech Creek children. No doubt such an emphasis contributed to the frustration of those who failed to build upon their inheritance, over and above the economic position enjoyed by their parents, but it was also the source of a driving strength, a spirit of optimism, and a faith in the ultimate "rightness" of democracy.

### Traditionalism: A Pattern of Patterns

In the preceding pages we have briefly discussed some of the more basic orientations or dominant configurations in the social organization of Beech Creek. We chose to describe the Beech Creek pattern of culture, as it was, in terms of three major, summarizing themes: familism, which distinguished the patterns of social interaction in these neighborhoods; puritanism, which represented the basis of the belief system; and individualism, which characterized the personality structure of Beech Creekers. These cultural themes of course were not mutually exclusive but, rather, they were interwoven and, in many ways and at many points, they reinforced each other; we have noted, for example, some of the more obvious linkages between puritanism and individualism.[35] To be sure, other important themes in the Beech Creek culture could have been stressed—the personalism of social relationships, or the particularistic orientations of Beech Creekers in their dealings with others, or the localism and provincialism that characterized the Beech Creekers' world view. Our brief treatment of this complexity of cultural values and beliefs nevertheless should suggest the cultural foundations of Beech Creek's social organization and the basic normative orientations of Beech Creekers. That Beech Creek was a traditionalistic sociocultural system, is clear.

Traditionalism lay back of every aspect of the Beech Creek culture, sanctioning and accounting for the behavior, attitudes, and valued ideals of the Beech Creek people. Most of the beliefs and practices in these mountain neighborhoods were handed down relatively intact from one generation to another, and because they were the beliefs and practices of one's father and forefathers, they were deemed right; they were prescriptions to be followed. Traditionalism, in short, served as the standard of standards, the legitimating principle integrating the various elements of culture and social structure and thereby tending to protect the integrity of this system, maintaining stability, and warding off the system-disturbing influences of modernization.

# BREAKDOWN OF ISOLATION

It is surprising how few "big events" can be discovered in the history of the Beech Creek area from the time of its settlement to the time of the Civil War. Life was changing, to be sure, as it always does, but the changes were minute, all but imperceptible, and nothing so striking as the coming of a railroad or the founding of a school passed down to the people of today from those earlier times. Instead about all that was remembered is that Daniel Johnson had two sons, and his two sons had many children, and they built log cabins up this branch and up that branch, and Joshua and Dick Johnson didn't get along, and "Old Dick" Johnson was a fine fiddler and "mighty wicked to boot," and Amos Andrews' father was a Revolutionary War veteran and so mean that he was said to have cut off his wife's breasts. In other words the early history of the area that lived in the minds of Beech Creek people was a web of personalized, localized events, little concerned with the events of the outside world.

Beginning with the Civil War, the geographic and cultural isolation began to break down at an accelerated rate. Like many other eastern Kentuckians, Beech Creekers were aligned on the Union side. No battles were fought in the area, or even nearby, but some old people could remember small groups of both Union and Confederate soldiers marching up and down these valleys, stealing some horses, carrying off food, and burning a few houses. At least one prominent citizen, Amos Andrews, was killed by the Confederates. The Beech Creek men who went off to Union armies were more than likely never far away from home, but they probably had been stationed outside of the mountain region and undoubtedly came home with vivid stories of the "outside" and with some new ideas of their own. Indeed, the part that Beech Creek families played in the Civil War still has significant influence upon the lives of Beech Creekers today. For years pensions granted to Civil War veterans and their dependents were the main cash income for several Beech Creek families, and two people, even in 1942, still received pensions as dependents of ex-Civil War soldiers. Another more obvious and sociologically significant consequence of the Civil War experience has been the unshaken allegiance of almost all Beech Creek families to the Republican Party.

Lumbering, which began in earnest in eastern Kentucky only after the Civil War, touched Beech Creek in the 1880's. Most of the land in the area was in the hands of local farmers, but at that time land companies were busily patenting land in all parts of Appalachia, and some Beech Creek land came into their possession. "Blanket patents" were issued to these companies which gave them ownership of all land not already patented and surveyed, and in the Beech Creek locale, as in so many other mountain localities, some people who had been living in the area for years suddenly discovered that they did not legally own as much land as they had supposed, for their surveys did not cover portions of their holdings. Much hard feeling was generated over these boundary disputes, and an attitude of suspicion toward outsiders' intentions was developed which lingers even today.

Of course some Beech Creek families cut their own timber, floated it out, and then gathered the logs into rafts for the long trip down the river. But most of the private timber holdings in the area seem to have been cut by contractors who bought a "stand"—sometimes acquiring scores of magnificent trees at twenty-five cents each—and supervised its cutting and removal by locally-hired labor, which may have included the original owner! Outsiders also came into the area from the late 1880's to 1920 to work in the log-woods or in a local sawmill, and while most of these people moved on after the timber was out, a few remained, marrying into Beech Creek families.

Several families secured an important part of their income from selling timber and working in the forest during this period, but none became rich or even moderately well-to-do. Indeed, lumbering left Beech Creekers worse off economically than they had been before, for their great natural resource, the fine hardwood forests, had been stripped from the hills, and the process of erosion, already far along, was hastened. Moreover, with the coming of lumbering and the consequent influx of cash money, the old style of self-sufficiency, already affected by outside influences and internal circumstances, was also subjected to a more intensified process of erosion as Beech Creekers became more and more dependent upon store-bought goods. Soon the old crafts of spinning, weaving, and shoemaking were forgotten; the growing of flax was no longer necessary; and the raising of sheep became less important (partly also because of county laws requiring that stock be kept fenced). When store-bought flour and sugar became popular and cash was available to purchase such commodities, wheat became an almost unknown crop, and the hard job of making sugar was gladly dropped from the homemakers' agenda of chores.

As Beech Creekers absorbed new desires, learned new wants, and began to sense a growing need for more money, ways to get money had to be found. When available, "public work" (that is, off-farm work which brought in cash money, whether it was from private companies or public agencies) attracted more and more men from work on the farm. An irreversible process, indeed a snow-balling effect, had been set in motion with the development of a lumbering industry in the region and the concomitant introduction of a money economy, the stimulation of demand for goods and services, and the growth of towns, trading centers, and local stores. But the coal mining developments of eastern Kentucky did not affect the area around Beech Creek, and few Beech

Creekers ever went off to work in the mines in other parts of the mountain region.

Since World War I, the outside world has been pushing closer toward the Beech Creek locality and deeper into the very foundations of Beech Creek's traditionalistic social organization. During and following the war years, when a demand for unskilled labor existed in the industrial centers to the north, many Beech Creekers—often entire families—moved out of the region; they became the forerunners of a great wave of out-migration, as we shall make clear in subsequent chapters. They also, through continuing communication with kinsfolk in Beech Creek, became effective advocates of change within the neighborhoods, jolting Beech Creekers in a most convincing manner into an awareness of the main currents of change in American society.

We have mentioned the great improvements that were being made in the area's roads and schools during this period. Since World War I, as the occupational structure of the region changed and as a greater variety in sources of income emerged from what had previously been a self-sufficient agricultural economy, an increasing amount of cash money became available to Beech Creek families. Logging, work in sawmills, raising cattle for sale, growing tobacco as a cash crop, WPA work (usually road construction), school teaching, delivering mail, old-age pensions, war veteran pensions, the earnings which members of some families made in the defense industries of southern Ohio—all contributed to the growing cash income of families in the area. This proliferation in the sources of income accelerated a demand for goods and services, so that one could find, in the Schooltown of 1942, such symptoms of modernization as juke boxes, a beauty parlor, a movie house, daily newspapers, magazines, fresh meat and vegetables, citrus fruits, and scores of other things which would have been difficult, if not impossible, to find in the area only a few years before.

At the outbreak of World War II, then, the traditionalism of Beech Creek was already in confrontation with and exposed to, the cogent forces of modernization; the sociocultural foundations of Beech Creek were already "being rocked"; malfunctional trends were already present. The deprivations of a frontier existence could no longer be tolerated, and the stage was set for a massive response by Beech Creek families to economic opportunities, generated by the mobilization of American manpower and industry for war, that existed elsewhere. Beech Creekers looked toward new frontiers.

# PART TWO
# EXODUS

# 4 BEECH CREEK MIGRATION
## and The Kinship Factor

Implicit in our approach to the study of rural Appalachian migration is the notion that migration functions as an adaptive mechanism by which the local sociocultural system, through the kinship structure, responds to changing environmental circumstances in the area of origin. We aim to elaborate this thesis more fully by exploring the interconnections between kinship structure, migration process, and the processes of adjustment to "new" situational circumstances encountered by Appalachian migrants in the areas of destination.[1]

Our inquiry, which focuses upon the case of an eastern Kentucky mountain people, will not be wholly applicable to migration in and from all other areas. We believe, nevertheless, that the frame of reference formulated in the course of our study suggests a conceptual approach that has wider application. Almost by definition, folk cultures are characterized by strong familistic bonds that unite kin members in cohesive family groups and fit individual desires into a framework of family needs.[2] The eastern Kentucky subculture, a part of the Southern Appalachian regional complex, has been, and still is, an area dominated by traditionally sanctioned, particularistic value orientations: even today, in rural Appalachia, the *extended family* plays a highly functional role. An understanding of how kinship groups facilitated Beech Creek migration should be useful in building toward a more general understanding of the patterns of migration and the transitional adjustment of persons who move to urban areas of industrial opportunity from similarly strong familistic folk cultures in other parts of the world.[3]

# SOCIO-DEMOGRAPHIC HISTORY OF THE BEECH CREEK NEIGHBORHOODS

### Beginnings of Out-migration

Actually, migration is an integral part of Beech Creek history. The earliest settlers, Daniel and Richard Johnson, accompanied by their sisters, fleeing from an epidemic of yellow fever in Virginia, established a small farm at the mouth of Beech Creek shortly after 1800. One of the sisters, Kate, soon left and apparently was not heard from thereafter; she, in effect, was not only one of the first in-migrants, but also was one of the first out-migrants.

By 1850 there were three households in the area with twenty-six persons, all Johnsons. By 1880 there were seven households with forty-nine persons, all Johnsons or Johnson "connections," and all residing in and around the basin and mouth of the creek. Land on the creek in 1880 was owned exclusively by members of the Johnson family group. Nevertheless, by this time a number of Johnsons native to Beech Creek had moved away, settling mainly in neighborhoods nearby.

During the forty years from 1880 to 1920, the land monopoly of the Johnsons in the Beech Creek basin neighborhood was broken through the sale of land to "outsiders," primarily by Johnson heirs who had moved away, and often before they had secured clear title.[4] This made possible the in-migration of a large number of new families. Most of these settlers were native born Americans from North Carolina, Virginia, Tennessee, and from other parts of the Southern Appalachians. They were attracted to Beech Creek for a variety of reasons: cheap land was available; lumbering operations were beginning in the area; lumber companies were buying up land at high prices in the areas they had left. Others came because they wanted to be near a brother or sister who had married a Beech Creeker. By 1920 the population in the basin neighborhood had jumped to one hundred sixty-four persons in thirty-one households.[5]

Meanwhile, however, more and more Beech Creek people were leaving.[6] Although most of them relocated nearby, within the mountain counties, migration to industrial areas in southern Ohio became increasingly common, especially during the war years.[7]

From 1920 to 1942 the total number of persons residing in the basin neighborhood remained about the same (see Table 4.1). Since the birth

Table 4.1. Estimated population and number of households in the Beech Creek basin neighborhood, 1810–1942.

| Year | Number of Persons | Number of Households |
|---|---|---|
| 1810 | 6 | 1 |
| 1850 | 26 | 3 |
| 1860 | 34 | * |
| 1870 | 47 | * |
| 1880 | 49 | 7 |
| 1900 | 86 | * |
| 1920 | 164 | 31 |
| 1942 | 162 | 33 |

* Reliable estimates not available for these years.

rate continued to be high and some in-migration had occurred, it is clear that the flow of out-migration was heavy.[8]

On July 1, 1942, then, there were one hundred sixty-two persons in thirty-three households residing in the basin neighborhood.[9] All told, the 1942 population of the three-neighborhood locality to which we now refer as "Beech Creek" was three hundred ninety-nine persons in seventy-nine households.

**Mass Exodus**

After the outbreak of World War II, migration from the neighborhoods assumed large-scale proportions. Virtually all able bodied young men entered the armed forces, usually after a short period of work in Ohio. Many young women, older people, and whole families moved to industrial towns in the Ohio Valley for work in war plants; a large number of Beech Creekers found their first employment in a gunpowder factory which had employed a large number of Beech Creekers also during the First World War period. Quite often these migrants joined relatives and friends who had preceded them and who already had established households in the areas of destination. On the other end of the migration stream, the Beech Creek neighborhoods, in which every house bulged with people during the depression years, became "lonesome country," and empty houses became common. The population of the neighborhoods dropped to three hundred fifty-three in 1943, and to two hundred ninety-three in 1945.

The mere listing of changes in the number of people living in the area, however, does not give any real notion of the shift of persons that had taken place during the war years. For instance, our records show that only 57 percent of the three hundred ninety-nine residents in 1942 were still residents of Beech Creek in 1947; five of the original residents had died, the rest had moved out to nearby neighborhoods or had migrated to Ohio or elsewhere.

World War II, then, instigated great changes in the personnel make-up of Beech Creek, and these changes had tremendous repercussions directly and indirectly upon neighborhood life and activity. Within the area, for example, large scale out-migration made possible a great amount of inter- and intra-neighborhood residential mobility as numerous farms were vacated and available for sale, tenancy, or rent. Church attendance and support decreased, and schools were disrupted by the decrease in enrollments as whole families migrated. The smaller number of employable adults of working age had a larger proportion of children and old people who were dependent upon them. Many older people who had expected to be surrounded by their children and grandchildren, as was the traditional familistic pattern, found themselves alone. Local roads were not kept up; paths formerly well-trodden became overgrown with bushes. Fields became thickets of sassafras and locust, and neglected houses began to fall apart.

But at the same time, of course, there was another, somewhat brighter side to this dark picture. Cash money was not as scarce as formerly; sons in the military service, for example, or employed in war industry, sent part of their incomes back to help maintain the family homestead. On some farms new houses and barns were built. Some houses were repaired and painted until they looked better than ever. The main roads were being improved. And, more important, electricity was brought into the area by the REA in 1947.

Though the immediate aftermath of World War II saw a slight resurgence in population growth (to three hundred thirty in 1947), this proved to be temporary. The migration trend was too deeply ingrained in the Beech Creek sociocultural system and in the economic circumstances dominating the eastern Kentucky situation. As the American economy pulled out of the postwar slump, as industry was stimulated by cold war re-armament, and as the Korean conflict again effected a massive mobilization of America's manpower, out-migration to the Ohio Valley from Beech Creek and eastern Kentucky again increased in volume. By 1952, the population of the neighborhoods had declined to two hundred eighty-five persons. This trend continued so that, by 1961, the total population of Beech Creek was only one hundred ninety-six persons.

One of the dramatic contemporary changes in the Beech Creek neighborhoods, then, has been their rapid decline in population. Only about half as many persons resided in the neighborhoods in 1961 as in 1942 (see Table 4.2). The number of households decreased from seventy-nine in 1942, with an average size of 5.1 persons, to forty-four in 1961, with an average of 4.5.

Table 4.3 presents data on the components of population change for 1942–52 and 1952–61. Although out-migration was extremely heavy during those years, the in-migration of families, mainly from nearby neighborhoods, had a considerable countering effect. In both periods,

**Table 4.2.** Population of Beech Creek neighborhoods, 1942, 1952, 1961.

|  | 1942 | | 1952 | | 1961 | |
|---|---|---|---|---|---|---|
|  | No. | % | No. | % | No. | % |
| Basin neighborhood: | 191 | 47.9 | 121 | 42.5 | 82 | 41.8 |
| Laurel: | 134 | 33.6 | 117 | 41.1 | 79 | 40.3 |
| Flat Rock: | 74 | 18.5 | 47 | 16.4 | 35 | 17.9 |
| Total, Beech Creek: | 399 | 100.0 | 285 | 100.0 | 196 | 100.0 |

**Table 4.3.** Components of population change in Beech Creek 1942–1952 and 1952–1961.

| Period | Births | Deaths | Net Increase | | In-Migration | Out-Migration | Net Migration | |
|---|---|---|---|---|---|---|---|---|
|  | No. | No. | No. | Rate | No. | No. | No. | Rate |
| 1942–1952 | 60 | 23 | 37 | +9.3% | 100 | 251 | −151 | −37.8% |
| 1952–1961 | 25 | 12 | 13 | +4.4% | 47 | 149 | −102 | −35.8% |

nevertheless, Beech Creek experienced a net loss through migration of over one-third of the previous decade's population, which was only slightly compensated for by natural increases.[10]

## The Regional Situation

These population statistics for the Beech Creek locality in many ways reflect the regional situation.[11] Since the turn of the century, eastern Kentucky lost more migrants than it gained. Prior to 1940, nevertheless, the loss through net migration and death was lower than the gains through high birth rate, so that population gains of from 17 to 23 percent were made during each of the four preceding decades. In the 1940's, however, with the outbreak of World War II, the stream of migrants from the region became so great that even the continued, though somewhat decreasing natural increase was surpassed by migration losses, and for the first time in its history the region's population declined (a 4 percent decline from 751,000 in 1940 to 721,000 in 1950). The net loss through migration in that decade, 1940–50, was 223,000 persons, a figure roughly equal to 30 percent of the 1940 population.[12]

In the small-scale commercial, subsistence agricultural area of eastern Kentucky (State Economic Area 8), in which the Beech Creek neighborhoods lie, this pattern of gradual population decline with a high rate of loss through migration continued during the 1950's. The net loss through migration in the 1940's was the equivalent of 34 percent of the 1940 population, and in the 1950's the equivalent of 25 percent of the 1950 population. During those two decades the population in the agricultural area declined 19 percent.

In the coal mining area (State Economic Area 9) of southeastern Kentucky, the pattern of continued growth through the 1940's, which was contrary to the regional trend, came to an abrupt halt in the early 1950's. The rapid introduction of mechanized mining fostered large-scale unemployment which, in turn, generated a mass exodus. Between 1950–1960 the population of these mining counties declined 22 percent, and the net loss through migration was 42 percent of the 1950 population. Where once the coal camps afforded job opportunities within the region for the unemployed and underemployed from subsistence agricultural counties nearby, since 1950 this has no longer been an available alternative.

By 1960 the population of eastern Kentucky was down to 584,000. During the two decades 1940–60 this area, with only three-quarters of a million persons, made a *net* contribution of nearly a half million persons (about 490,000) to other parts of the country; the latter figure represents more people than were residents in 1960 of Kentucky's largest city, Louisville! If one views these simple statistics about regional trends from the perspective that population decline and high rates of out-migration are indicative of regional economic "trouble" and social disorganization, then the larger picture appears depressing indeed.

Even more strikingly similar to the Beech Creek case are the population statistics for the county in which the neighborhoods are located; the rate of loss through net migration here was 35 percent and 34 percent in the two decades respectively. In other words, the large stream of out-migration which characterized the population situation of the Beech Creek neighborhoods from 1942 to 1961 was not a unique phenomenon, but rather it reflected demographic adjustments that were taking place in the region as a whole.

## Perspectives: Locality and People

Here then, we have a concise socio-demographic history of the Beech Creek neighborhoods from the very beginnings of settlement in the basin area by the Johnson family through the more recent phenomenon of mass exodus. Exposed to system-disturbing influences introduced from the outside which, coupled with changes of great consequence in the social organization and cultural foundations of this traditionalistic frontier society, in turn stimulated an irreversible process of "rising expectations," Beech Creekers, in order to climb above the level of living that small-scale, semi-commercial, and subsistence agriculture can support, have had to look elsewhere for job and economic opportunities. From the very beginning, the complementary processes of out-migration and in-migration were woven into the pattern of life in the neighborhoods. The story of Beech Creek, in large measure, is the story of population movement—individuals and families and, in effect, the neighborhoods themselves, responding to changing environmental circumstances through the adaptive mechanism of migration.

To the sensitive reader who recalls and values the earlier frontier traditions of the Southern Appalachians, the tremendous volume of migration from the neighborhoods during recent years and the concomitant population decline suggest a rather pessimistic picture that seems to be painted in black, ominous, and sad statistics. Almost by definition progress implies growth, and, as we have noted, the Beech Creek neighborhoods have not grown, nor have they seemed to prosper, at least relative to other segments of American society; to the contrary, if trend lines are any indication of direction, the neighborhoods appear to be in a state of final disintegration and headed toward virtual extinction as locality groups.

But there is yet another side to the Beech Creek story that should be considered. One inevitably generates pessimism about the future of rural Appalachian people by focusing attention on their neighborhoods and the depressing statistics of population decline. To be sure, an understanding of what has been, and is happening in the region is of vital importance not only to the well-being of people who make their homes in these coves and hollows but also to the ultimate development and integrity of American society as a whole. Our concern with the locality group per se, however, should be tempered with a similar concern and understanding of what has been and is happening to those individuals and families who at one time or another had lived in the mountain area. Where did they go? What are they doing? How are they getting along?[13] In the answering of such questions a more meaningful basis may emerge for judging the character and consequences of social changes occurring in contemporary Appalachia than that to which one is led by viewing only the startling trend of population decline in the mountain neighborhoods.

We should take into account, for example, that former Beech Creek residents, spatially dispersed over the years, carried with them and to some extent retained a sociocultural heritage that is uniquely "Beech Creek." In effect, then, the Beech Creek sociocultural system has extended its geographic locale and has been "transplanted" to other areas. The implication is that, though the tremendous exodus of people from the area is jeopardizing the very existence of the neighborhood system, Beech Creek as a sociocultural system is not being destroyed but rather appears to be making an adjustment to changing conditions.

We shall come back to the Beech Creek mountain neighborhoods in the concluding chapter. Let us focus our attention now more fully upon the migration process and the migrants. Our aim in the remainder of this book is to explore, through a modification of Frederic LePlay's stem-family concept, the manner in which kinship structure facilitates the Appalachian mountain migration process.

# KENTUCKY MOUNTAIN MIGRATION AND THE KINSHIP FACTOR

A few pertinent observations about the patterns of eastern Kentucky migration may be useful, at this point, to establish the general nature of our research problem:[14]

(a)  Eastern Kentucky is a chronically depressed area by most standards. From 1940 to 1960 many more economic opportunities were available in the more prosperous urban areas nearby, and tens of thousands of mountain people have moved to take advantage of these opportunities.

(b)  The pattern of the streams of migration from the area has been remarkably consistent over the years. For example, the proportions of migrants moving (1) within eastern Kentucky (that is, to other counties within State Economic Areas, 5, 8, and 9), (2) to contiguous areas, or (3) to noncontiguous areas were very similar for both the periods 1935–40 and 1949–50 (Table 4.4), though there is a discern-

**Table 4.4.** Out-migration: intra-area and to contiguous and to noncontiguous areas, 1935–40 and 1949–50, eastern Kentucky.[a]

|  | 1935–40 | | 1949–50 | |
|---|---|---|---|---|
|  | Number of migrants[b] | Percent | Number of migrants[b] | Percent |
| Intra-area: | 37,524 | 34.9 | 17,615 | 34.9 |
| Contiguous area: | 32,741 | 30.5 | 12,500 | 24.8 |
| Noncontiguous area: | 37,212 | 34.6 | 20,330 | 40.3 |
| Total: | 107,487 | 100.0 | 50,445 | 100.0 |

[a] "Eastern Kentucky" in 1935–40 includes Kentucky State Subregions 5 and 9. For the counties included, see Donald J. Bogue, Henry S. Shryock, Jr., and Siegfried A. Hoermann, *Streams of Migration Between Subregions*, Volume I of *Subregional Migration in the United States, 1935-40*, Scripps Foundation Studies in Population Distribution, Number 5, Oxford, Ohio: Miami University, 1957.

"Eastern Kentucky" in 1949–50 included Kentucky Metropolitan Area C and State Economic Areas 5, 8, and 9. For the counties included, see Donald J. Bogue, *State Economic Areas*, U.S. Bureau of the Census, Washington, D.C.: U.S. Government Printing Office, 1951.

[b] A "migrant" is defined as a person who has moved his residence across county lines. Intra-area migration is migration among the counties of eastern Kentucky. Contiguous area migration is migration to areas adjacent to eastern Kentucky. Noncontiguous area migration is migration to areas not adjacent to eastern Kentucky.

ible trend for a higher proportion to go longer distances and for a lower proportion to go to contiguous areas.

(c) The great stream of migration from the subsistence-agricultural area of eastern Kentucky (State Economic Area 8) to noncontiguous areas has been to areas in Ohio and, secondarily, to areas in Indiana. Out-migration from eastern Kentucky other than in these well-established streams has been to widely scattered destinations (Table 4.5).

(d) Countercurrents of in-migration, which generally accompany all streams of migration from an area, exhibit a pattern almost identical with that of out-migration. In other words, the proportion of all migrants from eastern Kentucky moving *to* a particular area "out-

Table 4.5. Percentage of out-migration to and in-migration from state economic areas not contiguous with Kentucky State Economic Area 8, 1949–50.

|  | Out-migration[a] | | In-migration[b] | |
|---|---|---|---|---|
|  | Number | Percent | Number | Percent |
| Total number of migrants to and from noncontiguous areas: | (6,130) | 100.0 | (4,410) | 100.0 |
| Kentucky, total: | (590) | 9.6 | (330) | 7.5 |
| Kentucky A (Louisville): | | 3.3 | | 1.9 |
| All other Kentucky: | | 6.3 | | 5.6 |
| Ohio, total: | (2,410) | 39.3 | (1,800) | 40.8 |
| Ohio C: | | 10.0 | | 6.8 |
| D: | | 6.4 | | 6.5 |
| K: | | 6.8 | | 9.0 |
| 3: | | 5.4 | | 2.8 |
| 4: | | 4.5 | | 4.2 |
| All other Ohio: | | 6.3 | | 11.6 |
| Illinois, total: | (150) | 2.4 | (90) | 2.0 |
| Indiana, total: | (945) | 15.4 | (540) | 12.2 |
| Michigan, total: | (305) | 5.0 | (355) | 8.0 |
| All others: | (1,690) | 27.6 | (1,295) | 29.4 |

[a] The total number of out-migrants during this period was 10,815, of whom 43.2 percent moved to contiguous areas.

[b] The total number of in-migrants during this period was 8,115, of whom 45.6 percent came from contiguous areas.

side" has been about the same as the proportion of all migrants into eastern Kentucky coming *from* that specific "outside" area. The net flow, of course, has been out; more people moved from than moved to the eastern Kentucky area during a specified time period (Table 4.5).

These data from demographic studies lead to some basic questions, in the answering of which knowledge of the kinship structure seems particularly relevant:

*First, why has the directional pattern of out-migration from eastern Kentucky been so consistent over the years that we could almost say the streams of out-migration were running in well-worn riverbeds?*

The generalization that labor tends to flow in the direction of greater economic opportunity is, of course, well-founded.[15] However, geographical, historical, and other factors must also be considered in understanding these streams of migration. Although Stouffer's hypothesis of "intervening opportunities"[16] helps explain what at first glance might be regarded as certain deviations from a more "normal" pattern (e.g., the "leap" over the largely agricultural counties of central and northern Kentucky to the industrial counties of southern Ohio), we believe that kinship also is a factor of some importance in the explanation of this consistency in the directional pattern of out-migration.[17]

The kinship structure, for example, undoubtedly provides a highly persuasive line of communication between kinsfolk in the home and in the urban communities. It channels information about available job opportunities and living standards directly, and most meaningfully, to eastern Kentucky families and, therefore, it tends to orient migrants to those areas where their kin groups are already established.[18] This effective line of communication among kin (which is, in our experience, overwhelmingly more important than the communication network of State employment offices) helps also to explain the fact that the rate of out-migration is so immediately responsive to fluctuations in the rate of unemployment in migratory target areas.[19]

Because of ascribed role obligations, it is also plausible that the kinship structure serves a protective function for new migrants to an area—a form of social insurance and a mechanism for smoother adaptation during the transitional phase of adjustment.

*Second, why do streams of in-migration exhibit patterns that are practically identical to the patterns of out-migration from this area?*

Individual reasons for moving back are of many kinds, as Peter Rossi observed in his study of "Why Families Move."[20] Knowing that eastern Kentucky has long been an area with heavy net losses through migration, that it has not, especially in the last two or three decades, attracted many outsiders, and knowing also from observation over more than twenty years that most persons migrating into the area are former residents, we can assume, until more systematic data are available, that most in-migrants to eastern Kentucky are former residents and their families. Some of them could not adapt themselves to "outside" circumstances and decided to move back to their "home" areas. Others are persons who are of retirement age or are drawing pensions of one sort or another and feel they can live better and at less expense in their "home" areas. Most persons who migrate into the area, then, have "roots" in eastern Kentucky.[21] This suggests that kinship ties tend to draw former residents back to a specific area from areas to which they migrated and, as a consequence, helps to explain the nature of countercurrents of migration (Table 4.5).

We also believe that the particular type of kinship structure characteristic of Appalachian Kentucky tends to encourage heavy out-migration. In considering this possibility, we have found Habakkuk's discussion of the effects of rules of succession upon population growth in nineteenth-century Europe suggestive. Habakkuk points out that "the single-heir system tended to retard population growth and [the system of equal] division to promote it."[22] Eastern Kentucky has had a system of equal division of property among heirs, and here, too, this system seems to have promoted great population growth; so much so, indeed, that equal division of land in recent years seemed somewhat less common and alternative plans more widespread (e.g., one heir's buying the shares of other heirs, or of all the heirs giving up their shares to one, often the youngest child, on condition that he take care of the old parents until they died).

Another of Habakkuk's findings is pertinent: the rules of equal division of property in Europe tended to promote long-distance migration for seasons or short periods, such migration being "not an escape from the peasant family but a condition of its survival. The peasant went, not to acquire a new occupation in a different society, but to improve his position in the old. . . . [But] the inhabitants of division areas were not likely in the absence of . . . severe pressure to respond readily to demands for permanent industrial labor in regions distant from their homes."[23] From our study of the history of the Beech Creek mountain neighborhoods, and from less systematic observation of eastern Kentucky's agricultural areas as a whole, we find that this same pattern seems to have been common until recently, when pressure became so great as to sweep out whole families and almost whole neighborhoods. The earlier pattern of a man's leaving his family in the home neighborhood while he worked in "public works" out in Ohio has become much less common as whole families have migrated.

Another function or set of functions performed by the kinship structure in the process of migration is that surplus population has been drained off which, if allowed to "dam up," might well have brought such strain that this society dominated by the family-kinship system would have broken up completely. Actually, the gradual migration characteristic of eastern Kentucky for decades has led to the formation of patterns enabling it to absorb the shock even of very heavy loss. The situation is similar to that found by Arensberg and Kimball among the small farmers in Ireland, where ". . . the forces operative within that structure are of such a nature as to allow the society of which they are a part to continue to function in essentially similar fashion through the welter of economic, political, and other events which have impinged upon the human beings who have successively filled the structure. Likewise, the structure is capable of continued and virile existence in the present, governing the lives of its component individuals and modifying itself to take in 'new influences.' "[24]

A crucial aspect of the eastern Kentucky situation, confronting any student of this Appalachian mountain area, is the importance attached to kin relationships in the everyday life of its people. Familism, as a value-orientation, tends to permeate the local society and stamps all institutions with its mark.[25] To discover the significant effects of heavy out-migration on the social institutions in the area, therefore, and to build an understanding of the meaning and social consequences of migration, one would certainly want to begin by exploring the role of the kin group in the migration process.

# BEECH CREEK MIGRANTS:
## The Kin Clustering Effect

Let us now examine more specifically the relationship of the kin structure to the process of migration in the Beech Creek case. Loss through migration, as we have indicated, is an old pattern for the Beech Creek neighborhoods but, during the two decades, 1942–1961, the loss was

**Table 4.6.** Persons living in Beech Creek neighborhoods, 1942, by residence location, 1961.

| Residence Location, 1961 | Number of Persons | Percent |
|---|---|---|
| Beech Creek neighborhoods: | 68 | 25.1 |
| Town nearby: | 15 | 5.5 |
| Neighborhoods adjacent to Beech Creek: | 22 | 8.1 |
| Other neighborhoods, nearby, in same counties: | 4 | 1.4 |
| Other places within eastern Kentucky: | 1 | — |
| Places outside eastern Kentucky: | 161 | 59.4 |
| Totals: | 271[a] | 100.0% |

[a] These data refer to the study population, i.e., those Beech Creekers who were included in the 1961 survey.

unusually heavy. Only about 25 percent of the 1942 population still resided in the neighborhoods by 1961. About 15 percent had moved to nearby neighborhoods, and nearly 60 percent had established residence outside of eastern Kentucky (Table 4.6). About three-fourths of the Beech Creekers who had left the region had settled in Ohio (Table 4.7).[26]

Two southern Ohio towns which are close to each other (here referred to as X-town and Y-town), their immediate vicinity, and three or four hamlets in the same general area, had drawn about 40 percent of the Beech Creekers who had migrated from eastern Kentucky. Also, about 14 percent of the migrants were living in a big city (City A), about 15 percent were residents of a smaller city (City B), and about 6 percent located in an industrial center (City C); these cities are not far from X-town. The rest of the migrants tended to form smaller congeries in other towns and metropolitan suburbs in the Ohio Valley (see Table 4.7).

These data show the tendency of migrants from Beech Creek to cluster in certain areas of destination. In fact, nearly all of the Beech Creek migrants to Ohio resided within an area that could be encompassed by a circle with a radius of about thirty miles. What part did kinship ties have in this clustering? We can pursue that question from several angles.

(a) *Members of the same family group in 1942 tended to migrate to the same places.*[27] Of the fifty-eight persons, for example, who in 1942 were in the Andrews-Barnett family group, five had died and fifty-three were still living as of July 1, 1961. About one-half of the original members of this family group still lived in Beech Creek or nearby. The migrants, according to our records, clearly tended to concentrate in two specific areas: (1) City B, a small city in southern Ohio, had drawn twelve members, or nearly half of the migrants, and (2) a small metropolitan area in Kentucky had drawn six members of one Beech Creek family-household that earlier had belonged to this family group.[28]

Similarly, other examples can be noted of this tendency for migrants of the same family group to cluster. Our analysis of the migratory distribution of five family groups revealed: (1) of the seventy-six living members of these five family groups as originally delineated, thirty-two still

---

**Table 4.7.** Residence location of Beech Creek people who were living outside eastern Kentucky in 1961.

| Residence Location[a] | Number of Persons | Percent |
|---|---|---|
| Kentucky, excluding eastern Kentucky: | (21) | (13.0) |
| Bluegrass City: | 6 | 3.7 |
| Others, scattered: | 15 | 9.3 |
| Ohio: | (122) | (75.8) |
| City A: | 23 | 14.3 |
| City B: | 24 | 14.9 |
| City C: | 9 | 5.6 |
| X-town and vicinity: | 42 | 26.1 |
| Y-town and vicinity: | 14 | 8.7 |
| Others (near X-town): | 10 | 6.2 |
| Indiana: | (16) | (9.9) |
| City D: | 11 | 6.8 |
| Others, scattered: | 5 | 3.1 |
| Tennessee: | 2 | (1.3) |
| Totals: | 161 | 100.0% |

[a] Of the total study population, 110 persons or 40.6 percent were residents of eastern Kentucky as of July 1, 1961.

lived in Beech Creek or nearby neighborhoods, (2) thirty-six lived in "X-town," and (3) only eight lived elsewhere (Table 4.8).

(b) *Another way of showing the clustering of migrants who are kin is to analyze the kin relationships of migrants in a given town or city.* We found, for example, that Beech Creek migrants in City B were predominantly from two family groups, the Andrews-Barnetts and the Preston Johnsons. Only five of the twenty-four Beech Creek migrants in this smaller city were *not* members or had not married members of those two original family groups. And of these five, only two were *not* attached to these families by close kinship ties.

---

**Table 4.8.** Examples of the tendency for members of a family group to migrate to the same general location. (Based on persons who constituted five family groups in Beech Creek on July 1, 1942, by residence on July 1, 1961.)

1. The Barnetts (16 still living):
   5 in Beech Creek and nearby neighborhoods
   10 in X-town, Ohio
   1 elsewhere

2. The Carters (15 still living):
   5 in Beech Creek
   7 in X-town, Ohio
   3 elsewhere

3. The Cundiffs (10 still living):
   5 in Beech Creek
   5 in X-town, Ohio
   0 elsewhere

4. The Lamberts-Snows (22 still living):
   7 in Beech Creek and nearby neighborhoods
   11 in X-town, Ohio
   4 elsewhere

5. The Smiths (13 still living):
   10 in Beech Creek
   3 in X-town, Ohio
   0 elsewhere

Total, all five family groups (76 still living):
   32 in Beech Creek and nearby neighborhoods (42.1%)
   36 in X-town, a small town in southern Ohio (47.4%)
   8 elsewhere (10.5%)

In one of the small Ohio towns (X-town), the situation, though somewhat more complicated, reveals a similar pattern. Of the thirty-five Beech Creek migrants who were living there, twenty-two were members, or had married members, of two family groups, the Lambert-Snows and the Barnetts. Nearly all of the other thirteen Beech Creek people there were related in some way to the Barnetts or to the Lambert-Snows, and in a number of cases, to both.

Here we are perhaps being a bit "archaeological," sticking too closely to statistical bones. For actually we knew from many observations over the years that members of a family group in Beech Creek "peeled off" as they got old enough and joined their kinsfolk who had previously migrated to the area of destination.

(c) *The same clustering phenomenon is revealed when we analyze the distribution of migrants by 1961 residence and according to their*

**Table 4.9.** Residence location of Beech Creek migrants, 1961, by social class position in Beech Creek, 1942.

| | Class position in Beech Creek, 1942 | | | | | | | |
|---|---|---|---|---|---|---|---|---|
| | High | | Intermediate | | Low | | Unranked | |
| | No. | % | No. | % | No. | % | No. | % |
| Total (N = 182)ᵃ | 38 | 100.0 | 72 | 100.0 | 53 | 100.0 | 19 | 100.0 |
| *Residence location* | | | | | | | | |
| Kentucky, outside eastern Kentucky: | 9 | 23.7 | 4 | 5.6 | 6 | 11.3 | 1 | 5.3 |
| Ohio: | | | | | | | | |
| City A: | 3 | 7.9 | 8 | 11.1 | 12 | 22.6 | 0 | |
| City B: | 19 | 50.0 | 4 | 5.6 | 1 | 1.9 | 0 | |
| City C: | 0 | | 2 | 2.8 | 5 | 9.5 | 2 | 10.5 |
| X-town, Y-town, or vicinity: | 1 | 2.6 | 34 | 47.2 | 20 | 37.7 | 10 | 52.6 |
| Other: | 1 | 2.6 | 7 | 9.7 | 3 | 5.7 | 1 | 5.3 |
| Indiana: | 1 | 2.6 | 7 | 9.7 | 4 | 7.5 | 5 | 26.3 |
| All other states: | 4 | 10.6 | 2 | 2.8 | 2 | 3.8 | 0 | |
| Armed forces: | 0 | | 4 | 5.5 | 0 | | 0 | |

ᵃ Our data here refer to *all* Beech Creek migrants residing outside eastern Kentucky, rather than persons included in the study population.

*1942 social class positions in Beech Creek* (Table 4.9).[29] Half of all the "high-class" migrants lived in and around City B, Ohio. Only one "high-class" migrant lived in X-town. On the other hand, nearly half of all those migrants earlier designated as "intermediate-class" lived in X-town, while only four lived in City B.

These observations are in the expected directions when one recognizes that class lines in Beech Creek tended to follow kinship lines very closely. To a great extent, the family group was the basic (i.e., effective) social class unit in the stratification system of Beech Creek, as is the conjugal family in urban American Society. Furthermore, inter-class marriages were not common in Beech Creek, especially between persons of the "high" and "low" strata; the social classes, therefore, tended to be networks of kin relationships. Thus, the available migration data reveal a pattern that is probably more a kinship than a social class phenomenon.

# LE PLAY'S STEM-FAMILY CONCEPT AND BEECH CREEK MIGRATION

On the basis of these exploratory efforts discussed above, we conclude that kinship ties did influence the destination of migrants from Beech Creek.

For a long time we have been aware of the similarity of Appalachian Kentucky and the Ozark Mountain area, as reported by Zimmerman and Frampton.[30] In particular, the structure of the Ozark family, which they call "an uncodified variety of the stem-family,"[31] resembles in many respects the structure of the Beech Creek (eastern Kentucky) family as we have come to know it. Zimmerman and Frampton's imaginative use of LePlay's model in studying the Ozark family influenced our thinking and led us to consider carefully LePlay's discussion of the stem-family (*famille-souche*) and its pattern of emigration as well as other aspects of his work.[32]

Though LePlay's contributions to social science were many and important, and the interplay of LePlay's inquisitive mind, his many interests, and the social and historical circumstances in which his ideas evolved are fascinating, we will here discuss only a few of his more relevant ideas. We would emphasize, however, that LePlay lived in

Europe in a period when urbanization and industrialization were bringing about great social changes (born 1806, died 1882).[33] Both the period of transition in which LePlay lived and his attempts to understand
the social and economic phenomena of his day make his work particularly relevant to the problems undertaken in our examination of the
Beech Creek case. Let us, then, note briefly some of the main features
of LePlay's conceptual model of the *famille-souche,* the stem-family,
emphasizing, of course, what has been most useful to us.

LePlay considers the family the elementary and basic social unit.[34]
He held that there is only one general family type, though fluctuations
in the strength of the main form accounted for three major subtypes
of families—the patriarchal, the unstable, and the *famille-souche,* or
stem-family.

The *patriarchal-type* has as its theme the principle of continuity;
emphasis is on keeping the family group intact and preserving traditional family boundaries, rather than on encouraging individual initiative. Members are loyal to family tradition and the established social
order; strong familistic, religious, and moral beliefs are maintained. All
property and savings in this type of family are controlled by the household head. Married children reside near the parental homestead and
remain under the dominance of the family. If, however, economic conditions become difficult, the patriarchal family either migrates *as a unit*
or begins to break up under the strain.

The *unstable-type* of family, on the other hand, has as its theme the
principle of change; a high degree of individualism is encouraged by
freeing children from family obligations. Members of the family have
no particular attachment to the parental homestead; family history and
traditions have little importance. This type, according to LePlay, is
found primarily in new, growing, and unstable industrial orders. The
individual member of an unstable family, write Zimmerman and Frampton, "depends more upon himself for a standard of living, and, in case
of serious accidents, unemployment or other calamities, he suffers unless
some extra-family agency, such as the government, takes care of him, or
unless he has accumulated sufficient property to take care of himself."[35]
Cyclical periods of unemployment and economic recession can, therefore, cause much physical and psychological hardship.

Finally, the *famille-souche,* which LePlay conceived as the type *best*
able to adjust to the changing conditions of an industrial society, incor-
porates some of the characteristics of both the patriarchal and unstable
types, emphasizing both the principles of change and of continuity
within the same structural framework. Zimmerman and Frampton describe this type as follows:

This stem-family consisted of a parent household (*the stem*) which preserved the organic basis of society, and of a number of individuals (*the branches*) who leave the parent household in order to fit into industrial organizations and urban environments where high but fluctuating money incomes were produced. The stem of the family helps to preserve the society and to insure that the branches which fail in their adaptations to contractual relations have havens of safety to which they may return. Thus, the stem part of the family reduces to a minimum the needs for public charity for the unemployed. At the same time, the successful branches contribute to the embellishment of society by their rapid adjustment to new opportunities, by the development of industrial areas, and by the increase in new types of production.[36]

In his conceptualization of the structure and functions of the *famille-souche,* LePlay, we must emphasize, was describing an "ideal type," deriving this abstraction from his studies of concrete families. Zimmerman and Frampton note this in saying: "This stem-type form is only a common manifestation of many strong families and does not necessarily appear in all or in most families of an area predominantly familistic. In the Ozarks it is far from being manifested in all families."[37] Consequently, we would not expect all Beech Creek families to manifest the characteristics of the stem-family form.

The *famille-souche,* as described by LePlay, maintains a homestead for its immediate members and sends other members elsewhere to make their own livings. The ancestral home, built by the founder, is managed by an heir, thus guaranteeing a continuous head to the family and assuring that family traditions are preserved. Family homestead in Beech Creek (or the "homeplace," as it is generally called) usually means the parental household. However, often it may refer simply to a piece of land, a presently abandoned or temporarily rented house, or close kinsfolk in the old neighborhoods who offer migrants a "haven of safety" in time of need. The LePlay *homestead concept* appears in the Beech Creek case as a configuration of elements blending land, neighborhood, parental household, kinsfolk, and the like, into, as one Ohio migrant put it, "a *place* to go to if things get rough out here." Zimmerman and Frampton hint at this point when they suggest: "It seems that the spirit and not the form, the strength and not the mould, is the dominating characteristic of this family."[38]

Family headship in the Beech Creek case, however, is *not* automatically ascribed to an heir who maintains the ancestral home. Nor is there a formal pattern of succession of the family leadership role, although on an informal level family leaders can be identified. Migration from the area has been so great over the years that family leadership is often held by one of the branches rather than by the stem. In this respect, the branches may, then, have as much to do with preserving family traditions and continuity as does the stem.

In case of misfortune, according to LePlay, the branches may secure temporary subsistence and aid from the stem or may draw back to the protective cover of the parental homestead. Thus, serving as a "haven of safety," the stem-family reduces to a minimum the need for public charity for the unemployed. Numerous examples from the Beech Creek case suggest this protective function of the kinship structure during the process of migration. Often migrants who have lost their jobs in Ohio, for instance, move back to their home neighborhoods until employment opportunities are again favorable in the Ohio area. LePlay, however, could not foresee such broad governmental programs of assistance for the unemployed as we have in the United States today, and these programs have done much to modify the stem-family form as found in eastern Kentucky. Nevertheless, although the protective function of the stem-family system, so far as the economic aspects are concerned, may not be as important as during LePlay's time, the social-psychological aspects, especially in terms of the migration process within a complex society, may be even more important.

LePlay's central concern was with the stem of this type of family and what it does for its branches in two ways: on the one hand facilitating and encouraging migration when conditions demand it, and on the other hand providing "havens of safety" to which the branches could return during crises such as unemployment. From this point on we attempt to elaborate LePlay's model, though we should note at once that the variation described here is implicit in LePlay's writings.

The stability of the directions of migratory streams from eastern Kentucky and the clustering of class-oriented family groups in certain areas during migration are *both* suggestive of the supportive role played by the "branch-families" within the migration system (that is, the migrants' family and kin in the new communities). Numerous researchers have noted that the new migrant is not necessarily alone or a stranger in the new community,[39] and indeed most Beech Creek migrants have many kinsfolk in the communities to which they go. To extend LePlay's model, these kinsfolk form a network of "branch-families" which serves important supportive functions during the transitional period of adjustment. Our observations of the Beech Creek migrants indicate, for example, that kinsfolk in the areas of destination often provide the newcomers with temporary housing, help in finding jobs, and assistance of many other sorts during difficult times.[40] Furthermore, it seems reasonable to expect that these networks of branch-families function as a socio-psychological "cushion" for the migrants during the transitional phase, and it is this cushioning function of the branch-families that will be our concern during the remainder of this book.

# FURTHER THEORETICAL NOTIONS

At this point, let us briefly explain two notions that occupy key positions alongside LePlay's stem-family concept in the development of our research theory.

*Migration System:* Migration is here defined as the ecological movement of people, involving residential changes that (1) remove them from the immediate interactional systems of which they have been a part and to which they are accustomed, and (2) place them in new interactional systems to which they are not accustomed.[41] A *migrant,* therefore, is a person who has moved spatially from one system (or subsystem) of interaction to another.[42] The interactional system within which a migrant is socialized is called his "donor subsystem." The interactional system at the place of destination is called the "recipient subsystem."[43] The implication is that the two subsystems together form the interactional system in which we wish to consider the adjustment of a given group of migrants, individually and collectively. We have, then, *one migration system* to consider, namely the Beech Creek-Ohio migration system.

We recognize that Beech Creek itself comprises a number of interactional subsystems and so, even more obviously, does Ohio (or Indiana or some other place of destination). The important point is that we are not dealing with the adjustment of a given group of migrants only in the place of destination; instead we are concerned with the adjustment of a given group of migrants, collectively and individually, in relation to two subsystems of interaction in which they are forced to participate *in the normative sense.*

The nature of the linkage between the two subsystems—between both ends of the migration system—is, of course, an empirical question that must be pursued through further research. It is clear, however, that the flow of migration between Beech Creek and Ohio and the kin clustering effect observed in the area of destination suggest a functional interrelationship; i.e., a sociological phenomenon rather than an accident of history.

*Adjustment:* From our definition of a migrant, it follows that migration means the shifting of an individual, or a group of individuals, from one relatively stable set of normative patterns of behavior (norms governing institutionalized ways of acting in a given specific social situation) to another. This shift necessarily entails stresses on individuals and on groups. The strains thus produced have psychological, sociological, and cultural dimensions. The resolution of these strains in a manner that enables individuals and groups to function adequately in terms of the demands of the interaction (migration) system is what we are calling adjustment, without restricting its meaning to any *one* of the three dimensions. As we conceptualize it, it is a holistic notion, defined as "a dynamic state in which individuals in a given society are able to live in relation to the members of their significant membership groups, satisfying their basic needs, fulfilling the responsibilities of their major roles, and maintaining the identity and integrity of their individual selves."[44]

Having thus somewhat clarified the notions of "migration system" and "adjustment," let us return to consider the relationship between our modified notions of LePlay's *famille-souche* and adjustment in the migration system.

According to LePlay, the stem-family encourages individual initiative while at the same time exerting moral control over its members. The individual who is unhappy with his present circumstances and wishes to advance socially and economically is offered an "escape mechanism" through the family structure. He is both assisted in his quest for opportunity and encouraged to go out "on his own." Further, branches that are already established in the areas of destination, as well as the stem at "home," provide a supportive structure and socializing agency for the individual during the process of migration. This support facilitates his adjustment to new circumstances in the migration system and helps to stabilize the migrant, in whom two interactional subsystems meet during the process of migration.

The foregoing arguments have led us to an over-all working hypothesis as the basis for our study of the Beech Creek migrants out of eastern Kentucky:

The greater the functional adequacy of the stem-family (modified to include the network of the associated "branch-families") of the Beech Creek sociocultural system in responding to the changing needs of the Beech Creekers, the more adjusted the migrants will be both as individuals and as families, under specified conditions.

The functional adequacy of the stem-family can be perceived in terms of status-roles. Social change entails modification of, and increase in the number of status-roles in the sociocultural system that is undergoing change. In other words, one significant pattern alteration that is associated with social change is differentiation in the status-role system. Further, some loss of function occurs with respect to some of the roles that continue even after change. This loss of function and modification of the status-roles will be reflected in the adjustment of the migrants.

# MIGRATION AS A SYSTEM-MAINTAINING PROCESS

One familiar with the Southern Appalachian region would surmise that over the years the way of life of people in the Beech Creek neighborhoods has changed. The most significant changes have taken place in the form of system-disturbing elements introduced from the outside. For example, the REA program brought electricity to every household in the neighborhoods, state and county aid helped in putting a road through the area, missionaries built a church, and federal and state welfare programs assisted the aged and needy. These programs, in turn, have been instrumental in introducing new ideas, new values, and greater awareness of the world external to the family and neighborhood. The "rhythm of life" characteristic of the Beech Creek neighborhoods in 1942 has changed and is changing. Beech Creek is becoming ever more closely linked with the mainstream of American society.

A readily observable consequence of the Beech Creek locality system's adjustment to these disturbances is the great exodus of people and families during recent years. Though loss through migration is an old pattern for the mountain area, out-migration was encouraged by the Second World War and Korean War mobilizations; jobs for unskilled and semi-skilled workers were plentiful in the industrial areas of the Ohio Valley. Without a comparable countering stream of in-migration, the draining away of people from the neighborhoods generated further and very drastic structural changes within the neighborhoods. In fact, continued erosion of its population base appears to threaten the very existence of the Beech Creek locality as a viable social entity.

In the normative sense, however, the boundaries of a sociocultural system tend to be maintained despite the territorial dispersion of unit carriers of that system. It would be rash to assume that an individual or family that moves spatially from one system of interaction to another at once severs all sociocultural ties with the donor system. Cultural orientations, for example, are learned, and learning (and re-learning) involves a period of time before it is manifested as structural changes within the system.

Furthermore, the individual or family that migrates may find itself, in the area of destination, in an interactional system that has many cultural elements in common with that of the area of origin. This, in turn, would tend to reinforce the patterns of behavior characteristic of the donor subsystem which the unit carrier brings to the "new" situation; where system-disturbing influences are minimal, change within the system is slow. We know, for example, that migrants from Beech Creek tended to cluster residentially in certain areas of destination; dispersion of the original Beech Creek population over the years was not random. Moreover, as we shall show in subsequent chapters, close interactional ties were maintained by Beech Creekers residing in the same general urban locale, and these clusters were located within what can be technically termed "cultural islands," but which are more descriptively labeled "little Kentuckies." Through the process of migration, therefore, the Beech Creek sociocultural system has been "transplanted," so to speak, to areas in Ohio and elsewhere. To the extent that the system itself is isolated from the eroding influence of direct contact with the host culture, the system tends to be maintained. The implication is that, although the tremendous exodus of people from the Beech Creek locality appeared to jeopardize the very existence of the neighborhood system, Beech Creek as a sociocultural system was not being destroyed, but rather appeared to be making an adjustment to changing conditions.

In other words, we are making a very real distinction between a sociocultural system (a system of interaction in the normative sense) and a locality group (the neighborhood system). In the process, of course, our interest shifts from what has happened to the neighborhood situation and its social structure to what has happened to the families and their sociocultural orientations and behavioral patterns. Students of the changing rural scene often fail to make this distinction and, consequently, their observations tend to lead to a somewhat distorted picture of what is happening in low income rural areas like eastern Kentucky.

It has been suggested by Slotkin and others that a necessary precondition for migration to occur is a "cultural inadequacy" of the source culture.[45] Slotkin, for example, emphasizes the idea of migration as an "escape valve" for those individuals who find their own sociocultural system inadequate for their own role expectations. From this perspective, we tend to look upon migration as an "unnormal" event, i.e., as deviant behavior by an individual relative to the normative structure of his society. Regional migration statistics, however, and an examination of the pattern of migration from Beech Creek area lead us to believe that the migration process is an adaptive mechanism somehow tied in with the sociocultural system and functional in maintaining the Beech Creek family structure. If this perspective is valid, then the large-scale migration from the Beech Creek neighborhoods and from other parts of rural Appalachia represents a patterned reaction by family-kinship groups to preserve traditionally sanctioned cultural values and to maintain group integrity in confrontation with environmental circumstances over which they can exercise little control. Frederic LePlay recognized this possibility many years ago.

# 5 OUTMIGRATION:
## Group Patterns
## and the Big Move

The general patterns of outmigration of Beech Creek people from the Beech Creek neighborhoods and from the Appalachian mountain region are explored here in greater detail.[1] We also focus more specifically on the social structuring of the migration "event." Our intent is to provide an illustration and further elaboration of the conceptual framework proposed in the previous chapter.

## INTERREGIONAL MIGRATIONS:
### General Perspectives

Beech Creekers migrated from the mountain region in great numbers during the two decades, 1942–1961. Of the original residents, only about a fourth did not at some time in this period reside outside eastern Kentucky for at least a month or longer.[2] And, after once having moved away from the mountains, approximately 60 percent remained in the areas of destination as "permanent migrants," a fact which lends some credence to the notion of "stability" in the motivational causes undergirding this massive exodus.[3] Nevertheless, some Beech Creekers, whom we might label collectively as the "betwixt and between" segment,[4] had moved out and back one or more times; many of these "migrations," however, were of relatively short temporal duration.

Conceptualized as a sociological phenomenon, migration involves a change in the interactional system to which an individual must re-orient himself.[5] It does not seem reasonable, therefore, to suppose that a Beech Creeker who leaves eastern Kentucky to "settle" in Ohio for a few months—with relatives, for example—and then returns to the family homestead in the mountains, in effect, has migrated (i.e., in a social psychological sense). To eliminate those migrations that were more like extended but temporary visits than anticipated permanent changes in region of residence, we imposed a more stringent temporal criterion of "six months or longer." This more permanent type of migration we have come to call a "big move." When we use the label "first big move," we mean nothing more than the first occasion after 1942 when the individual Beech Creekers moved from eastern Kentucky to reside outside the region continuously for at least six months. The accompanying table (Table 5.1) reports the migratory experiences of Beech Creekers during

**Table 5.1.** Interregional migrations of Beech Creekers, 1942–1961: cross-classification; number of migration from eastern Kentucky,[a] by region of residence 1961, "big move" experience,[b] and sex.

| | Region of residence 1961 | | | | | | | | | |
| | Within eastern Kentucky | | Outside eastern Kentucky | | | | | | | |
| Number of migrations from eastern Kentucky,[a] 1942–1961 | Never Made a Big Move[b] | | Returned After Big Move | | Returned After First Big Move | | Never Returned | | Marginal total | Marginal total as % of study population |
| | Number of persons, by sex | | | | | | | | | |
| | M | F | M | F | M | F | M | F | | |
|---|---|---|---|---|---|---|---|---|---|---|
| None: | 32 | 38 | | | | | | | (70) | 25.8% |
| One move out: | 2 | 2 | 9 | 16 | | | 63 | 59 | (151) | 55.7% |
| Two moves out: | 2 | 1 | 4 | 1 | 11 | 11 | 3 | 3 | (36) | 13.3% |
| Three or more moves out: | | | 2 | 1 | 5 | 6 | | | (14) | 5.2% |
| Total, by sex: | 36 | 41 | 15 | 18 | 16 | 17 | 66 | 62 | | |
| Column total: | (77) | | (33) | | (33) | | (128) | | (271) | |
| Column total as % of study population: | 28.4% | | 12.2% | | 12.2% | | 47.2% | | | 100.0% |

[a] A continuous residence for one month or longer outside eastern Kentucky.
[b] A continuous residence for six months or longer outside eastern Kentucky.

these two decades and compares the effect of a one-month vs. a six-month residence criterion.[6] In general, the interregional migration pattern for females was like that for males.

In the case of males, "short migrations" of less than six months were usually no more than extended visits to kinsfolk for the purpose of exploring work opportunities in the areas of destination.[7] Almost always the man was young, made the trip alone or with buddies, had not made any plans to move away from the mountains permanently, and simply regarded this event in his life as a "work visit." The situational circumstances surrounding such temporary migrations from the region were more varied in the case of females; nevertheless, similar conclusions may be drawn. Almost always, the woman was joining or accompanying her spouse, who had landed a temporary job or had decided to explore work opportunities in the area of destination. In a few cases the young unmarried girl was simply visiting her relatives for a few months with no thought of a permanent residential change, even though she might have taken a temporary job. For the most part, then, as we discovered from our examination of individual case histories, such "short" migrations were indeed "work visits" or extended "kin visits" made in the spirit of an exploratory venture that did not involve a meaningful separation of the Beech Creeker from his or her family homestead in the area of origin. To be sure, if the young man or young woman found situational circumstances favorable in the area of destination, the work visit may have evolved into what we have labeled "a big move."

Temporary migrations of relatively short temporal duration, such as described above, tended to precede the first big move out of the region even in those cases in which individual Beech Creekers subsequently returned to remain in eastern Kentucky. Rarely was an "unsuccessful" first big move followed by an "unsuccessful" second big move; generally these individuals and/or their families either decided to remain in the mountains after their initial migration experience, or they planned more firmly to make a go of it the second time, in which case the probability of their successful manipulation of situational circumstances was substantially increased. There is some evidence, then, to suggest a motivational stability underlying this massive exodus. Migration from the region was, on the part of Beech Creekers, purposeful, systematic, and once attempted, relatively permanent.

We also considered the cumulative length of residence outside eastern Kentucky by individual Beech Creekers over the twenty-year period. Among those who had never made a big move, only two persons had accumulated as much as one year's total residence outside the mountain region. These were men who, while young and single, spent a couple of summers traveling alone and working at odd jobs on the West Coast, in the South, and in Ohio; they never actually intended to move permanently from the mountains.[8]

On the other hand, Beech Creekers who had made a big move but subsequently returned to live in eastern Kentucky appear, for the most part, to have been firmly resolved, at least in terms of temporal perseverance, in their effort to establish themselves outside the mountains. Over half had accumulated two or more years residence in Ohio or elsewhere. Why they returned is an important, but exceedingly complex, question.

# PATTERNS OF OUTMIGRATION

We turn attention now to such questions as "when," "why," and "how" migration from the Appalachian region took place, and whether "stages" or patterns can be discerned. Our inquiry focuses on the individual Beech Creeker's first move away from the neighborhoods after 1942—many of these migrations were to towns and neighborhoods nearby—as well as the so-called "first big move" out of the region—many of these originated from the nearby towns and neighborhoods.

### Time patterns: When did Beech Creekers move?

The movement of persons out of Beech Creek (i.e., the study population) followed a fairly consistent but declining trend over the years (see Table 5.2).[9] The decline, of course, can be explained in large part by the "aging" of this specific population. It is evident from our data that the flow of people leaving, which swelled to its peak during the years immediately following the outbreak of World War II, subsided, then resurged again in the years immediately following the outbreak of Korean hostilities.

There is an evident similarity in the pattern of movement out of the Beech Creek neighborhoods and the pattern of migration of Beech Creekers out of eastern Kentucky (see Table 5.3). Interregional migration, however, appears to have been somewhat more consistent over the years. By the end of 1949, for example, one hundred thirty-one Beech Creekers had moved away from the neighborhoods for the first time, but only seventy-seven had made a first big move out of the region. On the other hand, from 1950 through 1961, only eighty-eight

Table **5.2.** Number of initial migrations from the
Beech Creek neighborhood,[a] 1942–1961, by period
of move.[b]

| Period of initial outmigration | Number of Persons | Percent |
|---|---|---|
| 1942–45 | 101 | 37.4 |
| 1946–49 | 41 | 15.1 |
| 1950–53 | 58 | 21.4 |
| 1954–57 | 21 | 7.7 |
| 1958–61 | 9 | 3.3 |
| Never moved | 41 | 15.1 |
| Total: | 271 | 100.0% |

[a] Includes first migrations from Beech Creek to nearby
towns and neighborhoods and also directly to areas in
Ohio or elsewhere (whether for a "work visit," an
extended "kin visit," or a more permanent type of residential relocation). It does not include those relatively
few cases of second migrations from Beech Creek by
individuals who had moved away, returned, then
moved away again at a later date during the period.

[b] From July 1, 1942 through July 1, 1961.

Beech Creekers had moved away from the neighborhoods, compared
with one hundred seventeen who had made a first big move during that
period. Although direct comparisons cannot be made from these data
for a number of reasons, it seems clear that the nearby towns and neighborhoods to some extent served as "collection points" in the process
of rural-to-urban migration: that is, *for some Beech Creekers, intraregional movement appears to have been a stage preceding interregional
migration.*

In terms of seasonal variations, we found that the rate of movement
out of Beech Creek was somewhat higher during the winter months than
at other times of the year. A third of all the initial migrations occurred
during the three winter months, when the tobacco crops had been sold
and new crops had not been planted.[10] Given the seasonal nature of
farming activity, without doubt winter is the more convenient time for
a residential change. One wonders, however, whether it is also an oppor-

**Table 5.3.** Number of migrations (first big moves)[a] from eastern Kentucky by Beech Creekers, 1942–1961, by period of move.[b]

| Period of initial outmigration | Number of persons | Percent |
|---|---|---|
| 1942–45 | 54 | 19.9 |
| 1946–49 | 33 | 12.2 |
| 1950–53 | 66 | 24.4 |
| 1954–57 | 28 | 10.3 |
| 1958–61 | 13 | 4.8 |
| Never moved out | 77 | 28.4 |
| Total: | 271 | 100.0% |

[a] The temporal criterion employed in defining a migration is six months or longer continuous residence outside the region. Excluded are those second migrations of individuals who, after having made a "big move," subsequently returned and then migrated out again. Included are Beech Creekers who had migrated to Ohio or elsewhere directly from Beech Creek (N = 144) as well as those who first moved to nearby towns and neighborhoods in eastern Kentucky before migrating from the region (N = 50).

[b] From July 1, 1942 through July 1, 1961.

tune time from the point of view of the job market situation in the industrial areas. (If not, then there is a greater risk that the rural migrant may become an added economic burden to kinsfolk or to community agencies in the receiving areas, or that he may be forced to return to the mountains after his own meager resources are used up.)

**Destination patterns: Where did Beech Creekers move to?**

Nearly two-thirds of the initial migrations from Beech Creek were directly to places outside of the mountain region, i.e., to urban, industrial centers in the Ohio Valley and elsewhere (Table 5.4). It is this interregional migration stream that interests us the most (on the assumption that the tensions, strains, and adjustment problems generated in the process of rural-to-urban migration are far more difficult to manage than those generated in the process of rural to rural movement of persons and families). Only about 14 percent of those Beech Creekers who first moved from the neighborhoods to destinations within eastern Kentucky settled in places more distant than their home counties; most families had simply moved closer to a good road, or closer to town. Hence, it does not seem reasonable to suppose that residential movement to nearby towns and neighborhoods means that the "migrant" severs ties with the old home neighborhood or experiences a basic change in his pattern of interaction with family and friends in the area. Nor does it seem reasonable to suppose that moving to another mountain neighborhood places the "migrant" in a new sociocultural situation to which he is not accustomed and to which he must adjust by altering his life style. In subsequent chapters, then, we shall be less concerned with this kind of intraregional migration, which is essentially an ecological realignment within the mountain society, than with migration out of the region.

Over three-fourths of the initial interregional migrations from Beech Creek were to places in the southern Ohio industrial area. The specific destination patterns as well as the "clustering" phenomenon were essentially similar to that observed in the residential location patterns of Beech Creek migrants in 1961 (see Table 4.7). It is readily apparent, then, why so many towns and residential districts around and in the major cities of southern Ohio became known, in time, as "little Kentuckies." There appears to have been a consistency in orientation to

Table 5.4. Destinations of initial migrations from Beech Creek, 1942–1961.

| Area of destination[a] | Number of Persons | Percent |
|---|---|---|
| Town nearby: | 26 | 11.3 |
| Neighborhoods adjacent to Beech Creek: | 34 | 14.8 |
| Other neighborhoods, nearby, in same county: | 14 | 6.1 |
| Other places within eastern Kentucky: | 12 | 5.2 |
| Places outside eastern Kentucky: | 144 | 62.6 |
| Totals: | 230 | 100.0% |

[a] Of the total study population, 41 persons or 15.2 percent never residentially moved away from the Beech Creek neighborhoods during the period under consideration.

particular areas of destination by persons caught up in this massive stream of migration.

Nevertheless, after initial settlement in an urban area, subsequent residential changes and further relocation were quite common. For example, of the one hundred sixty-one former Beech Creekers who were living outside eastern Kentucky in 1961, over half had changed their residence three or more times after their first move out (excluding any moves back to the mountains). A pattern of residential restlessness is normal in American Society and represents, we believe, the striving of families to upgrade their living conditions. What is more significant, however, is the fact that over 45 percent of these residence-changing Beech Creekers remained in the same general *community* they had moved to at the time of their initial migration, and only about 33 percent had made two or more community shifts.[11] This, we submit, indicates a considerable degree of stability in terms of orientation or attachment to the initial area of destination.

That nearby towns and neighborhoods tended to serve as "collection points" for some Beech Creekers in the process of migration from the region is further indicated when we compare the initial destinations (Table 5.4) with the 1961 residence location of Beech Creek migrants (Table 4.6). Whereas nearby towns and neighborhoods absorbed about 37 percent of the initial migrations, by 1961 only about 21 percent of the Beech Creekers not living in the original neighborhoods were living nearby. For some Beech Creekers, intraregional residential movement was a stage in the process of migration from the region.[12]

**Motivational patterns: Why did Beech Creekers move?**

Eastern Kentucky, a part of the Southern Appalachian Region, is an economically depressed, rural area. People from eastern Kentucky, by and large, migrate to Ohio and elsewhere in search of employment or more lucrative work opportunities than are available in the mountains. The wives and children who accompany family breadwinners are also caught up in the complex web of economic circumstances which, over the years, has generated a great exodus from the region.

Economic considerations are reflected in the Beech Creekers' own reasons as to why they moved away from the region. Over 78 percent of the males and 28 percent of the females left to "get" or "look for" work; most of the women who were looking for work were young and unmarried at that time. About 40 percent of the women wanted to "move with" or "join" their spouses who were looking for work. Over 12 percent of both men and women (who were children at the time) had to accompany parents who were looking for work. Thus, one or the other of these reasons, each of which is linked directly with economic considerations, was the expressed motive in about 85 percent of the cases of Beech Creekers who had moved from eastern Kentucky. Other reasons included "to join" grown children, siblings, or parents who were already living in the area of destination; one would be rash indeed to rule out economic motives in these cases, even though verbal responses make no mention of seeking "work opportunities." Rarely did any Beech Creekers see the motive for migration as an interpersonal "push" factor, such as trying to get away from a feuding situation, a messy family problem, and the like.

After initial migration from the region, many Beech Creekers moved again, at a later time, to another urban community. Such urban-to-urban migrations appear to have been prompted by the desire to find housing and neighborhoods more commensurate with enhanced status, as well as for reasons of seeking out more lucrative job opportunities in other areas.[13]

"Returned migrants," both men and women, offered a variety of reasons why they had returned. Males more frequently explained that they were either "laid off" from work or simply "not satisfied" with living in Ohio. Females, on the other hand, tended to explain their return in terms of "to be with kin," or because of "marital difficulties."

For some, of course, the initial move away from Beech Creek was not directly out of the region, but rather to nearby towns and neighborhoods. In general, these were family migrations instigated on the one hand so that the head of the household could be closer to his work (e.g., in the coal mines) or could gain access to better farm land, and on the other hand so that the family could be closer to better roads and community services such as schools, doctors, churches, and so forth. However, although economic considerations were important in the decision to move to areas nearby, they by no means dominated the motivational pattern, as in the case of migrations from the region. Of course, an adequate explanation would have to take into account differences between the two types of migration in terms of age and stage in family life cycle at the time of moving. Even then, however, we suspect that the perceptions of individuals as to why they moved would reveal decided differences in orientation for intraregional and interregional migrations.

At this point, let us digress and explore an additional factor which is tangential to motivational aspects per se but which, nevertheless, may have some bearing upon the topic. Did military service influence young male Beech Creekers to migrate?

Although a third of the male Beech Creekers were in the military service at some time during this twenty-year period, military service immediately preceded the first big move in less than a fifth (19 percent), and the initial residential move from Beech Creek in less than a fourth (23 percent), of these cases. It does not appear, then, that military service was in and of itself directly instrumental in residentially relocating many Beech Creek men. Generally speaking, after release from the military the young man returned to the family homestead in the mountains for, we assume, a period of "readjustment" to civilian life. When the situational factors influencing eastern Kentuckians to consider outmigration were perceived in their realistic context, most of these returned servicemen (all but three) moved away from the mountains for, we assume, much the same reasons as their neighbors who had not been in the military.

**Influence patterns: Who was involved in the decision-making process?**

Beech Creekers who had moved out of eastern Kentucky—and the pattern is quite similar for intraregional moves—tended to view that decision, in retrospect, as an individual matter that was not influenced by persons other than their spouse or (if they were unmarried) their parents (Table 5.5).

Manifestations of a patriarchal cultural orientation can be observed. Nearly a third of the married females, for example, said that their husbands alone made the final decision for them to migrate. If the wife claimed that it was solely her decision, she was usually referring to a situation in which the husband was already working and residing in the area of destination, and in which it had been left up to her to make the choice of joining him at that time, or remaining behind a bit longer at the family homestead. Although nearly half of the women and a third of the men regarded it as a joint decision, we also noted that in both cases most Beech Creekers saw the male head of the family as the *main* decision-maker.[14] This patriarchal pattern in the process by which married couples decided to migrate is not surprising. In his role as the principal breadwinner, the male head of a family household, presumably with the advice and consent of his spouse, was obligated to make those decisions which enhanced the economic well-being of his family; to migrate was one such decision.

Unmarried migrants regarded this decision as having been an individual matter except in those instances in which they and the parental family had moved away together as a unit. If they were less than sixteen years of age at the time they invariably moved with parents and had (and felt they had) very little to say in making that decision.

**Table 5.5.** Who made the final decision to migrate from eastern Kentucky (first big move)?[a]

| | Male | | Female | |
|---|---|---|---|---|
| Decision-makers: | Number | Percent | Number | Percent |
| In the case of married migrants, | | | | |
| Husband only: | 24 | 64.9 | 18 | 31.0 |
| Wife only: | — | — | 11 | 19.0 |
| Both husband and wife together: | 13 | 35.1 | 28 | 48.3 |
| Other: | — | — | 1 | — |
| Totals: | 37 | 100.0% | 58 | 100.0% |
| In the case of unmarried migrants, | | | | |
| An individual decision: | 44 | 89.8 | 15 | 71.4 |
| Migrant and parents together: | 3 | 6.1 | — | — |
| Parents only: | 2 | 4.1 | 5 | 23.8 |
| Other: | — | — | 1 | — |
| Totals: | 49 | 100.0% | 21 | 100.0% |

[a] Persons who were less than sixteen years of age at the time of initial migration (N = 29) were excluded from this table. In almost all cases (86 percent) they moved with parents.

Most Beech Creekers did not perceive or recall that anyone had encouraged or, for that matter, discouraged them in their plans to move. Of those who had received some encouragement (about 31 percent), nearly half felt it came from siblings, mainly in the form of "suggestions" about employment opportunities available in the areas of destination, "help" or the promise of help in securing employment, or simple "urging" to join them. Of those who had received some discouragement (about 26 percent), over half felt it came from parents, mainly in the form of "warnings" about how dissatisfied they would be away from home or, particularly in the case of women, "urging" them not to break up the family and kin group or, particularly in the case of men, "suggesting" that they could do as well to stay and work at home.

**Unit patterns: Did Beech Creekers migrate alone or in groups?**

Beech Creekers who moved to other places in eastern Kentucky rarely moved alone (Table 5.6). This kind of intraregional migration involved entire families. Almost half of those who made such a move went with parents and/or siblings and no one else; they invariably were children or adolescents at that time. Some who were married also moved along with their parents or older siblings. In most other instances, the move was solely a nuclear family migration. That the migration unit in this form of intraregional migration tended toward a large, extended family group becomes more dramatically evident when we observe the total number of persons who composed the unit. The median number of persons who accompanied the Beech Creeker was six; in 65 percent of the cases they were accompanied by five or more other people. (These facts suggest that, from a sociological perspective, the appropriate unit of analysis in studies dealing with this phenomenon of intraregional migration is the extended family or family-household group.)

On the other hand, nearly half of the Beech Creekers migrated "alone" when they moved out of the region (Table 5.7).[15] About a third made this big move with their spouses only or with their spouses and children only. The remainder reflected a variety of patterns that can best be summed up as having involved mainly young unmarried persons who had accompanied their parents and/or older siblings.[16] Rarely were fringe relatives or friends included in the migration unit.

It is clear that the social units which characterized the patterns of migration from the region had a basically different structural composition from the social units which characterized the patterns of residential movement within the region. These differences become more strikingly evident if we compare the two types of "migration" in terms of the number of persons who constituted the migration unit. In only 9 percent

**Table 5.6.** Persons accompanying migrant on initial move from Beech Creek to other places in eastern Kentucky, 1942–1961.

| Persons accompanying migrant | Number of Cases | Percent |
|---|---|---|
| No one else: | 3 | 3.5 |
| Spouse only: | 7 | 8.1 |
| Spouse and children, or children only: | 25 | 29.1 |
| Spouse and/or children, plus members of parental family: | 3 | 3.5 |
| Parents and/or siblings only: | 42 | 48.8 |
| Other: | 6 | 7.0 |
| Totals: | 86 | 100.0% |

**Table 5.7.** Persons accompanying migrant on initial migration from eastern Kentucky (first big move), 1942–1961.

| Persons accompanying migrant | Number of Cases | Percent |
|---|---|---|
| No one else: | 93 | 47.9 |
| Spouse only: | 22 | 11.4 |
| Spouse and children, or children only: | 41 | 21.1 |
| Spouse and/or children, plus members of parental family: | 2 | 1.0 |
| Parents and/or siblings only: | 30 | 15.5 |
| Other: | 6 | 3.1 |
| Totals: | 194 | 100.0% |

of the cases of interregional migration did five or more persons accompany the migrant, compared with 65 percent of the cases in residential shifts from Beech Creek to other eastern Kentucky locales nearby. Many of the latter, of course, were children. Nevertheless, it appears that migration from the region was a much more individualistic phenomenon involving a more "nucleated" migration unit than intra-area movement. But the structure of a migration unit is only one aspect in the social structuring of the migration process; for a more meaningful understanding of that process as a whole, the nature of the social situation immediately preceding and following the actual movement of migrants from one area to another must be considered.

# THE BIG MOVE: A Familial Event

## Family situation and migration: Overview

It is well known that migrants from rural low-income areas to urban industrial areas tend to be young people. This generalization is valid also in the Beech Creek case; the median age was about twenty-one years (Table 5.8). Because they were young, it is not surprising that most Beech Creekers were either unmarried, or at an early stage in the family life cycle when they moved from the mountains. In this respect, however, the pattern, or "strategy," of males differed somewhat from that of females (Table 5.9). Women were generally more advanced in the family life cycle at migration. Conversely, a considerably larger proportion of the men were unmarried. One explanation may be that females marry at an earlier age than males. Then, too, we know that many young, unmarried males had moved to Ohio in search of work. After having enjoyed the experience of an extended work visit, they returned to the mountains for a period of time, married mountain girls and, confronted with breadwinner responsibilities, decided to move "permanently" to Ohio with their spouses. Likewise, a similar extended work visit strategy seemed to prevail among the male heads of larger households.

In most cases (61 percent), Beech Creekers had been residing within "complete nuclear" family-household situations prior to migration. That is, they were living in households which consisted of a male head and his spouse, with or without unmarried children, and no other persons.[18] Other patterns were of course manifested[19] but, surprisingly, extended family situations were not common in these low income rural mountain neighborhoods; family boundaries were defined strictly along close kinship and immediate family lines despite economic deprivation. If other individuals in addition to nuclear family members were present in the household, they were generally immediate or parental family members; only occasionally were other close kin part of the household structure. If the migrant was married, he normally had been living with spouse and children and separate from parents, except in the case of some female migrants whose husbands had already left on extended work visits to Ohio.

We must also consider an additional factor that bears directly upon the family situation of the migrant, the structural strains concomitant with migration, and the adjustment problems confronted by Beech Creekers in the area of destination. Prior to migration, most Beech Creekers (88 percent) had been living in close proximity to their parental families. Some, of course, were living in the parental household, while many others were "only down the road" from the family homestead. In the process of migration, therefore, parental family ties had to be modified; this was an obvious "situationally-induced consequence" of migration.[20] Given the familistically-oriented character of the Beech Creek sociocultural system, it was an extremely important factor in the eventual adjustment of migrants to situational circumstances in the area of destination.

Upon arrival in the area of destination, only a small proportion (38 percent) found themselves involved in and part of a complete nuclear family situation. The pattern for males, however, was somewhat different in this respect from that of females. Only about one-fifth of the male, compared with over one-half of the female, migrants moved into

**Table 5.8.** Age of Beech Creeker at initial migration from eastern Kentucky (first big move), 1942–1961.

| Age, in years | Males No. | Males % | Females No. | Females % | Totals No. | Totals % |
|---|---|---|---|---|---|---|
| Less than 16 | 11 | 11.2 | 18 | 18.5 | 29 | 14.9 |
| 16–20 | 34 | 35.1 | 35 | 36.1 | 69 | 35.6 |
| 21–25 | 25 | 25.8 | 17 | 17.5 | 42 | 21.6 |
| 26–30 | 6 | 6.2 | 7 | 7.2 | 13 | 6.7 |
| 31–40 | 10 | 10.3 | 9 | 9.3 | 19 | 9.8 |
| 41–50 | 5 | 5.2 | 6 | 6.2 | 11 | 5.7 |
| 51 or more | 6 | 6.2 | 5 | 5.2 | 11 | 5.7 |
| Totals: | 97 | 100.0% | 97 | 100.0% | 194 | 100.0% |

**Table 5.9.** Marital status and nuclear family situation of Beech Creeker at initial migration from eastern Kentucky (first big move), 1942–1961.

| Marital status and nuclear family situation[a] | Males No. | Males % | Females No. | Females % | Totals No. | Totals % |
|---|---|---|---|---|---|---|
| Not married: | 49 | 57.0 | 21 | 26.6 | 70 | 42.4 |
| Married, no children: | 7 | 8.1 | 20[c] | 25.3 | 27 | 16.4 |
| Married, one or more children, youngest child under 6 years:[b] | 21 | 24.4 | 26 | 32.9 | 47 | 28.5 |
| Married, one or more children, youngest child between 6–10 years: | 4 | 4.7 | 5 | 6.3 | 9 | 5.5 |
| Married, one or more children, youngest child 16 years or older: | 5 | 5.8 | 7 | 8.9 | 12 | 7.2 |
| Totals: | 86[d] | 100.0% | 79 | 100.0% | 165 | 100.0% |

[a] Excludes those who were less than sixteen years old at migration (N = 29).

[b] One-third of these people reported only one child.

[c] Ten of these were young women who migrated "to get married."

[d] Subsequent analyses exclude three unmarried males and two married males who entered the armed forces and for whom further situational information was lacking or inappropriate.

what then became or already had been a complete nuclear family-household; male migrants were often "loners" (20 percent of the cases). One reason, of course, is that many married men moved to the area of destination alone, rented a room, and then, after getting established in a job and with housing, called for their spouses and families to join them. The latter, upon arrival, completed the nuclear family structure. In addition, many men (38 percent) moved with and/or joined kinsfolk, who then constituted a household that had the characteristics of an "extended family group."

Often female migrants also became part of an extended family or joint family household situation. That is, they moved with and/or joined others who, together, formed a larger family group within which a complete nuclear family served as the stabilizing core. Occasionally a woman found herself in an incomplete extended family situation; i.e., with kinsfolk, but not in a complete nuclear family situation. But never was the female migrant "alone." There was, then, a striking difference between the sexes in terms of the family-household situation they confronted upon arrival in the area of destination.

**Family situation and migration: Systemic patterns**

A detailed case-by-case analysis was made to explore how the family-kinship structure was linked with the migration of Beech Creekers.[21] (The findings are reported in appendix tables B.1 to B.7) This enabled us to view simultaneously both ends of the migration stream and to observe the patternings of familistic support which stabilized and channeled the great exodus from Beech Creek and Appalachia over the years. Our analysis was organized in terms of the migrant's marital status and sex. These two factors, more than any others, were closely linked with the major patterns of migration and, we believe, the major dimensions of individual and family-related needs associated with and generated by the process of moving from one geographic locale to another. Our attention focused upon three structural aspects of the migration event: (1) with whom the migrant lived prior to moving from the mountains, (2) with whom he moved, i.e., the composition of the migration unit, and (3) whom he joined at the place of destination. These situational factors must be taken into account in order to view the migration event in its entirety or, at least, to approximate a holistic conceptualization of "what happened." Only then can we begin to see this type of rural to urban migration as a socially organized phenomenon, and only then can we begin to approach an understanding of migration as a social process.

*Males, unmarried.* The majority of Beech Creek males were young and unmarried when they migrated. For the most part they had been living with their parents, had moved alone or with friends, and generally had joined kinsfolk or rented a room near kinsfolk in the area of destination. Theirs was the classic pattern of chain-migration (or "stem-family migration"), in which the kin network at the receiving end of the migration stream plays an important part in facilitating the "absorption" of the newcomer into the host community.

About a third of the unmarried male migrants eventually returned to the mountains, usually after less than two years of residence in the area of destination. Of course many again moved out at a later time, usually with a mountain girl for a wife.

*Females, unmarried.* Generally, unmarried female migrants had been living with their parents, moved alone, and in all cases joined kinsfolk or members of their parental family in the area of destination. The extended family group, in subtle and perhaps not so subtle ways, did not permit a single girl to "drift" by herself in the urban environs.

About 40 percent of these girls later returned to the mountains. Those who remained generally lived with kinsfolk until an opportunity for marriage was accepted; more often than not, they married an eastern Kentuckian.

*Females, just married.* An important pattern which must be considered as a distinct category is the case of girls for whom migration and marriage were simultaneous events. Whether girls migrated "to get married" or vice versa is irrelevant; what is relevant is that the two events were concurrent.

These girls were generally living with their parental families prior to migration and wedding. Almost always their suitors were either Beech Creek migrants in Ohio who had carried on weekend courtships while visiting their parents, or "outsiders" who for one reason or the other had been introduced into the family circles. After the wedding, the girl moved with her new spouse to the area of destination and, almost always, they established their own separate household in close proximity to kinsfolk who helped them with furniture and the like.

This pattern of migration appeared relatively stable; less than a third of these young women eventually returned to the mountains.

*Males and females, married, no children.* Prior to migration, the young childless couple generally lived with *his* parents in a joint family situation. Rarely did they live with *her* parents. (This fact suggests that a patrilocal pattern existed in these Appalachian neighborhoods.) Because the normative orientation in Beech Creek was toward separate households and conjugal family independence, the joint household situation may have been a factor stimulating migration.

The young couple almost always migrated as a unit. Generally, they established their own household in the area of destination but, depending upon circumstances, some found it necessary to accept temporary residence with members of their family already there. Although in about half the cases the couple returned to the mountains, many eventually migrated out permanently.

*Males and females, married, with children.* If a man with a family decides to migrate, the implementation and organization of that plan are a great deal more complex than, for example, in the case of a bachelor. Individual circumstances and problems are compounded, and the strategy of migration, from the point of view of his immediate family, must be tailored to these specifics. It seems far more useful, therefore, to view the migration of the male head of a family (and so, too, of the principal homemaker) not as an isolated happening but as a coincidental part of the larger event, namely, the migration of a nuclear family unit.

In such cases, the man and his family have at least two alternative courses of action available. Either he can take his wife and children with him to the area of destination, or he can "go it alone" for a while and send for them later "if things work out." In the latter instance the male breadwinner usually becomes a weekend commuter. Of course, it may sometimes happen that the routine of commuting becomes institutionalized as a normal pattern of behavior; i.e., the form of the family is altered so as to adapt to commuting.

A Beech Creek family that migrated as a unit usually moved into an apartment or small house near kinsfolk in the area of destination or, in some instances, temporarily joined the household of another member of the family, such as an older son who had moved to Ohio earlier. Perhaps because the migration of a nuclear family is a relatively complex affair, only a few of these families eventually returned again to the mountains.

In cases in which the man had moved first and in which his extended work visit had turned out to be successful and the prospects for a more permanent relocation looked good, he had his wife and children join him.[22] Arrangements for adequate housing were usually made by him prior to their arrival on the scene. For a nuclear family following this strategy of migration, relocation was a two-step process: kinsfolk helped the breadwinner get established in the host community and he, in turn, prepared the situation for the arrival of his spouse and children. Some of these families later returned to the mountains (about a third) after residing for a while in the urban area. More often than not, returned migrants were older persons or young couples who had not found adequate housing or secure jobs in the area of destination.

**Family-structured migration: Summary**

Our analysis demonstrates that the migration of Beech Creekers over the years (a total migration universe) was structured along family-kinship lines. How one conceptualizes the phenomenon of migration, to be sure, has much to do with the conclusions reached about the nature of that phenomenon.[23] We chose a sociological approach, from the point of view of family units or groups involved in the processes of residential relocation. Taking into account the migrant's family-of-origin situation in eastern Kentucky, with whom he moved, and the family-household situation at the place of destination, we found that the migration of Beech Creekers in most cases was a group phenomenon. Conversely, we concluded that the migration of Beech Creekers, as individuals, seldom occurred as an event isolated from the family-kin network and, therefore, that in the Beech Creek case the "big move" was indeed a familial event.

In no instance did an unmarried Beech Creek girl move into a non-kin situation or attempt to "go it alone" in the area of destination. Indeed, most of these girls had moved with or joined siblings, parents, or other close kin. Though unmarried males in some ways appeared more independent of kin ties, relatively few had ventured to establish (or perhaps could have financially afforded to establish) themselves in a household situation separate from kinsfolk; even then, as we noted, the "loner" lived in close residential proximity to kinsfolk.

For some Beech Creek girls, marriage and migration had been concomitant events. In these cases, of course, the pattern of migration was similar to that of conjugal family units.

The young married couple or older childless couple had generally migrated as a unit and either had joined kinsfolk (siblings, parents, close kin) or, if they were financially able, had established households of their own near kinsfolk in the area of destination. To view this kind of migration as an "individual event" would be quite inappropriate. Furthermore, this unit was part of a larger structure of relationships, namely, the family-kin group of each of the marriage partners; these kinsmen undoubtedly helped the conjugal pair in the process of adjusting to the circumstances of migration.

The migration of a nuclear family unit was a more complex phenomenon. It directly involved and affected the lives of a number of persons who had a variety of needs, and it therefore became, so to speak, a difficult logistical problem. We have observed that Beech Creek families manifested, essentially, two distinct patterns or strategies of migration. On the one hand, there was what we might call the "uprooting pattern."

In these cases the nuclear family had migrated as a unit and, as a unit, either joined other members of the family or established a new household in the area of destination. On the other hand, there was what we might call the "two-phase pattern." Here the male head of the family, as the principal breadwinner, had migrated to the area of destination on an "extended work visit" and, if circumstances proved favorable, in due course called for his spouse and children to join him. At the first phase of this pattern, the man often moved in with kinsfolk until he could become established with a secure job or until he had decided to return.

That the kin system performed an important function in facilitating the migration of nuclear family units is clear. Even when a nuclear family moved and relocated as a unit in a new household separate from kin, it seems reasonable to assume that the kin network provided a measure of social and psychological support during the migration process.

In the Beech Creek case, then, the event of rural-to-urban migration was not as big a sociocultural change as one may have assumed. To be sure, moving from a mountain locale in eastern Kentucky and settling in an urban, industrialized area of Ohio did indeed represent a "break" with the old and, for the Beech Creek migrant, a change in his normal rhythm of life. The event, without doubt, was a physically and mentally taxing chore even for those who were eager to "get out." Yet, as we have suggested and as we propose to demonstrate more convincingly, *the two ends of the Beech Creek migration stream were systematically linked via the kinship structure.* And the "new" situation toward which the migrant was directed was not necessarily "strange," nor socially and culturally differentiated from the social context at the point of origin. To the contrary, the geographic mobility of Beech Creekers, for the most part, occurred *within* a familistic structure; the kin system facilitated, stabilized, and channeled the migration stream. It is granted that, over time, the relocation of a Beech Creeker became a "culturally significant event" with important consequences for him and for the system which he represented and of which he was a part. Nevertheless, it is somewhat of an exaggeration for us to call that specific event—that incident in the course of a Beech Creeker's life when he packed up some belongings and took off for Ohio—a tremendous sociocultural event. And by no means can we view this migration in the same way as (or even as belonging to the same class of phenomena with) those migrations that brought the original settlers over the mountains to the mouth of the Beech Creek basin.

# PART THREE
# CONFRONTATION
# AND ADJUSTMENT

# 6 BEECH CREEK FAMILIES in Ohio

Through the process of chain-migration over the years, Beech Creekers and their families relocated in areas of Ohio and elsewhere. They were seeking to enhance their economic lot in life, for Beech Creek and the Appalachian mountain region no longer offered them the means to satisfy their needs and newly acquired wants. Like the earlier European immigrants who turned to America, they looked toward the promise of work opportunities in the Ohio Valley. They settled in or near the centers of industry in urban or suburban localities that were often populated, for the most part, by similar migrants from Appalachia. Invariably, as individuals or family groups, they joined kinsfolk who had preceded them to the area of destination. They arrived in the host community as unit carriers of a traditionalistic mountain culture that emphasized familism, individualism, and puritanism. Beech Creekers and the sociocultural system which they represented were, so to speak, "transplanted." Over the years, of course, in confrontation with the urban sociocultural system, they were subjected to forces of change and modernizing influences that affected the very foundations of their way of life. The individual Beech Creeker found himself adjusting to, and having to adjust to, environmental circumstances in the area of destination, and so also to the requisites of living as a participating member of mainstream America.

This adjustment phase of the migration process, an integral part of the Beech Creek story, is our main concern in this section. To understand the functions performed by the family-kin network in the resolution of tensions within the Beech Creek migration system, it is useful and perhaps even necessary to begin by exploring the social context in the area of destination and the Beech Creekers' reactions to those circumstances.

# INITIAL SITUATION

It was a rare Beech Creeker who arrived in the community of destination as a complete stranger. Many (over half) had visited that community at least once before moving there to stay. Some joined relatives in established households, and most had numerous "close kin" who were already living in the area (Table 6.1).

---

**Table 6.1.** Number of kin and friends in receiving community when the Beech Creeker migrated from eastern Kentucky.

| Number of families** in receiving community | Male | Percentage* Female | Total |
|---|---|---|---|
| *Close Kin* | | | |
| None: | 20.0 | 30.4 | 25.0 |
| One or two: | 41.2 | 41.7 | 41.4 |
| Three to five: | 21.2 | 22.8 | 22.0 |
| More than five: | 17.6 | 5.1 | 11.6 |
| Total: | 100.0 | 100.0 | 100.0 |
| *Distant Kin* | | | |
| None: | 39.3 | 53.8 | 46.3 |
| One or two: | 13.1 | 17.9 | 15.5 |
| Three to five: | 21.4 | 15.4 | 18.5 |
| More than five: | 26.2 | 12.9 | 19.7 |
| Total: | 100.0 | 100.0 | 100.0 |
| *Friends* | | | |
| None: | 29.4 | 54.4 | 41.5 |
| One or two: | 18.8 | 12.6 | 15.9 |
| Three to five: | 22.4 | 19.0 | 20.7 |
| More than five: | 29.4 | 14.0 | 21.9 |
| Total: | 100.0 | 100.0 | 100.0 |

* N = 85 males and 79 females.

** Information refers to number of family units whom the migrant regarded as "close kin," "distant kin," or "friends." Hence, the number of individual units represented are far more than the number of families indicated.

---

As a rule, they brought few household possessions with them. Kins-folk and friends were quick to supply the newcomers with essential furniture and the necessary equipment for housekeeping. Kinsfolk also helped them find a place to live (in more than half the cases) and helped the principal breadwinner of the migrant family find a job (in more than a third of the cases).[1] In addition, kinsfolk assisted the new arrivals in getting oriented to the city—instructing them on how to get around, what buses to take, where and how to shop, how to cook with gas or electricity, how to establish credit, and so forth. In effect, the kin system functioned as a "natural" advisory service for new-comers.

Those who did not join an established household usually located in the immediate vicinity of kinsfolk and friends. The first residence, gen-erally speaking, was a temporary arrangement of some kind, often a small, rented house (in 55 percent of the cases) or a small apartment (in 30 percent of the cases). Within a year the migrant family was in-clined to move again (in over 50 percent of the cases) to more perma-nent housing. This change of residence usually occurred after the bread-winner felt assured of a fairly steady job. Then, pressured by "rising expectations" and fortified by a newly acquired sense of financial secur-ity, he and his wife began seeking out modern conveniences and new furniture. Credit-buying was quickly accepted as a means of getting things.

Some Beech Creekers initially located in urban "inner-city" tenement house situations. A number of families, for example, had taken up resi-dence along one street in what was regarded as a "zone of transition" in City A. From their apartments on the hill they enjoyed a spectacular view of the river and the heart of the city's business district below. But neighborhood conditions—both physical and social—were far from ade-quate, and the disturbing atmosphere of "ghetto" life[2] tended to gen-erate tensions and to erode family stability. Buildings were shabby. Rats prowled around garbage piled in the dark alleys. Many families were on welfare, and economic and educational deprivation were neighbor-hood norms. These circumstances (and the conditions they symbolize) in turn fostered problems of truancy, delinquency, marital discord, and other behavioral manifestations of social disorganization.

Beech Creekers and other migrants from Appalachia who were located in such situations invariably wanted to get out and, if they could muster the necessary resources, they eventually did move to more favor-able residential environments. It was difficult, however, because those who initially settled in an urban depressed area or slum neighborhood more often than not lacked the requisite skills, training, education, and family resources to capitalize on their willingness to work. To be sure, they were drawn to that area of destination by kin affiliations. However, because they were generally from lower-class Beech Creek families, they not only had very little stem and branch family economic support, but also very little to go back to in the mountains had they decided to return. In effect, they were "trapped" by the initial circumstances of migration and by the situation they encountered in the area of destination; only by sheer determination and/or luck could they overcome those socioeconomic handicaps.

Some Beech Creek migrants, on the other hand, particularly those who were from "high-class" families in the mountains, settled in more established residential areas in and around the major metropolitan centers. They had the necessary financial resources and family connections to avoid inner-city tenement house situations and, perhaps because of their "class consciousness," they were inclined *not* to locate in the "little Kentucky" suburban communities of southern Ohio. Initially they may have lived with kinsfolk. Because of strong support from kin and because they were favored with some educational advantage over other Appalachian migrants, they were able to find and hold relatively high-paying jobs; they could save some money. After accumulating sufficient financial resources for houses of their own, they generally sought out modest places in middle-class residential neighborhoods that invariably included many native Ohioans.

The majority of Beech Creekers, however, initially moved into a more suburban locale or metropolitan fringe community, such as X-town, where they enjoyed a semi-rural atmosphere that was in some ways comparable to life in an eastern Kentucky town. Many had gardens from which they could harvest bumper crops of beans, tomatoes, sweet corn, and "greens," and this added immeasurably not only to their family "incomes," but also to their personal sense of well-being and independence. Some lived with kinsfolk at first, but many, soon after arriving in the area, rented houses or apartments in duplexes or "bought" small places through some kind of land contract arrangement (e.g., $500 down on an $11,000 house, to which they would receive title only after an agreed upon portion of the selling price, usually over a third, had been paid). The motivation to own a place was strong, and those who rented or who resided with kinsfolk were usually not satisfied until they could save enough money for a down payment. Then, if they could manage to keep up payments on house and furniture, they soon became integrated into the social life of this "little Kentucky" community. For, like many of the smaller urban-fringe communities in the southern Ohio area, X-town had a population composed of well over 90 percent Kentuckians, and its social and cultural life was not unlike that of county-seat towns in Appalachia. It was essentially a "bedroom community;" men worked in the factories nearby (e.g., General Electric, Frigidaire, Ford Body Division, Proctor & Gamble, etc.), but the residential community itself was relatively free from the industrial atmosphere, and its tempo of life was for the most part suburban and in many ways quite "rural."

The residential settings initially encountered by Beech Creek migrants varied. Where they settled, after having been drawn to the general area by job opportunities and for other reasons, depended somewhat upon the prior settlement pattern of their kinsfolk, the financial resources available to them, as well as upon their own values, motivations, and aspirations acquired earlier within the context of their family groups. Some, by reason of circumstances rather than choice, found themselves in an urban-slum situation that was in sharp contrast to the rural (though also poverty-stricken) atmosphere of the mountain neighborhoods they had left. Some, through family ties, located in an enclave of mountain people near the big city and the industrial heartland of Ohio—where community life was by and large "Kentucky." Others melted very quickly into the mainstream of suburban middle-class American society. The specific situations encountered by the migrants, of course, had much to do with their eventual patterns of adjustment.

In almost all cases, however, Beech Creekers located within relatively short distances of each other. Most had acquired an automobile or access to one soon after, or even before, their arrival in the area of destination, and this permitted a great deal of contact with kinsfolk and old friends who resided nearby. On long weekends they also could visit the family homestead back in the mountains.

# INITIAL REACTIONS

We have no way of really knowing the individual migrants' initial reactions to the circumstances encountered through migration; the quality of human experience is elusive and time itself had erased many memories from the minds of our subjects. However, we can explore their retrospective point of view regarding initial "difficulties" or "botherations."

Many Beech Creekers, thinking back over the years to when they first arrived in the community of destination, conclude that under the circumstances they really had not experienced any botherations worth recording (and their arguments are rather convincing). Apparently, some even consider it morally wrong to admit to having had "problems." Nevertheless, various dimensions of botheration could be gleaned from our discussions with them.

A major area of perceived difficulty has to do with "factors of city life." Two foci were distinguished: (1) physical characteristics of city life, such as the traffic, noise, distances from work, inadequate housing, use of electricity and gas, differences in food and water, and so forth; and (2) urban-type "interpersonal relationships," such as the fact that social life runs on formal rules and not on informal relations, as in the mountains, and that the mountain style of life and manner of speech are conspicuous to others in the urban context. Indeed, for both sexes, the initial "strangeness" of city life seems to dominate their memories of "what happened."

Some difficulties are associated with the work situation; e.g., getting a job and becoming accustomed to the industrial work routine. It is surprising that this does not receive more emphasis, for one would think that entering the urban labor market from a low-income rural background would be a formidable undertaking and a source of great tension for the mountaineer and his family. However, most Beech Creekers migrated North *only* after they had received word via the kin communication network that specific jobs were available or that the labor market situation was favorable.

Financial difficulties seem to have plagued some families initially. In a situation in which regular expenses for gas, electricity, water, and rent are high, and bills arrive each month, newcomers, who simply are not accustomed to handling large amounts of money, often encounter household management problems.

Few Beech Creekers appear to have been disturbed by the idea of bringing up children in the narrow confines of an urban environment. Being away from family and kin in the mountains bothered some, of course. Yet it is paradoxical, given the familistic qualities of their normative patterns of behavior, to observe the minor part such concerns occupy in the experience world of the Beech Creeker. If we recall that they invariably joined kinsfolk and maintained close ties with the family homestead in the mountains despite geographic distances, this phenomenon becomes plausible.

For some families, the various botherations, difficulties and frustrations encountered in the area of destination prompted a decision, usually made by the male breadwinner in collaboration with his spouse, to return to the mountains. They either moved back to the Beech Creek neighborhoods, to Schooltown, or to neighborhoods nearby.[3] Their reasons for moving back vary, but the final decision was often crystallized during an extended "lay-off" period in the automobile industries of southern Ohio. Others, however, were simply reacting to a general and pervasive feeling of dissatisfaction with the rhythm of urban life and the pace of industrial work. A few were running from debt collectors. In general, those who had returned do not regret their decision now.

However, most Beech Creek migrants (72 percent) hold the opinion that people who have moved from eastern Kentucky to Ohio, Indiana, and elsewhere are better off, particularly in economic terms, for having moved. Indeed, a large proportion (69 percent) feel that most of the Appalachian migrants they know—neighbors, friends, and kinsfolk—are satisfied with their new way of life in the urban area. They recognize, nevertheless, that "homesickness" or "nostalgia for the mountains" is a factor with which many Appalachian migrants must contend.

# MUTUAL AID
# AND FAMILISTIC SUPPORT

We have suggested that the kin network in the area of destination performs a supportive function during the transitional phase of adjustment and that kin group members may help the newcomers in various ways. Of course, when a migrant arrives on the scene in the host community he does not seek help from *all* kinsfolk in the area (and he probably does not need to). He can often manage most of the problems encountered very well by himself. Furthermore, there is usually an informal leadership structure among the various family groups that have relocated or are in the process of relocating, and one or the other of the group members—perhaps an older "aunt," for example, who happens to be a sister of the family's patriarch in Beech Creek—frequently assumes the mantle of responsibility for the welfare of newcomers in Ohio. Then too, because mutual aid and norms of reciprocity are a "natural" state of affairs, i.e., the modus operandi within a familistic social organization, and not at all recognized as anything unusual or noteworthy by family group members, incidents of assistance are quickly absorbed into the experience world of the migrant and readily "forgotten."

We found, nevertheless, that 62 percent of the Beech Creek migrant families remembered having had at one time or another provided some form of assistance to other newcomers from Appalachian Kentucky. The form of aid varied, of course, depending upon the circumstances. In general, those who had arrived earlier were instrumental in helping newcomers find jobs and places to live, in getting them acquainted with people in the area, and, in a variety of ways, in helping them to become stable members of the migrant community.

More important than these kinds of facilitating aid during the relocation process are the functions performed by the kin network toward the maintenance of the migrant's personal stability during periods of crisis in the years following the event of migration. Here, reinforced by norms of reciprocity, the pattern of mutual aid takes the form of "social insurance and assurance" woven into the structure of interpersonal relationships as a "kin obligation." To a migrant family running into financial difficulties, "help" from kinsfolk is important, to be sure, and undoubtedly is welcomed as a means for overcoming the immediate problem and stabilizing the situation. However, in the normal course of life—i.e., of life between personal crises—the knowledge that aid and assistance from family members will be forthcoming in the event of a major disturbance in and of itself performs an important stabilizing function with many psychological ramifications. For "need" is a variable thing, and normative obligations associated with the mutual aid function of the kin network are, generally speaking, manifested only in situations defined as "trouble."

Thus, aid of a material nature exchanged between family members during any one year, if at all, may be trivial or "merely" symbolic-in-kind. But, if the "promise" of substantial material aid in the event of crises exists as a normative obligation (coupled with the assurance of an intimate and understanding social group upon which one may rely), then the stabilizing function of the kin network may be regarded as an empirical reality.[4]

We found that a third of the Beech Creek migrant families had helped some other migrant family or families in some way during the year preceding our discussions with them. This aid was extended to siblings, in the main, or to parents and sometimes to other kin. It was generally for the purpose of supplementing family living expenses during periods of financial hardship such as occur from long "lay-offs" or sickness (e.g., to pay an electric bill, to satisfy a finance company collector, to buy some necessary clothing, to take care of the rent, to help with medical expenses and hospital bills, and so forth). Almost always, the "help" given was in the form of money (other kinds of "help" are generally not regarded as anything noteworthy in the minds of Beech Creekers).

Twenty-two percent of the migrant families were recipients of help given by others. Usually these were younger families or single persons, and the help they received came from parents or siblings and sometimes from other kin. It often included non-monetary aid in the form of food, clothing, or furniture.

One or two individuals or families generally play a leading role in managing such affairs within the kin network. For example, about two-thirds of the Beech Creekers specified some member of their family group in the area of destination as the person upon whom they and other members of their household can rely in time of trouble. These people are usually members of the migrant's parental family or, occasionally, secondary kin such as great-aunts, older cousins, and so forth. A leadership structure is evidenced by the fact that the response patterns of individuals within a family group tend to converge. In short, through normative obligations and group organization, the branch-family network stands ready to help the individual Beech Creeker.

Then, too, the family homestead in the mountains also provides the migrant with an additional sense of assurance that during crises he could return to a haven of safety in time of stress. Indeed, over two-thirds of these migrant families perceive a place to go back to in eastern Kentucky *if it ever became necessary.* Yet, few hold title to or retain possession of any real property in the mountains (only 17 percent). Those who do are generally heir to a virtually worthless parcel of un-worked, eroding land and an unoccupied, dilapidated (and usually abandoned) house.

Hence, when Beech Creekers say they have "a place to go back to in eastern Kentucky," they invariably mean that if circumstances forced them, they could join parents or other kin. To the Beech Creeker, then, the concept of family homestead connotes the kin network in the area of origin.

Although they cling to the notion of the family homestead as a haven of safety, most Beech Creekers would be reluctant to avail themselves of the opportunity to return to eastern Kentucky if economic conditions become unfavorable in Ohio (37 percent of the family spokesmen said they probably would return if things got tough, 20 percent said "maybe," and 43 percent said "no"). For some migrants, return to the family homestead exists as a real and meaningful alternative to waiting out a prolonged period of unemployment and economic recession in the city; for many, however, the family homestead notion serves principally as a psychological "cushion" during the transitional adjustment process.[5]

In any case, it is clear that the stem and branch-family network functions as a social mechanism which enhances the Appalachian migrant's chances for social and psychological survival in the industrial area of destination.

## THE KIN NETWORK
## AND VISITING BEHAVIOR

Typically, the migrant's household is a complete nuclear family unit composed of husband, wife, and their children.[6] Extended family arrangements are uncommon at this later stage in the history of the Beech Creek people. Nevertheless, nuclear family units tend to be linked together (in some instances it may be more appropriate to say "locked together") into larger social groups through interactional bonds invariably formed along kinship lines. For the individual Beech Creeker, this kin network or family group serves as an arena for meaningful social relationships with significant others.

Interaction with parents and members of the parental family are by far the more important of these bondings. A few families, of course, have married children living elsewhere, but the children generally reside close by and are able to maintain a pattern of frequent visiting. As a matter of fact, over half of the migrant families who have children elsewhere see them daily.

At this stage in the Beech Creek migrant's life cycle, at least one parent is usually still living. Rarely are both parents of both the husband and wife deceased (only 14 percent of the cases). Hence, the migrant family inevitably has one, and very often two (the husband's and wife's) parental "homesteads" to which it owes some allegiance and to which it is obligated and oriented in the mountains or, because the parents too have migrated, close by in the area of destination (often in the same urban neighborhood). We found that only about one-third of the Beech Creekers have parents still residing in eastern Kentucky—a fact which explains a great deal about the mountain visiting patterns of these families. In many cases the stem of the family has been drawn toward the branches, and the family group has thereby been totally "transplanted."

If the parents live nearby, visiting exchanges are quite frequent, often daily or at least on a weekly basis. If the parents reside in the mountains, visiting exchanges are, of course, less frequent; but this does not necessarily mean that parental family ties are any less strong in a psychological sense.

Also, both the husband and wife in a migrant household generally have siblings living close at hand with whom they, as a family, are socially involved. And since most Beech Creekers come from rather large families, they are very likely to have some siblings who continue to reside back in the mountains, perhaps managing the old family homestead.[7] Because familial ties among siblings are strong, interactional contact within the sibling network is frequent. To be sure, any one migrant family may have closer social relationships with some siblings than with others; but rarely is a migrant family isolated from meaningful communication with every member of the family group.

The Beech Creeker and his spouse, then, are bound into two large kin networks which, by their marriage, have been joined together. As a family unit, they maintain visiting ties with each of these networks. There does not seem to be a pattern of favoring one over the other, except insofar as the migration pattern itself tends to be patrilocal. Through interaction with members of the family group, which reinforces family solidarity, come responsibilities and obligations as well as a feeling of belonging and security.

Let us now consider the extent to which migrant families maintain social ties with kin and friends back in the mountains.

The stereotype is well known, and it is often the chuckle point of some humorous anecdotes that, when an opportunity presents itself and without a great deal of contemplation, the Appalachian migrant will jump into his car and head for home to hunt, fish, visit, and loaf. A systematic observer, such as a compulsive noter of automobile license plates, if stationed at one of the main arteries into eastern Kentucky at the beginning of a long weekend, could not but be impressed by the large percentage of out of state traffic, only a fraction of which can be rationalized by the drawing power of the mountain tourist industry. This phenomenon, abstracted into sociological terms, is, we believe, a manifestation of the personality system of the migrant straining to maintain interactional ties with persons in the area of origin, i.e., with the interactional system with which it is in accord.

How often do Beech Creek migrant families visit back in eastern Kentucky? We found that 23 percent had not been back the year previous to our interview, 39 percent had made one or two visits, 26 percent had made three to six visits, and 12 percent had been back seven or more times. This averages 3.4 visits per year or, if we exclude those families who had made no visits (on the assumption that they have severed all ties with kin and friends in the mountains), 4.5 visits per year per family.[8] Considering the distance, the relatively poor road conditions, and the difficulties often involved in getting into the mountain neighborhoods, one may regard this as a great deal of visiting.

Generally speaking, these visits are on such holiday weekends as Labor Day, the Fourth of July, Christmas, and Easter, and they are made by the nuclear family unit to parents and siblings still living in the mountains. Longer visits are rare and, because of the distance and difficulties involved, one-day trips are rather uncommon (and practically impossible because of the logistical problems).

On occasion, of course, migrant families also receive visitors from the mountains. In this case, 78 percent had received at least one, and the average family had received about 3.0 visiting units (i.e., groups of visitors) per year or, excluding those who had received none at all, 3.9 per year per family. These tend to be short, overnight visits from siblings, parents, and other kin. Nevertheless, with respect to visiting behavior, a norm of reciprocity seems to be well established.

Exchanging letters also seems to be an active form of communication. Although some migrant families (28 percent) confess that they write to kinsfolk in eastern Kentucky only once a year or less often, about a third write at least once a week, and over half write at least once a month. Frequency of receiving letters, as we all know, is highly correlated with frequency of writing. The news as well as the attitudes conveyed by these letter exchanges, or by visiting exchanges, is quickly diffused among members of the family group and, subsequently, to almost all segments of the Beech Creek community, whether in Ohio or eastern Kentucky.

In short, the two segments of the Beech Creek migration system are integrally bound together through communication via visiting or letter exchanges within the various kin networks.

# SOCIAL ACTIVITIES
# AND FRIENDSHIP TIES

The social life of the Beech Creek migrant is attuned to the family. On weekends, for example, the men like to putter around the house, work in the garden or on the car, relax with their children, and watch T.V. Their wives, who have similar home-centered interests, place a bit more emphasis upon religious activities. Kin visiting, of course, is important, and in many respects it is a weekend ritual.

Leisure time activities during the week are also generally confined to the home. Many Beech Creekers (about half) claim hobbies of one kind or another; women prefer handicrafts while men like outdoor activities such as hunting, fishing, and other sports.

On holidays or vacations, the migrant families are inclined either to visit in eastern Kentucky or to stay at home and perhaps to visit with relatives and friends in the urban area.[9] Vacation trips other than to kinsfolk in the mountains are only an occasional event and not an integral part of the life style, as it is among some segments of American Society and among working-class families in many parts of Europe. Indeed, the entire pattern of social activities of Beech Creekers bears the stamp of a familistically-oriented cultural tradition. We expect that this is characteristic of rural Appalachian people in general.

To what extent do Beech Creekers participate in the formal organizations of the host communities? We know they were drawn from a mountain society that regarded lightly formalized social activities of any kind. Hence, there is little reason to suppose that they would feel comfortable as participants of organized groups in the urban area.

To be sure, the mountaineer takes his religion seriously, and church membership is considered important. Yet 45 percent of the men and 24 percent of the women do *not* belong to a church or sect group in the area of destination. (One might compare this with 57 percent of the male and 22 percent of the female Beech Creekers still living in eastern Kentucky who do not belong to a church.)

The only other formal organizations that seem to occupy some space in the interest world of the migrant are the labor unions. These are relevant mainly for the male segment of the population. Only 46 percent of the men belong to any labor union, and those who do generally take only a pragmatic interest in union affairs (66 percent of the union members actually attend union meetings).

Beech Creekers rarely participate in any other organizations. A few men (15 percent) may belong to the Masons, and some women (13 percent) will on occasion attend PTA meetings. By and large, however, the variety of special-interest groups, such as the American Legion, VFW, League of Women Voters, and so forth, which are woven into the fabric of American urban and suburban life, are of little concern to the Beech Creeker. In fact, 38 percent of the men and 77 percent of the women do *not* belong to any formal secular organization. (One might compare this with 75 percent of the male and 92 percent of the female Beech Creekers living in eastern Kentucky who do not belong to any secular organization.)

Although participation in formal organizations is not an integral part of the social life of Beech Creekers at either end of the migration stream, this does not mean that migrants are completely isolated from face-to-face communication with persons native to the urban area. Many feel they have at least some social contact with non-eastern Kentuckians; relatively few feel they have none (Table 6.2).[10] These social contacts generally take place at work, in the neighborhood, or at church.

The non-kin visiting pattern of males is composed primarily of eastern Kentuckians—from the neighborhood (42 percent), the work crew (27 percent), and the church (17 percent). On the other hand, the females' visiting circle is made up largely of non-eastern Kentuckians— yet, likewise, from the neighborhood (52 percent), the work crew (21 percent), and the church (21 percent).[11] This difference in composition of non-kin visiting networks may be the result of two situational factors: (1) Beech Creek women who are employed outside the home generally work in situations that include many native Ohioans, whereas the work situation commonly encountered by men tends to be composed largely of eastern Kentuckians; (2) Beech Creek women who are full-time homemakers are generally confined to the immediate neighborhood during the day and, except in the case of families living in a "little Kentucky" settlement such as X-town, the neighborhoods often include many Ohioans. Their husbands, on the other hand, generally have control over the use of the family automobile, and therefore possess greater mobility to seek out acquaintances with similar interests and from similar backgrounds. In short, the picture that emerges is that Beech Creek women, far more than men, are cut off from social interaction with persons who share similar cultural traditions. While the processes of social absorption into the urban community may be more rapid in their case, as compared with men, they may also feel more alienated from the mountain way

Table 6.2. Amount of social contact Beech Creek migrants feel they have with people who are native to the area of destination.

| Amount of Contact | Percentage | |
|---|---|---|
| | Males (N = 82) | Females (N = 79) |
| None: | 6.1 | 16.5 |
| Very little: | 32.9 | 24.1 |
| Some: | 36.6 | 19.0 |
| Great deal: | 24.4 | 40.4 |
| Total: | 100.0 | 100.0 |

of life. In that sense they encounter greater, or at least different, adjustment problems from those encountered by men.

Furthermore, although Beech Creek women have numerous visiting
acquaintances from "outside" the Appalachian migrant community,
meaningful communication ties may be tenuous. This is indicated by
the fact that 29 percent of the women but only 13 percent of the men
can *not* count any native of the urban area as a "close friend" with
whom they meet in each others' homes. Indeed, the average female has
only about three such friends, whereas the average male has about six.[12]
The Beech Creek woman, it seems, is in many ways more isolated
socially than her husband.


# TRADITIONALISM IN RELIGION
# AND POLITICS

Beech Creekers, as we have mentioned, are a religious people in spite
of the fact that only about half of the male and three-fourths of the
female migrants belong to some kind of church or sect group in the
host community. Like southern highlanders generally,[13] although they
shy away from organized group activities of any sort and have a strong
aversion to rigid ceremony and conventional modes of religious expression, spiritual matters play a prominent part in their lives. Almost all
Beech Creekers who are not actively involved in an organized church
group nevertheless profess some kind of denominational interest and
loyalty (only four percent do not) and, with few exceptions, this interest
tends to be of a fundamentalistic variety.

We found that 28 percent of the migrants identified with the Baptist
Church; 23 percent with the Church of God, Holiness, and similar sect
groups; 21 percent with the Church of Christ; 20 percent with the
Christian Church; and 8 percent with the Methodists and Presbyterians.
This pattern of religious preference is much like that of Beech Creekers
residing back in the mountains.

Can we distinguish any changes in the pattern of church affiliation
and preference as a result of migration and subsequent exposure, over
time, to urbanizing influences in the area of destination?

Before moving out of the mountains, many Beech Creekers had been
associated with one or the other of the religious groups in or near the
Beech Creek neighborhoods (10 percent of the women and 24 percent

of the men had *not*). Only about half of them (45 percent of the men and 55 percent of the women who had belonged to a church prior to migrating) continue to manifest interest in, or maintain affiliation with, that specific denomination in the host community; the others have "switched" their allegiance.

We observe a similar pattern of change when comparing the migrant's present denominational interest with that of his or her parents. Only about 43 percent of the men and 50 percent of the women continue in the same denominational tradition as their fathers, and only 45 percent of the men and 58 percent of the women cling to the denominational affiliation of their mothers. (The pattern is similar among Beech Creekers back in the mountains.) It is clear, then, that some changes have occurred and that the individual Beech Creeker does not necessarily follow in the religious footsteps of his parents; the family group seems to tolerate religious diversity of a kind.

Indeed, most Beech Creekers believe that an individual has the inherent right, freedom, and privilege to choose for himself in matters of religion and that, rather than family tradition, an individual's preferences, beliefs, and interpretation of the Bible should be the basis for his convictions and choice. In other words, they are inclined to argue the legitimacy of individual choice-making based upon personal sentiments and to disregard the social determinants of those sentiments; individualism, not familism, is the ideological foundation in this case.

Even so, there exists a latent attitude among Beech Creekers that church going ought to be a family affair and that "togetherness" and family traditions in such matters are "good things." Furthermore, the "differences" we have noted in the religious preferences of Beech Creekers before and after migration, and between migrants and their parents, are far from meaningful in magnitude. That is to say, the theological distinctions between the various denominational categories are, from a sociological point of view, of minor import. What, for example, does it mean for a migrant to have switched from Baptist to Christian Church, or from Church of God to Church of Christ? To be sure, there are doctrinal differences, but because the emphasis upon a congregational, sectarian, fundamentalistic, literalistic-interpretation of the Bible type of religious orientation seems to have been retained, the observed changes are, for the most part, of minor significance. Indeed, the changes in denominational affiliation may be more an artifact of the immediate neighborhood situation than of any basic shifts in religious philosophy.

We can say, then, that the migrants brought a frontier faith with them into the areas of destination, that church and sect groups in the receiving communities had been organized around various dimensions of that faith, and that these groups, in turn, tend to reinforce the traditionalistic religious orientations characteristic of the mountain folk culture.

What does religious fundamentalism of the mountain variety proclaim and to what extent do Beech Creekers adhere to its teachings? The following statements suggest certain beliefs often associated with fundamentalism;[14] consider the migrants' pattern of response:

(1) *The Bible is God's Word and all that it says is true.* Ninety-two percent of the women and seventy-nine percent of the men believe this; few believe that the Bible was written by men inspired by God.

(2) *Gambling is always wrong.* Ninety-seven percent of the women and ninety-three percent of the men believe this; few believe that it is only sometimes wrong.

(3) *Drinking is always wrong.* Ninety-two percent of the women and eighty-six percent of the men believe this.

(4) *A call to preach is more important for a minister than training.* Sixty-nine percent of the women and sixty-eight percent of the men believe this; some believe that both a call and training are important.

(5) *Card playing is always wrong.* Fifty-nine percent of the women and fifty-seven percent of the men believe this.

(6) *The world is soon coming to an end.* Fifty-one percent of the women and forty-three percent of the men believe this religious teaching to be true.

If we regard agreement with at least five of these statements as indicative of an extremely fundamentalistic position, 63 percent of the female migrants and 38 percent of the male migrants can be so classified. Women are far stronger advocates of fundamentalism than men; they, it seems, are the guardians of the frontier faith.

Comparatively, Beech Creekers living back in eastern Kentucky, i.e., non-migrants, tend to be much more absolute in their fundamentalistic beliefs (although a few feel that card playing may not always be wrong): we find that 80 percent of the women and 69 percent of the men agree with at least five of the items. Hence, if we dare to make comparisons, there is some evidence of an erosion of traditional, fundamentalistic beliefs among the migrant segment, and especially among the men who, in various ways, are in more direct contact with the urban industrial culture.

It would be quite presumptuous, given the nature of our data, to suggest the effects that the Beech Creekers' religious orientations had upon their patterns of adjustment in the area of destination. The problem is very complex. We have some reason to suspect, however, that the extreme fundamentalistic orientation and the particular kind of notion of God's will that tends to prevail among these people have important behavioral consequences in their struggle to enhance their lot in life and to achieve some measure of upward mobility.[15]

In political behavior as in religion, Beech Creekers tend to employ an individualistic rather than a familistic ideology to legitimate their choices. For example, only 21 percent of the men and 16 percent of the women feel that a person should support the political party favored by their parents and kin. They will argue that "kinsfolk should stick together," that "it's the right thing to do if one is raised that way," and that "one usually does anyway." But the larger majority feel that "voting should be one's own decision," that people should "vote for the best man, not the party," that "an individual has the right, freedom, and privilege to choose for himself," and that "you might not agree with your parents." There is little doubt that most Beech Creekers regard voting behavior as a matter of individual conscience.

As with religion, Beech Creekers are inclined to take their politics seriously. We found that 61 percent of the men and 63 percent of the women were registered to vote, and that 58 percent and 59 percent, respectively, had actually voted in the previous presidential election. This record compares favorably with the national average. It is interesting, however, and perhaps indicative of traditionalism, that those who voted (in the 1960 Kennedy-Nixon campaign) feel they did not have much difficulty in making up their minds (only 15 percent confess to having had a "little trouble").

Most Beech Creek families, through traditions tracing back to the Civil War, have been and are Republicans.[16] Even today, for instance, about 90 percent of the Beech Creekers living in the mountains consider themselves Republicans. It is noteworthy, therefore, that among the migrants we find only about 65 percent identifying with the Republican Party; about 13 percent regard themselves as "independents," and the remainder (22%) are Democrats. Perhaps the urban experiences of these people have had a liberalizing effect.[17] In any event, there is some evidence to suggest that individualism has become a bit stronger as a basis for political choices, and that family tradition in such matters has been weakened.

It is also clear that Beech Creekers retain a firm belief in the "rightness" of the democratic process. Their valued traditions—in politics as well as in religion—have by no means been shattered or replaced through their encounters with the urban, industrial world.

# BETWEEN TWO WORLDS

Let us now consider the interplay and balance between the satisfactions these people have attained within the context of the host environment and the factors or forces that draw their thoughts back home to the mountains. Beech Creekers and similar rural-to-urban migrants in other parts of the world are in many ways caught between, and the products of, two worlds, and the resolution of tensions generated by this dualism is one of the fundamental problems in the study of migration.[18]

Some Beech Creekers (23 percent) are chronically homesick, often experiencing periods of great longing for the old home neighborhood. Others harbor only a slight degree of nostalgia, which may be manifested especially on occasions when things just aren't going the way they should. Many more, however, "rarely" or "never" miss their former friends and the eastern Kentucky mountain area (about 42 percent); they, in effect, have made a complete transition, wiping from their minds all sentiments of attachment to the old. Among Beech Creekers, then, nostalgia is a variable thing—a psychological condition that undoubtedly has its roots in the social circumstances associated with the process of migration.

Do Beech Creekers ever regret having moved away from the mountains? Normally, their answer will be a flat "no" (in over 85 percent of the cases). A few may, at times, feel homesick enough to want to move back, but in general, most Beech Creekers recognize and appreciate the advantages that have accrued to them as a result of migration and, although some cannot shake off their nostalgia, most have firmly resolved to make a go of it in the urban, industrial world.

Their way of life, of course, has changed and is different from that of Beech Creekers in eastern Kentucky. They feel they have been blest with greater economic prosperity and with more conveniences and material things than they would have enjoyed had they remained in the mountains. (Women tend to see this material advantage in terms of "conveniences," whereas men see it in more basic terms, as, for example, better income and job security.) Some prefer to focus their notions of satisfactions on the social and recreational advantages of urban life, on the more modern institutional services that are available, and on the obvious fact of being less isolated. Only a few feel there have been no real differences or that the differences experienced stack up as "negative" against the new situation. Indeed, almost all Beech Creek migrants are quite satisfied with their new way of life. The few who are somewhat dissatisfied are mainly men who for one reason or the other do not appreciate the urban environment and the routinized demands of industrial work.

Furthermore, these migrants from Appalachia do not feel discriminated against by other people in the host communities. It is a rare Beech Creeker who will admit to having experienced some form of social injustice within the urban milieu. In fact, almost all of the men (over 90 percent) and even most of the women (about 70 percent; most of the others "don't know") adamantly insist that eastern Kentuckians have the same chances of getting and holding jobs as persons native to that area (i.e., as Ohioans). Beech Creekers are reluctant to talk about such things; the thought of social discrimination runs against their equalitarian grain, and a good mountaineer would never allow himself to admit to having been "victimized" in any shape, form, or manner by others. If the urban, industrial communities of the Ohio Valley discriminate against "Briarhoppers" from Kentucky, it is a phenomenon that Beech Creekers do not, or perhaps will not, recognize as a problem.

Yet despite this general, pervasive feeling of satisfaction about their new way of life and about circumstances in the host communities,[19] Beech Creekers as a collectivity evidence signs of divided loyalty. At this point in their history they appear to be in a stage of transition—betwixt and between the old and the new. Indeed, there are many indications that the migration system links together two periods of time, two ways of life, two worlds. Consider, for example, how Beech Creekers respond to a series of questions designed to tap various dimensions of their orientation to, or identification with, the host community and area of origin:

*Would the Beech Creek migrant prefer to live elsewhere?* If given a free choice, many of course would. It is interesting that women are less willing to entertain ideas of moving again than men (37 vs. 58 percent, respectively), and few women, as compared with men, favor the thought of returning to the mountains (9 vs. 33 percent, respectively). Men, it seems, have an affinity for the mountain way of life; women tend to shy away from it, perhaps because they have accomplished the difficult chores of creating a new home, now enjoy the amenities of urban life, and are inclined to see the old way of life as offering them very little.

*Where would the Beech Creek migrant prefer to retire someday when too old to work?* This question attempts to rule out all consideration of differential employment opportunities. Again we find, however, that men are more oriented toward the mountains, while women are more content to remain in the urban community even in their later years.

(About 60 percent of the men and 22 percent of the women would like to move back to eastern Kentucky; 24 percent of the men and 51 percent of the women would like to stay where they now live; and the remainder would prefer to retire elsewhere, such as in Florida or California, where the climate is more favorable.) In many cases, obviously, certain reality factors other than work opportunities have helped tip the scales of residential aspiration away from the object of nostalgia, namely, the Beech Creek neighborhoods.

*Where does the Beech Creeker feel is home?* Here we explore a slightly different dimension, for the concept "home" has deeper meanings than simply residential location. Our data clearly reveal the dualistic nature of the migration system at this point in time. (About 38 percent of the women and 49 percent of the men regard the Beech Creek neighborhoods as "home"; 56 percent of the women and 43 percent of the men think of the host community as "home"; only a few feel attached elsewhere.) As a matter of fact, with only two or three exceptions, those who regard the mountain neighborhoods as their "real home" sincerely believe, and emphatically state, they will *always* feel that way.

Does time itself play a role in the formation of such distinctive attitudes and orientations? Perhaps. And perhaps the migrant's age when he arrives in the host community and the stage in the migration process of his family group are also important factors. In some cases a change in orientation, i.e., in community identification, may never occur. In other cases the change may be experienced almost immediately after arrival in the host community. For example, of those Beech Creekers who feel at home now in the urban area, about 51 percent believe it took less than six months for them to assume that attitude; on the other hand, 15 percent believe it took more than five years.

*Where would the migrant prefer to be buried when the time comes?* For some, of course, it matters little (16 percent), but for many, this ultimate question is of very great concern and poses an issue they would rather resolve themselves while they are still able. Of those who care 43 percent would prefer to be buried in or near the urban community they now regard as home, whereas 57 percent would prefer to be laid to final rest in or near the Beech Creek neighborhoods (e.g., in the Andrews family cemetery, the Laurel neighborhood cemetery, and so forth). Again, there is little doubt that the male is more oriented toward the mountains than the female (68 percent of the men prefer the Beech Creek area as compared with 46 percent of the women). It may be that these differential attitudes reflect the patrilocal character of the mountain culture, and that this tendency is present even in the choice of a burial site (women, of course, would want to be buried near their husbands and, since some had married outside the Beech Creek community, their ultimate wishes would be affected).

A pattern of attitude begins to emerge. Some Beech Creekers seem perfectly content with, or resigned to the idea of regarding the host community as their permanent "home." Some simply cannot shake off their nostalgic identification with the Appalachian area. In either case, however, they feel the decision to migrate had been a proper response to economically depressed circumstances in the mountains and that they are better off for having migrated. As a collectivity, then, the migrants are "caught" between two worlds. But because the process of transition was stabilized within a stem-family system of migration, the possible tensions and strains have been minimized and the well being of the individual Beech Creeker maximized. As compared with Beech Creekers residing back in the mountains, for example, the migrant segment suffers far less from feelings of anxiety and despair.[20] Nostalgia, it seems, is something most migrants have learned to cope with and perhaps have internalized into a dimension of their personality. Although they may be unable to overcome the nagging feeling of being more at home in the mountains, that aspect of deprivation is more than compensated for by the material advantages they have attained and enjoy in the area of destination.

# WORK AND MATERIAL STYLE OF LIFE

Beech Creek families migrated in order to enhance their economic lot in life. They were seeking work opportunities and, for the most part, they found them in the urban, industrial areas of the Ohio Valley.

But they came to the areas of destination generally ill-prepared for other than unskilled labor. Few had the advantage of any high school education. Only about 22 percent of the men had held some kind of full-time non-farm job prior to migration[21] and rarely had any of the women been employed outside the home. Although many of the men had been in the military service, few had been able to attend any special schools that might have prepared them for industrial work.[22] Hence, Beech Creekers usually entered the labor market in Ohio at an unskilled level.

Over the years, however, they exhibited a pattern of gradual upward mobility. Some men, for example, had availed themselves of opportunities to attend trade schools in the urban area or to acquire on-the-job industrial training; a few had taken night school courses (in the main, to become teachers). About 18 percent have achieved skilled, clerical, or professional status, and only about 19 percent are still at an unskilled level (Table 6.3). Although the change has not been dramatic, that an up-grading in the occupational status of the collectivity and, presumably, in the industrial proficiency of these men has occurred, is clear. Most of them, however, continue to be manual workers. About 59 percent are involved in the manufacturing industries, 15 percent in the building and maintenance industries, 10 percent in transportation and commerce, and the remainder in other kinds of occupations, such as teaching. The overwhelming majority of these men are "satisfied" with their jobs.

A large proportion of the women are also employed (32 percent). Some are in clerical positions, a few are school teachers or store managers, but most of those employed (67 percent) are in semiskilled or unskilled jobs.

Despite the low level of occupational status of Beech Creek migrants relative to the general occupational structure of American Society, the important fact is that most of them *are* employed and at reasonably

Table 6.3. Occupation of Beech Creek male migrants, 1961.

| Occupations | Number | Percent |
|---|---|---|
| School teacher: | 3 | 4.1 |
| Farm operator: | 2 | 2.7 |
| Clerical, sales, kindred: | 4 | 5.5 |
| Skilled worker, foreman: | 6 | 8.2 |
| Semi-skilled worker: | 44 | 60.3 |
| Unskilled, farm and non-farm: | 14 | 19.2 |
| Total:* | 73 | 100.0% |

* Nine cases are not applicable (3 going to school, 3 long retired, and 1 unable to work). For those who were laid off or unemployed (but employable) at the time (12 cases), these data refer to the last job held.

high wages. Few migrant families are on welfare or drawing social security benefits.[23] Their family incomes, on the average, are at or slightly below the national norm but far above those of Beech Creekers in the mountains (Table 6.4).[24] Indeed, 20 percent of these families had over $8,000 income in 1960, and only 17 percent had below $3,000. Obviously, some are poor—but perhaps not as poor as they might have been

**Table 6.4.** Level of living of Beech Creekers, 1961: comparisons between migrant and eastern Kentucky family-households.

| | Percentage of Beech Creek Households Possessing Item | |
|---|---|---|
| Item | Migrant families (N = 138) | Eastern Kentucky families (N = 64) |
| Mechanical refrigerator: | 99.3 | 95.3 |
| Radio: | 96.4 | 92.2 |
| Automobile: | 92.7 | 58.7 |
| Water piped into house: | 91.3 | 34.9 |
| Electric clock:* | 89.1 | 60.9 |
| Power washing machine: | 88.4 | 90.6 |
| Television set: | 88.4 | 20.3 |
| Indoor flush toilet: | 79.0 | 15.6 |
| Hot water system:* | 77.5 | 22.2 |
| Electric vacuum cleaner:* | 74.6 | 23.4 |
| Indoor tub or shower:* | 73.9 | 15.6 |
| Pressure cooker:* | 55.8 | 52.4 |
| Telephone:* | 54.7 | 4.7 |
| Daily newspaper: | 51.4 | 6.3 |
| Regular magazine: | 44.9 | 32.8 |
| Automatic washing machine:* | 26.1 | 0 |
| New model auto (2 years or less):* | 23.3 | 1.6 |
| Piano:* | 4.3 | 3.1 |
| Median level of living score (*), all families: | 4.6 items | 1.1 item |
| Median family income, approximate: | $5230 | $1340 |

* Note: Asterisks indicate the nine items included in the Cornell Level of Living Scale from which the median level of living score was derived.

had they remained in Appalachian Kentucky (where 37 percent of the Beech Creek families had less than $1,000 income in 1960). Monetarily, the migrants seem to be doing fairly well in the urban area.

Most of them reside in one-family houses. Only about 20 percent live in rented apartments or, in a few cases, trailers. About 50 percent of the families own their own homes.

In material terms they enjoy a modestly high level of living (Table 6.4). Compared with Beech Creek families in Appalachia, one could say that they live in material affluency, if not splendor. There is little doubt that migration gave them an economic advantage over their kinsfolk and former neighbors who chose to remain behind in the mountains.

## HAPPINESS: Past and Present

We may well ask, at this point, whether Beech Creekers are happy and content with their life situations in the host communities of the Ohio Valley. They have experienced a variety of difficulties over the years, not the least of which were the confusions associated with the process of relocation, and they retain many memories, both pleasant and unpleasant, of people and events long past. What are their foci of interest and how do they view the "scheme of things entire?" What are the pleasantries, tragedies and sources of consternation that permeate their lives and orient their actions?[25]

Most Beech Creekers will say that their happiest period of life was sometime in the past, when they were young, in school, and living back in the mountains of Kentucky. They nurture idyllic memories of the fun, freedom, and family-centered activities of growing up in the Beech Creek neighborhoods. Although the rational sector of their minds clearly recognizes the poverty of those earlier years, these memories of youth appear to be affairs of the heart little swayed by thoughts of material deprivations.

Despite this general idealization of the old way of life, most Beech Creekers nevertheless regard themselves as "very happy" nowadays. Few admit to being somewhat unhappy. Indeed, if survey findings are any sort of valid indication, they may be more content with their lot in life than the average American. For example, Gurin and his colleagues[26] found that one-third of the respondents in a cross-sectional sample of the U.S. adult population said they are "very happy" whereas, using similar interviewing tactics and procedures, we found almost two-thirds of the Beech Creek migrants choosing to respond in that highly positive tone.

In the immediate context, the Beech Creeker's realization of happiness is inextricably linked with conditions and factors associated with and affecting the well-being of the family, children, and home. For the male breadwinner, of course, work satisfaction and job security play a prominent part in this assessment; women, on the other hand, are more likely to consider matters of family health (Table 6.5).[27]

In contemplating the past, however, their notions about sources of happiness take on a decidedly different slant (Table 6.5). The independence and freedom of early childhood and adolescence in the mountains becomes the focal point of their imagination and, in many respects, the object of their nostalgia. This is especially so in the case of men. Obviously, the mountaineer considers himself deprived of that which he once had. He feels confined by the congested environs of the urban area, and he feels constrained by the demands of the industrial work situation. Consequently, and quite understandably, the freedom to wander in the hills of Kentucky and the sense of independence associated with and perhaps inherent in the mountain way of life—conditions

Table **6.5.** Sources of happiness, past and present, reported by Beech Creek migrants.

| Sources of Happiness | Past happiness | | | Present happiness | | |
|---|---|---|---|---|---|---|
| | Percentage of total sources mentioned | | | | | |
| | Male | Female | Total | Male | Female | Total |
| Family and children: | 13.8 | 34.5 | 24.1 | 33.4 | 51.6 | 41.6 |
| Economic and material: | 1.7 | 1.7 | 1.7 | 14.9 | 7.5 | 11.6 |
| Job and work: | 8.6 | 1.7 | 5.2 | 21.1 | 9.7 | 15.9 |
| Health, self, and family: | 1.7 | 3.4 | 2.6 | 9.6 | 15.1 | 12.1 |
| Church and religion: | 1.7 | 1.7 | 1.7 | 7.0 | 4.3 | 5.8 |
| Independence and freedom: | 70.8 | 46.6 | 58.7 | 8.8 | 7.5 | 8.2 |
| Miscellaneous: | 1.7 | 10.4 | 6.0 | 2.6 | 3.2 | 2.9 |
| None: | 0 | 0 | 0 | 2.6 | 1.1 | 1.9 |
| Total percentage: | 100.0 | 100.0 | 100.0 | 100.0 | 100.0 | 100.0 |
| (Response N = ) | (58) | (58) | (116) | (114) | (93) | (207) |

perceived by him—in retrospect become equated with "happiness past."

Yet, when comparing the present with the past, the observed deprivations seem to be balanced and compensated for by material gains experienced through migration. For family, kin, and home are primary concerns, and their well-being in large measure determines the Beech Creeker's sense of fulfillment. Lingering memories of what once was—of happier times in the past—seem to have little effect upon their assessment of the immediate context. Beech Creekers, by and large, regard themselves as quite happy.

But let us not create the impression that these migrants are immune from unhappiness. To the contrary, they are well aware of what unhappiness means and, like other human beings, they try to avoid those circumstances that tend to produce it. Although many migrants (a third) can think of nothing they are unhappy about at present (have they somehow achieved complete mastery over the forces that control their lives?), most can identify at least one source of consternation (Table 6.6). Women tend to focus on matters relating to the family and children and to management of the household budget. Men focus on things about job and work, about matters of money, and about community and world problems. In both cases, however, a variety of concerns is evidenced; misfortunes vary, and the objects of concern are determined by the vagaries of events affecting one's life.

The kinds of things Beech Creekers tend to worry about are similar, in pattern, to the kind of things they regard as sources of "unhappiness" (compare Tables 6.6 and 6.8).

In reflecting upon the past, however, the Beech Creeker's notions of what has constituted "unhappiness" are a bit different from their immediate objects of consternation (Table 6.7). Memories of a death or serious illness in the family are sharply impressed upon their minds; this is especially so among men. Furthermore, both men and women regard the problems associated with military service—whether it was to go off to war or to remain behind and wait for a loved one's return—as a source of past uneasiness and despair. Such events as death, illness, and military service threaten the fabric of interpersonal relationships that is their mainstay of life and their wellspring of meaning. Although some women, for perhaps the same reason, tend to think of the migration event as a period of "unhappiness," men do not. Neither men nor women, however, regard their migration experience as an especially pleasant affair, for it too, like a death in the family, separated them from persons to whom they were affectively bound.

Whether Beech Creekers are happier or unhappier now for having migrated is a question that can never be answered. From a strictly

**Table 6.6.** Sources of present unhappiness reported by Beech Creek migrants.

| Source of Present Unhappiness | Percentage of total sources mentioned | | |
|---|---|---|---|
| | Males | Females | Total |
| Family and children: | 3.4 | 17.3 | 10.0 |
| Economic and material: | 12.4 | 13.6 | 12.9 |
| Job and work: | 21.3 | 7.4 | 14.7 |
| Health, self, and family: | 4.5 | 4.9 | 4.7 |
| Community and world problems: | 16.9 | 3.7 | 10.6 |
| Dissatisfaction with new and longing for old way of life: | 1.1 | 4.9 | 2.9 |
| Miscellaneous: | 7.9 | 17.3 | 12.4 |
| None: | 32.5 | 30.9 | 31.8 |
| Total percentage: | 100.0 | 100.0 | 100.0 |
| (Response N = ) | (89) | (81) | (170) |

**Table 6.7.** Sources of past unhappiness reported by Beech Creek migrants.

| Sources of Past Unhappiness | Percentage of total sources mentioned | | |
|---|---|---|---|
| | Males | Females | Total |
| Death in family: | 50.0 | 29.4 | 37.9 |
| Economic and material: | 4.2 | 2.9 | 3.4 |
| Job and work: | 4.2 | 0 | 1.7 |
| Health, self, and family: | 16.7 | 26.5 | 22.4 |
| Military service: | 20.7 | 17.6 | 19.0 |
| Migration: | 0 | 11.8 | 6.9 |
| Family problems: | 0 | 2.9 | 1.7 |
| Miscellaneous: | 4.2 | 8.9 | 7.0 |
| Total percentage: | 100.0 | 100.0 | 100.0 |
| (Response N = ) | (48) | (68) | (116) |

Table 6.8. Sources of present worry reported by Beech Creek migrants.

| Source of Worry | Percentage of total sources mentioned | | |
|---|---|---|---|
| | Males | Females | Total |
| Family and children: | 14.0 | 23.8 | 18.8 |
| Economic and material: | 23.5 | 16.9 | 20.3 |
| Job and work: | 16.9 | 6.9 | 12.0 |
| Health, self, and family: | 14.7 | 18.5 | 16.5 |
| Church and morality: | 1.5 | 5.4 | 3.4 |
| World affairs: | 16.9 | 16.9 | 16.9 |
| Community and national problems: | 5.9 | 2.3 | 4.1 |
| Miscellaneous: | 6.6 | 9.3 | 8.0 |
| Total percentage: | 100.0 | 100.0 | 100.0 |
| (Response N = ) | (136) | (130) | (266) |

economic perspective, there is little doubt that their decision to relocate was a wise one, under the circumstances. Fortunately, the migration system contained within itself the social mechanism for managing this process with a minimum of tension and for assuring the personal stability of newcomers in the host community. Beech Creekers today seem to be fairly content and satisfied with their lot in life. As a people, they may be caught between two worlds. Nevertheless, they seem to have adapted well to the exigencies of the situation.

# 7 ADAPTATION TO Industrial Work Situation[1]

The process of adaptation to the industrial work situation encountered in the area of destination may be one of the more important sources of potential strain in the transitional adjustment of rural-to-urban migrants. This is even more probable if the migrants were reared within a familistically-oriented social organization and accustomed to the self-directed work routine that characterizes the patterning of economic pursuits in relatively isolated, subsistence farming localities of Appalachia. An individual migrant from rural Applachia, for example, has little opportunity prior to migration to acquire industrial-type work experiences. Upon arrival in the area of destination he seeks out and assumes a work role for which he may have very little, if any, preparation and which, moreover, is at once sharply differentiated from family activities. It seems inevitable that some kinds of strain result in the process of adaptation. To the extent that the family-kinship system is responsive to the changing needs of the migrant, serious adjustment difficulties are probably avoided. For a proper understanding of the adaptation process, however, it is also necessary to take into account the nature of the industrial work situation in the area of destination. Indeed, the social context in receiving areas, which includes the industrial work situation and other aspects of the local community situation, probably determines the effectiveness and, perhaps, the very form of response by the family-kinship system to the changing needs of the migrant.

The previous chapter provided an overview of Beech Creekers in the area of destination and their reactions to this confrontation with the host community. Our aim here is to explore more specifically and in greater depth the *male migrant's* pattern of adaptation and reaction to the requisites of industrial work.[2] We have noted that many Beech Creek male migrants (59 percent) are employed in manufacturing industries and generally at semi-skilled or unskilled jobs. It is toward this segment of our study population that we shall direct most of our attention.[3]

# FROM FIELD TO FACTORY

The work situation in the mountain area of eastern Kentucky was, and to a considerable extent still continues to be, the antithesis of the work situation encountered by migrants in urban Ohio. Prior to migration most male migrants from Beech Creek were engaged in farming, either on a full-time or part-time basis, and this work was very often a family endeavor with responsibilities divided according to age and sex, and clearly articulated with other life activities. Some men, to be sure, had held supplementary jobs in the log-woods, in the mines, or as laborers on county road construction projects, and a few had worked at one time or another in factories in southern Ohio; but the rhythm of work life was in the main organized around, and tempered by, the seasonal demands of subsistence agriculture. "Public work," as Beech Creekers called almost any kind of off-farm employment, required only a temporary separation of the individual from the family homestead, and a man's obligation to do his share of the farming remained foremost.

Male migrants in Ohio generally reflect back favorably and with considerable nostalgia on their early life and work experience in the mountains. "Farming," they feel, "was good to grow up on." They recall the independence and sense of security it accords and the fact that farming is an outdoor activity with a great variety of tasks. Many would agree with the Beech Creeker who said, "If I could take my present job and move it back to the hills, I'd go in a minute."

Of course, as the latter suggests, farming in the Beech Creek area did not and does not offer the possibility of an adequate cash income. The difficulties of "making it on the farm" and the lack of occupational alternatives in the mountain region function as important "push" factors in stimulating out-migration and, likewise, provide a subsequent basis for comparison with the work situation in the area of destination. Most Beech Creekers, consequently, are not unhappy with their new work situations. As one migrant succinctly put it: "Any job here beats hell out of pounding rocks in Kentucky."

Migration to Ohio is an old pattern for the Beech Creek neighbor-hoods. Contemporary migrants undoubtedly moved with the comforting knowledge that many before them—kinsfolk and neighbors—had been successful in making this transition and in adapting to the industrial work situation. Their predecessors' obvious mastery of the situation (relatively few returned permanently), coupled with the visible spoils of victory (many visited home with new cars and other symbols of affluence), bolstered the confidence and undergirded the fortitude of these "new recruits" to the Ohio labor market.

In his book dealing with new factory employees, Slotkin describes one type of migrant as the "permanently uprooted."[4] These migrants perceive the donor system (our terminology) in the area of origin as substantially and permanently inadequate, hence migration from the area is undertaken with expectations of permanency. We suggest that such "expectations of permanency" are directly tied in with the sup-portive functions performed by the kinship structure. From significant kin group members in the area of destination, for example, the potential migrant secures information about the kinds of jobs available, as well as some idea about the work expectations connected with these indus-trial occupation roles. In this way, the potential migrant is aided sig-nificantly in formulating an image of work requisites in the factory vis-a-vis those of the farm. His kin are often able to supply details about a specific job "opening." The Beech Creek migrant, therefore, who had fairly accurate information about the job situation in Ohio, was able at least partially to anticipate the industrial occupation role prior to migration; the event of migration was, from his point of view, the end result of a rational decision and the manifestation of a firm resolve to accept the "punishment" which would be entailed in pursuing the "re-ward." Our data converge upon this conclusion. Indeed, in numerous ways the transition from field to factory and the process of adaptation to the industrial work situation were begun long before the migrant left Beech Creek; the kin structure (i.e., the stem-family system) helped stabilize and manage the process.

### Initial Job Situation

Few if any Beech Creekers had kinsfolk in the area of destination who were in a position actually to hire them. Employers in Ohio, however, not only recognized the importance of kin ties among Kentuckians, but utilized the migrant kin network to secure an adequate labor supply, especially at the laborer and unskilled job levels. When job vacancies occurred, the word was passed along within the shop via the kin com-munication network and soon became common knowledge in the migrant community, quickly trickling down to families in the coves and hollows of eastern Kentucky. Such personalized appeals were, and continue to be, far more effective than the mass media for drawing job applicants from the mountain "labor pool." Moreover, a worker who is hired on the basis of references supplied by kinsfolk in that same factory is bound to be more reliable; family obligations are involved and family honor is at stake.

"We have special appeal for Kentuckians," said one company official, "because of our reputation for hiring many Kentuckians through the years and the fact that we have many family ties in the company over a period of three generations." Indeed, it is common knowledge among migrants that some employers favor job applicants who have family connections within the plant; "unless your brother or your brother-in-law is working for them," said a Beech Creeker bluntly about a high paying factory in the area, "there is no use in trying to get on." It is not unusual, therefore, to find many members of a family group working for the same firm; three brothers, for example, and some of their cousins from Beech Creek are employed in one of the larger factories.

A few managerial personnel are of the opinion that hiring along kin lines is less prevalent nowadays than formerly. It had tended to create certain unique problems. For example, as one informant put it: "We used to hire close relatives of our employees and, especially with Kentuckians, if there was some emergency back in the mountains we would have a whole group of workers who took off to visit a sick aunt. This paternalistic attitude can backfire on you." Nevertheless, kin-hiring still appears to be an important technique used to secure employees for lower-status jobs. As a result of this practice over the years, a type of homogeneity with respect to the workers' backgrounds and normative expectations was fostered in many work situations. Southern Appalachian migrants, for example, predominate in the light and heavy manufacturing industries around Cincinnati; in some plants the proportion of Kentucky-born workers is reported to be as high as 50 to 75 percent. It is not surprising, therefore, that few Beech Creekers encounter difficulties in getting along with native Ohioans in the work situation for, as they often exclaim, "there ain't no Buckeyes to get along with."

Beech Creekers generally, like most migrants from rural Appalachia, found their initial jobs in factories that did not require at the time of hiring any previous industrial experience or a high school diploma. This was fortunate, because they came to the areas of destination generally ill prepared for other than unskilled labor. Few had the advantage of any high school education. They were often hired to perform simple assembly-line tasks that were quickly learned with a minimal amount of on-the-job training.[5] For instance, one Beech Creeker recalled that, "the boss took me to the place where I'd work and told a guy there to explain what I'd do . . . he did . . . it took about ten minutes." Similarly, a foreman explained that his plant "doesn't require any polish or a lot of education, and Kentuckians know this by word of mouth and a lot of them come here." Another foreman reported that, "anyone can get a job here. They give an aptitude test, but hell, the whole thing depends on whether they have an opening or not." The type of work required by these industries seemed to have been designed to make use of the potential labor force in the nearby southern Appalachian region. One company official declared pointedly: "Our strongest appeal to the Kentuckian worker is our proximity to Kentucky."

This proximity to eastern Kentucky, which permits the Beech Creeker to maintain visiting ties with the family homestead, coupled with the supportive kin network in the area of destination and the minimal skill requirements demanded of the rural migrant by Ohio industry, facilitated the initial entry of Beech Creekers into the industrial labor market. To be sure, the work that newcomers were expected to perform (for example, punch press operator) and the job context (a factory or shop situation) constituted new experiences for most Beech Creekers. It was, nevertheless, a relatively simple transition under the circumstances. Indeed, most Beech Creekers seem to have been quite satisfied with their first jobs in Ohio. Although their starting wages were not high (ranging, for example, from $0.60 to $2.60 an hour, with a median of $1.25 during 1941–56 for thirty men specifically interviewed for this phase of our study) what they earned was a great deal more than they could have expected in the mountains. More important, they *were* employed. Management, at least in terms of its past policies, tended to be paternalistic in its dealings with Appalachian migrants and, perhaps because of this, Beech Creekers regarded the initial work conditions as quite satisfactory. Getting along with co-workers offered no special difficulties; after all, most of them were also "Briarhoppers" from the mountains. The initial situation, from the migrant's perspective, provided an effective mechanism for allowing him to adapt gradually, and with integrity, to the demands of a machine technology.

# ADVANCEMENT AND STABILITY

While the industrial work situation in southern Ohio was generally in accord with the needs and unskilled talents of beginning workers from rural Appalachia, these same initially favorable conditions made it possible, perhaps even necessary, for ambitious migrants after a year or so "to look around for better jobs." Some, to be sure, were encouraged to rise through the ranks within the factory where they had started. Seniority rules, however, and other factors tied in with a particular firm's organization of manpower made such movement difficult. Upward mobility toward higher-paying, more skilled jobs often meant seeking out new employers for the originally unskilled majority who had managed to acquire the basic industrial training and were eager to capitalize on that experience. The relatively high rate of job turnover, i.e., inter-plant mobility, by Appalachian migrants in Ohio and elsewhere (a phenomenon quickly noted by observers) should not be interpreted as a sign of occupational insecurity or instability (a trait often attributed to these newcomers). Rather, it is more likely a consequence of the migrants' desire to get ahead, a behavioral manifestation of the "maturing" workers' realistic appraisal of the situation, and an indication of the newcomers' adaptation to the demands and opportunities of the industrial labor market.

As a matter of fact, the Appalachian migrant is rather reluctant to change jobs, because it not only entails moving into an unfamiliar situation, but also means that he must give up the security of accrued seniority rights. A foreman explained: "They have a great value for security, and once they get to know their work group and boss they don't want to move. Also, they are sensitive about their lack of educational skills, which may be required in another job, so they tend to stay on the same job." To become upwardly mobile, however, the Appalachian migrant often must seek out a new job.

The general advancement in occupational status (and, of course, level of skill) over the years by Beech Creek migrants is striking. For example, of the thirty men whom we interviewed at length for supplementary information during this phase of our research, twenty-one had begun work in Ohio as unskilled laborers, four as semi-skilled, two as skilled, and three as farm workers. In 1962, ten were still at an unskilled level (one temporarily unemployed), but nine were semi-skilled (one temporarily unemployed), nine skilled, one a salesman, and one a pool room attendant (service). The proportion who were able to command more skilled jobs had tripled, and their wages reflect this increased status (ranging, in 1962, from $1.25 to $4.37 an hour, with a median of $2.67).

During their relatively short work careers in the urban area (from five to twenty years) these men had found it useful or necessary to make a number of place of work changes. One migrant, in fact, had worked for thirteen different employers during his fifteen years in Ohio; six migrants, on the other hand, were still in the same factory where they had started and were apparently quite satisfied. This median number of employer changes for this representative group of thirty male migrants is three. More significantly, the median length of time they had held their current (1962) jobs was over four years; in fact, the man (mentioned above) who had exhibited the most "unstable" employment pattern had worked for this current employer for more than two years.

Beech Creekers in Ohio, then, had manifested some degree of occupational "restlessness," but most of this seems to have occurred early in their work careers. Perhaps it was a function of youth or represented the rural migrant's way of "testing" his abilities on the urban labor market, or maybe it was linked with social-psychological changes that had come about as a result of migration. In any event, although relatively frequent job changes appear to have been the norm during the initial period of transition that followed migration from the mountains, the later period of a Beech Creeker's work career had become markedly stabilized. It seems he had found his place in the industrial order—a niche that was in reasonable accord with his talents and ambitions.

One additional point is especially relevant here: most male migrants from Beech Creek secured their initial jobs in Ohio through the aid or influence of kinsfolk. Those who subsequently changed jobs, and most of them did, probably did so "on their own" without help from kinsfolk. After having been exposed to the urban occupational sub-culture for a period of time and having become familiar with the industrial work situation, Beech Creekers were in a much better position personally to pursue and evaluate job opportunities in light of their own occupational mobility aspirations. Changing jobs at that time was not of the same order of crisis as finding the first job; individualism, not familism, was the appropriate orientation called forth in this situation.

### Reactions to Lay-offs

The threat of being "laid-off" (i.e., an involuntary, though temporary, loss of job for a period ranging anywhere from one week to six months or longer) is an ever-present fact of life among manual workers, especially those employed in manufacturing and construction industries. A great many Beech Creekers (over half of those interviewed during this phase of our study) had experienced a "lay-off" at some time during their industrial work careers. The economic recession of 1957–58 was a particularly difficult time. More commonly, however, lay-off periods were normally associated with massive retooling operations or production "change-overs" such as occur, for example, every two or three years in the automobile industry. To be sure, a Beech Creeker now and then "quit" or was "fired" for personal reasons or for reasons of incompetence. But the lay-off pattern, either as an actuality or as a threat, was a prevailing norm in the industrial work situation of Ohio during the 1950's and early 1960's, and we shall confine our brief remarks to this form of unemployment and the Beech Creekers' reactions to it. Their reactions (in retrospect) ranged from a deep sense of frustration on the part of a few, to the more typical attitude of regarding a lay-off period as a vacation and a chance to do some work around the house or to visit with the family in the mountains.

In general, Beech Creekers accept the threat of a lay-off as one of those annoying conditions of industrial work, like punching a time-clock and working indoors, that has to be tolerated much as the vagaries of weather have to be tolerated in farming. As a worker gains seniority on the job, of course, the threat is reduced; men hired last are the first to be "bumped." But even those with considerable seniority are attitudinally prepared for the eventuality: they, too, may be included in the next round of lay-offs. Most Beech Creekers feel fairly secure in the knowledge that unemployment compensation will hold them over in good stead; if a lay-off period turns into chronic unemployment, for whatever reason, they can always return to the mountains and wait out the crisis on the family homestead.

During a lay-off period, then, Beech Creekers try to make the best of it. They draw unemployment compensation, attempt to find other jobs (as they must under existing regulations) and wait for their old jobs to reopen. In the meantime, they have an opportunity to visit kinsfolk in Kentucky and in the surrounding Ohio communities, to do chores around the house, work in the garden, fix up the back porch, go fishing, or simply to loaf. There is no question that the Beech Creeker, in his own way, has found it rather easy to adapt to this potentially disturbing feature of industrial work life.

### Attitude Toward Unions

The Beech Creeker supports union activities in much the same way as do the majority of rank and file union members in American industry. His general opinion of union activities is on the whole favorable; his participation in union activities is in most cases minimal. The Beech Creeker's attitudinal support tends to focus on the "practical" functions of unionism, i.e., so-called "bread and butter unionism," such as protection of the worker from arbitrary acts of management that can result in loss of job or pay. In many ways he is like the American workingman described by Schneider, who "expects his union to secure for him (1) above all, better wages; (2) more favorable hours; (3) job tenure; and (4) congenial work rules and conditions of work."[6]

In spite of this basically favorable attitude, a general behavioral apathy nevertheless prevails. Practical issues are rarely regarded as sufficiently important for personal involvement. There appears to be an undercurrent of fear of managerial reprisal for active union involvement, especially among older migrants; as a matter of fact, one Beech Creeker had indeed lost his job as a result of union organizing activities. Moreover, Beech Creekers just aren't very good joiners; they feel uncomfortable in a formal gathering. Participation in union meetings and activities outside of the immediate job situation tends to interfere with home life, and most Beech Creekers are unwilling to allow this to happen unless such union activity involves and serves the needs of the whole family. One man, for example, reported that he used to take his family to all appropriate union events but had ceased to do so because these events often became "beer blasts." Of the thirty men interviewed for supplementary information during this phase of our field study, sixteen were union members, but only four were active in the sense of having attended a number of union meetings the previous year. For most Beech Creekers, union membership is a nominal status.

On occasion a Beech Creeker may voice some negative comments about unions: "You don't get anything for the dues you pay;" "You take a gripe to the shop steward and that's the last you hear of it;" "If you do your job right and work hard, you don't need a union;" "I think someone ought to crack down on both the union and management. They spend too much money fighting each other when they could be helping the worker."

Most Beech Creekers, however, do not seem to question the right or place of unions in the industrial work situation. Although generally apathetic about getting involved with union activities, Beech Creekers, like rank and file union members elsewhere, are passive advocates of pragmatic unionism.[7] They accept union membership in much the same way as they accept other, more discomforting aspects of factory work life, and they obey union dictums in much the same way as they obey shop regulations or the orders of a foreman. Whether a Beech Creeker's initial motivation to join derived from his employment in a factory that was bound by a union shop contract (in which case new workers must join the union within a stipulated time, usually thirty days after being hired) or from informal pressures by co-workers who insisted that "to be a union member is to be a right guy," further involvement (attending meetings, assuming a leadership role, proselytizing, and so forth) demands an emotional or intellectual commitment over and above that for which the Beech Creeker is prepared. In that respect the Beech Creeker is not very different from other Appalachian migrants and from the majority of American industrial workers. His apathy is mixed with allegiance. Indeed, one might say that he has adapted to the form of industrial work life without having become uncomfortably involved in its complexities.

### Job Satisfactions

Among American workers generally, the pattern of responses to such questions as: "Taking into consideration all the things about your job, how satisfied or dissatisfied are you with it?" invariably indicates a high degree of satisfaction.[8] Similarly, virtually all employed Beech Creekers in Ohio say they are quite satisfied with their current jobs. Of course, the meaning of "satisfaction" is inherently vague.[9]

Most Beech Creekers will emphasize that they like the kind of work they are doing because it is "interesting" or they are "learning something different." They talk a lot about the working conditions; it is "clean work" or they are working with a "nice crew." The amount of take-home pay, of course, and the degree of security accorded (in the form of seniority rights, adequate compensation during lay-off periods, and so forth) are important considerations in assessing the job situation. Pay and security factors are fairly standardized in terms of skill levels among the industries in southern Ohio; hence, if dissatisfactions about a particular job exist they usually focus upon specific working conditions and especially the interpersonal relationships among work crew members and with the boss. As one foreman explained: "They are very sensitive to the kidding from other workers. Then too, they seem to have a holy fear of the boss. After about six months they adapt to the kidding, but it seems to be a general characteristic that they are more afraid of the boss than other workers." Another foreman put it more strongly: "They don't like to be bossed, and they seem to be afraid or shy in front of the boss. Then too, you have to ask them to do the work rather than tell them." To the highly individualistic, personalistically-oriented Beech Creeker, social relationships with fellow workers and immediate supervisors are a major source of potential strain; the fact that most Beech Creekers work with other Appalachian migrants from similar sociocultural origins contributes to the stability and, from the Beech Creeker's point-of-view, satisfactoriness of the work situation.

Advancement opportunities would certainly be a factor in the overall evaluation of any job and here, too, Beech Creekers are quite satisfied. Few feel "trapped" or "held down" or that their jobs are "dead-ends." In general they seem aware of existing opportunities. Those who have attained skilled levels feel they might eventually move up to supervisory or "office" positions. Those who are at semi-skilled levels, although cognizant of opportunities and confident of their abilities to attain higher levels, say that they prefer to avoid the "headaches" and responsibilities that inevitably accompany higher paid jobs. Laborers, on the other hand, more often than not simply feel that further advancement is not important, especially if it means (as it often does) giving up the security of the moment for the uncertainties of occupational mobility. Beech Creek migrants, in these respects, are not unlike American industrial workers in general; over the years, undoubtedly, a sorting-out along the lines of relative ambition and talent has occurred.

The basic satisfaction with job and work situation is further reinforced on one hand by the migrant's favorable attitude toward management (a naive trust, the roots of which perhaps are to be found in the patriarchical tendencies of the mountain society) and, on the other hand, the migrant's conviction that employers in Ohio are satisfied with the work performance of Appalachian people. Indeed, most Beech Creekers feel that factory supervisors consider Kentuckians to be "better and harder workers" than native Ohioans. The personnel managers and foremen whom we interviewed tend to validate the Beech Creekers' own favorable self-image vis-a-vis hard work; but they add, often in the same breath, that the mountaineer appears to be a bit too docile for his own good in the industrial labor market.

# OCCUPATIONAL ADAPTATION IN CONTEXT

Beech Creek men who had migrated to Ohio had been able, over the years, to make a satisfactory and, as they themselves see it, satisfying transition from field to factory. In the process, it seems, they did not encounter, and therefore did not find it necessary to cope with, those difficult tension producing conditions that are so often associated with rural-to-urban migration and the phenomena of industrialization in other parts of the world. Their record of upward occupational mobility in the urban area, which we regard as impressive under the circumstances, and their relatively long tenure in current (1962) jobs, which we regard as a sign that stability has been normalized, attest to their confidence in and acceptance of the industrial work role and their successful adaptation to the industrial work situation.

Initially, of course, the migrants had encountered some difficulties as beginning workers. The formal schedule and rigid authority system of the factory, for example, were particularly irksome, and working with and around complicated machines was for many quite confusing and sometimes even frightening at first. Yet these men, reared in an isolated mountain locality of eastern Kentucky and few of whom had been fortunate enough to get beyond the eighth grade in school, were able, after a relatively short period of time, to master the technical details of their new jobs, to familiarize themselves with the industrial arts and the formalized procedures of factory work, and to feel comfortable in the midst of industrial complexity. Perhaps, during the transitional period, their frontier-bred fortitude and willingness to work hard had compensated in part for their initial lack of skills on the job. Such other factors as the labor market situation at that time must be considered in venturing an explanation of why the process of adaptation in this case was not more difficult and disturbing. However, we chose to focus our inquiry on the kinship factor, which we believe offers a valid, though partial, explanation of the relative "success" of Beech Creekers as industrial workers.

The stem-family form of kinship structure, we pointed out earlier, helped to stimulate migration from the mountains, directed and "cushioned" the relocation of Beech Creekers, and facilitated, in various ways, the entry of migrants into the industrial work situation. Through the kin network, information about jobs and working conditions in the area of destination were made known to potential migrants in the mountain neighborhoods. Kinsfolk in the host community assisted newcomers in finding the initial jobs and, thereafter, served as advisers and instructors in the process of urbanizing their "greenhorn" kinsmen. More important, the "branch-family network" in the area of destination, which is linked directly with the family homestead in the mountains, provided the newcomer with a measure of assurance that, in the event of some unforeseen crisis, he would not stand alone. The Beech Creek stem-family system, in short, served to stabilize the migrant's social world external to the factory and consequently helped to keep "off-the-job" problems and anxieties from entering into and disturbing the migrant's "on-the-job" performance. (If the Beech Creek kin system had been a nucleated form, the migrant worker, we believe, would have experienced greater difficulty in adapting to the industrial work situation and, as a consequence, factory managers in the area would have had many more labor problems and far greater labor costs. The contribution of Appalachian mountain families to the economy of Ohio, other states, *and* the larger society that resulted from extended family normative obligations "to take care of their own," if it could be measured, would undoubtedly stagger the imagination of many government officials.)

In the Beech Creek case, perhaps the most abrupt and immediate change (i.e., system-disturbing change) that occurred and was experienced by the Beech Creekers as a result of migration was the distinct separation of occupational activities from family activities. Many of the sociocultural elements characteristic of the Beech Creek neighborhoods had been transferred to (or recreated within) the area of destination via chain migration of kinsfolk and neighbors over the years. Furthermore, a kind of residential segregation has given rise to a number of "little Kentucky" neighborhoods in and around the major metropolitan centers of southern Ohio. The host neighborhood in the area of destination is, therefore, often structured in the image (sociocultural) of a Kentucky mountain community. Because kinsfolk are near at hand, the newcomer from Beech Creek is, in many respects, "at home" in Ohio.

For most Beech Creekers, then, the abrupt separation of family life from work life was, in the normative sense, the biggest change that had come about as a result of moving to Ohio. Some men had been employed off the farm in "public work" prior to migration. As we have explained, this was generally defined as a temporary activity, peripheral to the family work activity configuration and often undertaken on a seasonal basis; farming, for most of these men, continued to be the main enterprise, and management of the homestead and its lands the primary obligation. That attitude had to be modified in conforming to the industrial situation. After migration, work for wages in a shop or factory became the family's only means of support, and a man's job (about which his wife had little comprehension) became, without question, his primary responsibility.

Adaptation to an industrial occupational role, therefore, undoubtedy had some stress-producing potential, because Beech Creekers were not well prepared for this experience and its immediate and obvious consequences. Yet the potential, so far as can be discerned, was not manifested to any unusual degree (e.g., through instances of marital discord, criminal behavior, alcoholism, mental illness).[10] Supportive functions performed by the kin network, we believe, had much to do with keeping resultant tensions within manageable bounds. Moreover, because the kin network tended to isolate the newcomer from other segments of the urban community, it also tended to perpetuate the Beech Creek value system and to provide the migrant with a means for self-expression and for the satisfaction of culturally derived needs. Adaptation to the industrial occupation role required merely the acceptance of new standards in an isolated area of behavior, namely work; it had little effect upon other, and to them more important, areas of life. The tensions aroused by these "minor" changes in the migrant's life were more than adequately compensated for by the obvious rewards that were forthcoming. Over time, of course, these same "minor" changes may build into system-disturbing influences that effect more fundamental changes; at that point the Beech Creek sociocultural system will have been absorbed into the great "melting pot" of American society.

# 8 CLASS ORIGINS AND Economic Life Chances[1]

Casual observers as well as trained social scientists tend to think of rural low-income areas or neighborhoods as being composed of relatively homogeneous populations. They often fail to recognize that systems of social stratification exist within these locality groups. The families in depressed areas vary in their abilities to cope with the problems of survival and of assuring the well-being of family members in a situation of continual economic crises. Furthermore, for many persons in rural low-income areas, migration to areas of greater economic opportunity is the only feasible means available to enhance their lot in life. Individual responsiveness to the conditions stimulating migration and the ability to cope successfully with the circumstances encountered in the area of destination are also variable things. Too often we regard rural migrants as an undifferentiated group or category. This is perhaps especially true of migrants from the Southern Appalachians, whose people have been falsely assumed to be much more homogeneous culturally and socially than they actually are.

We know that some Beech Creekers have been more successful and have done materially better over the years than others. We believe that, in this rural low-income area with its characteristically high rates of out-migration, a family's social class position significantly influenced not only its pattern of relocation, but also its members' economic life chances in the area of destination. The relative success of migrants faced with the demands of the host society depends, in large measure, upon factors and conditions that were being shaped long before they left the area of origin. Moreover, to explain adequately the existing variations in levels of economic attainment among Beech Creek families, one must take into account differences in the "strategies and tactics" of migration associated with the various social classes.

# CLASS ORIGINS AND PATTERNS
# OF MIGRATION

From our follow-up after twenty years of persons who had been residing in the Beech Creek neighborhoods in 1942 (N = 271) we found
that about 60 percent had relocated in areas outside of eastern Kentucky, about 25 percent were still residents of Beech Creek, and the
remaining 15 percent were living in a small town or neighborhoods
adjacent to Beech Creek. The latter, generally, were persons from in-
termediate- or low-class families in Beech Creek. Few Beech Creekers
from high-class families settled in the nearby town or neighborhoods,
probably because the economic alternatives in the area were not sufficiently attractive to offer them any sort of relative advantage over
their already more favorable socioeconomic circumstances vis-a-vis
their neighbors.

There is little difference, however, in the proportions of persons from
each of the three social classes residing *outside the mountain region*
in 1961 (Table 8.1).[5] Except for a slightly smaller percentage from

Table 8.1. Residence location in 1961 of Beech Creekers, by social class origin
1942.

| Residence location 1961 | Social class origin in Beech Creek, 1942 (percentage distribution)[b] | | | | |
| --- | --- | --- | --- | --- | --- |
| | High | Inter-mediate | Low | Unclas-sified[a] | (Total N, all classes) |
| Beech Creek neighborhoods: | 33 | 23 | 30 | 0 | (68) |
| Town or neighborhoods near Beech Creek (within eastern Kentucky): | 7 | 15 | 18 | 29 | (42) |
| Outside eastern Kentucky: | 60 | 62 | 52 | 71 | (161) |
| Total %: | 100% | 100% | 100% | 100% | |
| (N = ) | (59) | (101) | (87) | (24) | (271) |

[a] The persons in the "unclassified" category are members of families not included in the
original delineation of social class.

[b] Proportions of males and females are approximately the same in all cells.

**Table 8.2.** Interregional migration patterns of Beech Creekers during period 1942 through 1961, by social class origin.

| Interregional migration pattern 1942–1961[b] | Social class origin in Beech Creek, 1942 (percentage distribution) | | | | |
|---|---|---|---|---|---|
| | High | Inter- mediate | Low | Unclas- sified[a] | (Total N, all classes) |
| Residing within eastern Kentucky in 1961 and: | | | | | |
| Never moved away from eastern Kentucky | 25 | 30 | 36 | 4 | (77) |
| Moved away but returned | 14 | 8 | 12 | 25 | (33) |
| Residing outside eastern Kentucky in 1961 and: | | | | | |
| Moved back to eastern Kentucky after first migration (but moved out again) | 7 | 12 | 15 | 17 | (33) |
| Never returned to eastern Kentucky after first move out | 54 | 50 | 37 | 54 | (128) |
| Total %: | 100% | 100% | 100% | 100% | |
| (N = ) | (59) | (101) | (87) | (24) | (271) |

[a] Only one person who was not classified in the original study remained a permanent resident of eastern Kentucky throughout the ensuing two decades.

[b] A temporal criterion of six months or longer continuous residence was employed in defining a "migration."

low-class families, there appears to have been no clearly discernible social class selectivity in the patterns (that is, in the net result of the process) of migration from eastern Kentucky over the years.

Since 1942, of course, some Beech Creek migrants had returned to Appalachia, and some returned migrants had moved away again. The pattern of interregional migrations during the two decades (Table 8.2) suggests a degree of relative stability in the overall trend and, we infer, a positive commitment to move away permanently on the part of most migrating Beech Creekers. Persons from different social classes seem to have behaved somewhat differently in this respect. Individuals from low-class families, for example, were less likely to have attempted to migrate from the region, and those who did were less likely to have been "successful" on their first attempt. Otherwise, the general pattern appears strikingly similar for the three social classes.

Although a Beech Creek migrant's first move from the mountains was, in 72 percent of the cases, also his first move from Beech Creek, some persons initially relocated in the nearby town or neighborhoods prior to out-migration. Here we discern notable class differences. Forty-three percent of the migrants from low-class families initially moved to a neighborhood or town near Beech Creek, compared with only 20 percent of those from intermediate-class families and 5 percent of those from high-class families.[2] For high-class families, then, the pattern was either to move entirely out of the region or to remain in Beech Creek; intervening opportunities nearby, however, provided low-class families with relatively favorable alternatives which, for many, resulted in a "two-stage" pattern of migration. (Our interpretation here attempts to link geographic with social mobility on the premise that the two phenomena are inextricably bound together in the process by which individuals and families decide whether or not to migrate.)

By dividing the years between our two surveys into three historically significant time periods, we find that the flow of migration out of the region during each period was dominated by a different social class grouping (Table 8.3). From 1942 through 1947, the World War II period, over half the migrants were from high-class families in Beech Creek; over two-thirds of the high-class migrants left eastern Kentucky during those years. From 1948 through 1953, the Korean War period, well over half the migrants were from intermediate families; nearly two-thirds of the intermediate-class migrants left in those years. From 1954 through 1961 over half the migrants were from low-class families in Beech Creek.

We surmise that this phenomenon was affected in part by the tremendous changes that had occurred in the structure of economic opportunity in Appalachian Kentucky and in the areas of destination (i.e., the Ohio Valley), and by differences that existed in the perception or awareness of opportunities among individuals and families from the various social classes in Beech Creek. We are quite certain, for instance, that the higher class families in Beech Creek were sensitive to and cognizant of the rapidly widening gap between economic circumstances in the mountains of eastern Kentucky and the opportunities that existed in the industrial areas to the north. Compared with their lower class

Table 8.3. Year of migrant's initial residence outside eastern Kentucky after 1942, by social class origin.

| Year of initial residence outside eastern Kentucky | Social class origin in Beech Creek 1942[a] (percentage distribution) | | | |
|---|---|---|---|---|
| | High | Inter-mediate | Low | (Total N, all classes) |
| 1942–47: | 68 | 23 | 23 | (59) |
| 1948–53: | 16 | 63 | 43 | (76) |
| 1954–61: | 16 | 14 | 34 | (36) |
| Total: | 100% | 100% | 100% | |
| (N = ) | (44) | (71) | (56) | (171) |

[a] Those individuals not classified as to social class position in Beech Creek in 1942 were omitted.

neighbors, they were already in advantageous positions in the rural low-income area and, consequently, perceived that little could be gained through residential or occupational shifts within the region. As they saw their situation, upward social mobility could be effected only through migration, and the immediately obvious method for them to enhance their own and their children's lot was to move out of the region. The lower class families, on the other hand, because of their positions within the Beech Creek social class hierarchy, were less influenced by status differentials vis-a-vis "outsiders" and more oriented toward neighborhood and the community norms in the process of formulating aspirations. Hence, lower class families perceived that some advantages would accrue from occupational and/or residential shifts within the area. Intervening opportunities nearby, in that sense, did exist for them, at least until recent years.[3]

Perhaps the Beech Creek case is unique. We know, however, that in earlier years a similar phenomenon occurred in the case of many immigrant groups to the United States. If the waves of migration at different times from rural low-income areas are selective of individuals and families from various social strata, we can expect concomitant differences in the problems and processes of adjustment of rural migrants in urban areas, as well as in the causes of strains that occur within rural communities experiencing large scale population decline.

Let us now consider the effect of social class origin on the destination of Beech Creek migrants. At the time of their initial migration from eastern Kentucky, over three-fourths of the migrants went to Ohio; only a few moved to central Kentucky, Indiana, or other states. Those who moved to the bluegrass area were all from one large family group. Likewise, migrants from two large family groups accounted for most of the movement to Indiana.

The pattern of settlement of Beech Creekers in Ohio, however, reveals some important differences that can be explained, in part, by social class origins. Most migrants from intermediate-class families settled in and around a small town in southern Ohio, while migrants from low-class families tended to settle in the Appalachian enclaves of City A and City B in Ohio. Migrants from high-class families initially migrated to City A and City B, but a considerable proportion of the City A group later moved to City B, which, by 1961, had become the residential nucleus for the high-class families from Beech Creek. Places of destination, therefore, were apparently associated with the migrant's social class origins. We believe, however, that the primary reason for the clustering of migrants from Beech Creek in various locations is to be found in kinship ties. Since close kin generally belonged to the same class, the migrant's choice of where he would move was probably based on a combination of kinship and class factors.

These observations about particular places of destination of persons of different classes apply, of course, only to this particular migration universe and should not be interpreted to mean that certain cities or towns tend to attract a certain class of rural migrants: that may be so, but it cannot be generally demonstrated from our findings in the Beech Creek case.

In analyzing the structure of the migration process, influenced by the migrant's social class, the following factors were considered: the migrant's age, marital status, and family-household situation prior to migration; the social structure of his migration unit; and his family-household and housing situation in the area of destination immediately after migration. Some social class differences in the migration process were observed. A much smaller percentage of migrants from high-class families migrated alone (30 percent as compared with 53 percent for the two other classes), and a considerably larger percentage migrated with their parents or siblings. A much larger proportion of migrants from intermediate-class families joined an already established household in the area of destination. Differences such as these can be explained, for the most part, by differences in strategies that seem to have been employed in the migration process by the three social classes.

Beech Creek migrants, generally, were young persons when they moved away from the mountains. Significantly, almost a third of the migrants from high-class families were under sixteen years of age at the time, compared with only about 9 percent from the other two classes. Excluding these youngsters, who simply accompanied parents, we found that migrants from high-class families tended to be older. Furthermore, adult migrants from high-class families, particularly males, tended to be more advanced in the family life cycle at the time of migration than those from the other classes. Although we have a relatively small number of cases, these facts suggest an important social class difference in the migration process: the high-class pattern was a "family-uprooting" type of movement, whereas the pattern for the other social classes, especially the intermediate class, tended to follow more along the lines of a stem-family type of migration. All our data about social class differences in the process of migration substantiate this conclusion. High-class families from Beech Creek moved away from the mountains as nuclear families and usually established new households as nuclear families in the areas of destination. Intermediate-class families tended to maintain family homesteads in the mountains, and young migrants from these families usually joined their older siblings or close kin who were already established in the areas of destination. Low-class families manifested a more diverse pattern which, we suspect, was a consequence of their ownership or non-ownership of homesteads in the mountains.

# CLASS ORIGINS AND ECONOMIC SUCCESS

In exploring the influence of social class origin on the Beech Creek migrant's economic success in the urban industrial area, we direct attention to a latter stage in the process of transition, the migrant's socioeconomic situation in 1961 when follow-up data were collected.[4] At that time, although the larger proportion of Beech Creek migrants had been residing outside eastern Kentucky for ten years or more, some were more recent migrants with less time and opportunity to become established in the urban occupational structure. Compared with the intermediate and lower class migrants, a larger proportion of the migrants from high-class families were youngsters when they first moved and, also important, they dominated, percentage-wise, the first "wave" of migration after 1942. Migrants from high-class families in Beech Creek, therefore, had distinct advantages over those from the other social classes, including better schooling and better knowledge of the social conditions at the areas of destination.

An individual migrant's social class origin in Beech Creek, we expected, would be indicative of a particular level of aspiration to achieve, a particular set of value-orientations, and certain kinds of social skills, as well as of the possession of economic means, such as savings, all of which would be directly related to the migrant's ability to cope with the problems of adjustment encountered in the process of migration. This relationship between social class origin and ability to cope with adjustment problems, we hypothesized, would be manifested in a direct relationship between the migrant's (i.e., his family's) social class position in the Beech Creek neighborhoods and his achieved socioeconomic status in the area of destination. Differences in economic life chances, a concept which implies prediction, were inferred from the empirical observations and our knowledge about the socioeconomic differences that existed among the Beech Creek social classes.[5]

We found a high, direct relationship between the social class origin of migrants and their level of living in the areas of destination in 1961 (Table 8.4).[6] From these data,[7] one can posit a convincing argument

Table 8.4. Level of living of Beech Creek migrants in areas of destination in 1961, by social class origin 1942.

| Level of living 1961 (scores)[a] | Social class of family of origin in Beech Creek 1942 (percentage distribution) | | | |
|---|---|---|---|---|
| | High | Inter-mediate | Low | (Total, N, all classes) |
| High (9–7): | 69 | 14 | 13 | (40) |
| Intermediate (6–4): | 28 | 56 | 33 | (60) |
| Low (3–0): | 3[b] | 30 | 54 | (44) |
| Total: | 100% | 100% | 100% | |
| (N = ) | (36) | (63) | (45) | (144) |

[a] The numbers in brackets refer to scores on the Cornell level of living scale.

[b] One case in low category. Percentage included only for consistency in reporting.

that the status hierarchy of individuals within a rural-to-urban migration system of this kind tends to maintain a reasonable degree of stability despite the seemingly disruptive process of migration. That is, though rural-to-urban migration is concomitant with changes in valuational criteria, and though the migration system itself undergoes a re-equilibrating process within the context of the larger society, the relative positions of individuals within that system tend to be remarkably stable over a period of time.

This finding is supported by a parallel analysis focusing upon family income and occupational prestige.[8] More important, the general conclusion is supported by our observations from intensive, quasi-participant field work with a number of selected families.

One reason why individuals tend to maintain their social class positions relative to other individuals within a given migration system, such as the Beech Creek case, may be the differential value placed upon education by the various social classes. Nearly two-thirds of the migrants from high-class families had completed high school (and one-third had at least some experience in college), compared with only 13 percent of the intermediate-class migrants and only one migrant from the low-class families. Migrants who were children when they first moved to urban areas had the considerable advantage of easy access to good schools, while migrants who were reared in the mountains did not; and most of this advantage accrued to the migrants from high-class families who, in general, had moved earlier.

Hence, we find that the social class system perpetuated itself not only through differences in value placed upon education and the behavioral consequences of these orientations, but also through differences in the form of migration and the resultant situational circumstances encountered by the migrants.

# SUMMARY PERSPECTIVE

In the Beech Creek case over the years, an individual migrant's social class origins influenced, to some extent, not only when he left the mountains, where he moved, and with whom, but also his economic success in the area of destination. The latter was affected, in no small part, by social class differences in the form or strategy of migration. By the very nature of the sequence of "irrevocable decisions" and events, the patterns of migration contributed to the maintenance and stability of the social class hierarchy within that migration system despite the seemingly disruptive phenomenon of mass relocation. Even for a rural low-income population, therefore, social class origin seems to have validity in predicting a migrant's abilities to cope with the external environment and, consequently, his chances of enhancing his own and his family's economic well-being in an urban area.

Whether such influences and effects are apart from or independent of kinship and factors associated within kinship can not be established here. Indeed, social class and kinship are empirically inseparable in the Beech Creek case.[9] For this reason especially, because these phenomena were and are inextricably linked, the stem-family hypothesis (or any equivalent hypothesis that posits the family structure as an important intervening variable between the forces of social change and the complementary processes of individual striving to become and individual yearning to be) gains support from the findings reported in this chapter. Clearly, the higher the social class position of families in the mountain neighborhoods, the greater their functional adequacy in responding to the changing needs of their members and, subsequently, the greater the economic attainment of migrants (an indicator of "adjustment") in the area of destination.

Degree of economic success, however important, is only one dimension of adjustment and only a crude indicator of the migrant's ability to cope with and manage the sundry problems and various circumstances encountered in the host community. Other aspects of adjustment must be considered, and in relation to the changing form of the Beech Creek family and the changing needs of the Beech Creeker, if one is to understand the complexities of the phenomena associated with the absorption of mountain people into the mainstream of American society.

# 9 ADJUSTMENT PATTERNS: Diversity and the Kinship Factor

The physical act of residential relocation is of brief temporal duration compared with the period of adaptation and adjustment that follows in its wake. Indeed, it may take many years before the resultant tensions are resolved and the individual migrant learns to cope effectively with his new environment so as to become a functionally significant and stable member of the recipient community. What are the factors that facilitate the social and psychological adjustment of rural migrants to the situational changes and the stresses and strains that accompany the processes of migration and adjustment? Most observers would agree that the extended family structure plays a part, and we have noted this to some extent in the Beech Creek case.[1] It is a far more complex problem to attempt to understand how and in what sense the kin network functions to facilitate or hinder the adjustment process over time, especially if we take into account the diversity of social needs that exists within a migrant population.[2]

Some Beech Creekers, for example, had migrated earlier and some more recently; there are many reasons to suppose that the problems of encounter of these two categories of migrants with the greater American society differ markedly. Likewise, the transitional adjustment difficulties of men undoubtedly differ from those of women. In the process of adjustment, then, the distinctive needs of a particular segment of the migrant population, coupled with the responsiveness of the family-kin network to satisfy, to provide for, or perhaps to block the attainment of those needs, determines the degree of tension generated within each segment and the personal stability and ultimate integrity of the migrants.

To explore the effects of social and situational differences (and hence, by implication, of diverse needs) upon the ad-

Table 9.1. Relationships between various aspects of migrants' interactional adjustment and certain specified conditions.

| Interactional adjustment variables | Sex | Social class origins* | Level of schooling | Level of living | Church membership | Age | Length of urban residence |
|---|---|---|---|---|---|---|---|
| | | | | Specified Conditions | | | |
| | | | | Direction of relationship and c̄* | | | |
| Size of nearby kin group: | | | | | | | +.21 |
| Frequency of visiting nearby kin: | | | | +.21 | | −.22 | |
| Social contacts with urban natives: | | .36ᵈ | +.45 | +.36 | +.29 | | |
| Friendship ties with urban natives: | .31ᵃ | +.26 | +.47 | + | +.28 | | +.38 |
| Visiting in eastern Kentucky: | .22ᵇ | | | | −.29 | −.21 | −.24 |
| Visiting exchanges with people in eastern Kentucky: | ᶜ | − | | | −.24 | −.21 | −.27 |
| Letter exchanges with people in eastern Kentucky: | | −.31 | | | | −.28 | −.25 |

* NOTE: For social class origins, a trichotomy, df = 2; in all other cases, df = 1. In this and subsequent tables, where c̄ is reported, P < .10; where only direction of relationship is reported, P < .20 but > .10.

ᵃ, ᵇ, and ᶜ Compared with male migrants, female migrants as a category scored lower.

ᵈ In this case, the relationship was curvilinear; intermediate-class migrants scored lower than either of the other two classes.

justment patterns of Beech Creek migrants, seven distinct factors were taken into account: (1) sex, (2) social class position of the migrant's family in the area of origin, (3) level of schooling attained, (4) level of living achieved by the migrant and his immediate family in the area of destination, (5) membership in a church or sect group, (6) age, and (7) accumulated length of residence in the urban area. We are concerned with the influence of these factors (specified conditions) upon certain aspects of the migrant's interactional and psychological adjustment (Tables 9.1 and 9.2) as well as upon the patterns of interrelationship between those dimensions of adjustment (Table 9.3 through Table 9.9).

Appropriate indicators were developed of three important aspects of the Beech Creek migrant's social interactional adjustment: degree of involvement (1) with kinsfolk in the area of destination (branch-family ties), (2) with natives in the area of destination (urban ties), and (3) with kin and friends in the area of origin (stem-family ties). These variables enable us to observe the "cushioning effect" and "functional adequacy" of the kin network vis-a-vis the particular needs of various segments of the migrant population. (Our methods and approach in tapping the selected dimensions of social and psychological adjustment are discussed at greater length in Appendix C.)

Similarly, we devised indicators of six aspects of the migrant's psy-

Table 9.2. Relationships between various aspects of migrants' psychological adjustment and certain specified conditions.

| Psychological adjustment variables | Sex | Social class origins* | Level of schooling | Level of living | Church membership | Age | Length of urban residence |
|---|---|---|---|---|---|---|---|
| | | | | Direction of relationship and c̄* | | | |
| Residential stability: | .26a | | | + | +.36 | +.33 | |
| Nostalgia for home: | .42b | −.27 | − | −.25 | −.23 | | −.23 |
| Expressed happiness: | | +.23 | | | | + | |
| Extent of worry: | | + | | | +.25 | | |
| Anomia: | | −.32 | −.54 | | | +.22 | |
| Anxiety: | .49c | d | | | +.25 | | +.28 |

* NOTE: In this case, df = 2; in all other cases df = 1.

a, b, and c Compared with male migrants, female migrants scored lower on nostalgia for home and higher on residential stability and anxiety.

d In this case, intermediate-class migrants scored lower than either of the other two classes.

chological adjustment: (1) identification with the urban locality (residential stability), (2) identification with the mountain region (nostalgia for home), (3) general assessment of life situation (expressed happiness), (4) degree of personalized concerns (extent of worry), (5) feelings of normlessness and despair (anomia), and (6) symptoms of psychological stress (anxiety). These attributes are indicative of certain facets of the migrant's personality structure—his state of mind, general orientation, and the like. By observing their variability in relation to the three aspects of interactional adjustment, we may delineate the nature and locus of basic disturbances or incongruities which, by inference, are consequents of rural-to-urban relocation and its aftermath phase, the processes of absorption of Beech Creekers and the Beech Creek migration system into the mainstream of urban America.

# SEX: Male and Female Patterns of Adjustment Differ

Beech Creek women are in many ways more satisfied and at ease with (or perhaps resigned to) the urban situation than men and far less likely to harbor feelings of great longing for the old home neighborhood or mountain way of life (Tables 9.1 and 9.2). Few Beech Creek women entertain notions about going back to live in Appalachian Kentucky; indeed, they even visit in the mountains less often, on the average, than men.

Yet it is more likely that the male migrant has acquired a large number of close friends from outside the normal social circle of kinsfolk and fellow eastern Kentuckians. In many respects, he seems to be the more socially active. Mountain women, nevertheless, also have a strong need (reinforced by cultural norms) for social acceptance and personalized interaction; they, too, like to visit, to exchange information with friends and relatives, to communicate. This observed discontinuity in the case of women suggests that their social interactional needs tend to be frustrated by situational circumstances in the host community which, in turn, may account for the higher incidence of anxiety symptoms among them.[3]

Male migrants will generally look toward their stem-families for aid and comfort in time of stress. If they are burdened with worries, for instance, they tend to visit more frequently with kinsfolk in eastern Kentucky (Table 9.3).[4] But these frequent visits to eastern Kentucky are

**Table 9.3.** Relationships between various aspects of migrants' psychological and interactional adjustment, by sex.

| Psychological adjustment variables | Branch-family | | Urban ties | | Stem-family | | |
| --- | --- | --- | --- | --- | --- | --- | --- |
| | Size of kin group | Freq. of visiting kin | Social contacts | Friendship ties | Visiting E. Ky. | Visiting exchanges | Letter exchanges |
| **Males (N = 82)** | | | | | | | |
| Residential stability: | + | | +.39 | +.31 | −.46 | −.30 | |
| Nostalgia: | | | | −.42 | +.37 | +.32 | |
| Happiness: | | +.29 | | | + | + | |
| Worry: | | −.34 | | | + | +.30 | + |
| Anomia: | | | −.35 | | | | |
| Anxiety: | − | | | | | | |
| **Females (N = 79)** | | | | | | | |
| Residential stability: | | | | | | | |
| Nostalgia: | | | | | | | |
| Happiness: | | | | | | | |
| Worry: | | | | | | | |
| Anomia: | | | + | | − | − | |
| Anxiety: | − | −.34 | | | | | |

not an unmixed blessing. These men have their family obligations back in Ohio and a need for interacting with family and friends there. Thus frequent visits to eastern Kentucky create new worries of a serious nature.

On the other hand, when they find themselves in situations in which frequent interaction can and does occur between them and their close kin nearby, i.e., with branch-families, male migrants are less prone to worry. In that case a high degree of kin involvement may serve to isolate them from extra-familial activities and from direct encounters with the "system" disturbances of an urban way of life, hence reducing the level of individual worry. Male Beech Creekers who are not closely bound into an interactional network of branch-families will have cause to worry more about their problems, because those problems and the associated responsibilities are not diffused within a larger group; as a consequence, they seek social and psychological support from the stem-family in the area of origin.

Although Beech Creek women are inclined to worry about somewhat different things from men, they do not seem to differ from men with respect to extent of worry. Yet extent of worry in their case is not affected by the degree of interaction they maintain with persons either in the area of origin, or in the area of destination. We surmise, therefore, that female migrants do not have the same kind of access to the supportive assistance from stem and branch families as men. They are more isolated situationally from the kin system and its "cushioning" mechanisms. In a typical Beech Creek migrant family, for example, it is the husband, not the wife, who makes the decision to visit in eastern Kentucky, and it is the husband, not the wife, who drives the car and decides where to go on a Sunday afternoon. Then too, we must take into account that, in the process of migration women were probably able to make the interactional adjustment of modifying ties with kinsfolk more rapidly and more decisively than men.

Because they tend to be more situationally isolated from the kinship system and its supportive mechanisms or have modified their ties with kinsfolk more than male migrants, we can begin to understand why there is a strong, positive association between the females' level of anxiety and degree of social contacts with urban natives. It also helps to explain why a larger proportion of Beech Creek women, as compared with men, express symptoms of psychological anxiety. This anxiety is probably a manifestation of stress in the system resulting from an inadequacy of the situational structure to fulfill the social interactional needs of these women.

Even so, male migrants are less likely to be residentially stable or "satisfied" with their situation in the host community, and more likely to be extremely nostalgic for home and the mountains. Obviously, if our reasoning is correct, there are things about the situation in the area of destination which, in the case of women, are sufficient to compensate them for unfulfilled social interactional needs and, hence, make them feel like permanent members of the host community. The technological conveniences in the household and other amenities of the urban industrial way of life to which they now have access and which they enjoy are major compensations for many of the botherations and frustrations they experience in the migration situation.

The contrary is true among male migrants. In spite of the "cushioning" effect provided by the stem family, there are things about the situation in the area of destination that make them feel somewhat dissatisfied with, and in some respects like transients in, the urban industrial community. Beech Creek men in many ways are more strongly oriented toward the extended family—the Grossfamilie—than Beech Creek women; they are happiest when they can enjoy frequent contacts with kinsfolk. Women, on the other hand, particularly when they become older, tend to build their social world more around their children, the nuclear family. Then too, males enjoyed a degree of independence and rugged individualism back in the mountain neighborhoods which they can no longer practice in the relatively restricted urban industrial situation; hence they tend to resist (psychologically) the putting down of permanent roots in the host community. In short, while Beech Creek women see in the urban industrial situation a chance to escape from the drudgeries that characterized or symbolize their earlier way of life in the Beech Creek neighborhoods, Beech Creek men see in that same situation a threat to their freedom.

Therefore, the male migrant who is in some degree dissatisfied with the urban way of life and who feels that he does not belong in that situation turns to the mountains, to the family "homestead," for support and assurance. Of course, the more a male migrant becomes integrated into the informal extrafamilial structures of the urban community, and the more friendship ties he establishes with persons who are natives of the host community, the more likely it is that he will be "satisfied"—feel he has become a permanent member of the host community, and manifest a sense of confidence about his ability to exercise some control over the impersonal social forces that affect the course of his life.

# SOCIAL CLASS ORIGINS:
## Intermediate-Class Patterns of Adjustment Are More in Accord with the Stem and Branch Family Model

Differences in interactional patterns as well as in moral standards and economic means had existed between the class groupings within the Beech Creek neighborhood context. As we have discovered, the social classes also differed in patterns of migration, especially in terms of where, when, and how individual migrants moved away from Beech Creek, and subsequently, too, in the level of material affluence the migrant families had been able to attain within the urban setting. These and other behavioral patterns and attributes associated with social class origin would have some bearing upon the processes of social and psychological adjustment of Beech Creek migrants in the area of destination.

We find that class seems to affect three aspects of interactional adjustment (Table 9.1).

If we take into account the history of migration from Beech Creek, a negative relationship between social class and degree of letter exchanges with people in the mountains is understandable. Migrants from high-class families tended to be in the earlier wave of migration, whereas migrants from low-class families dominated the later phases. This indicates that differences exist in the stage of migration of the various family groups composing the social classes. Whether or not close kin members of a migrant's family group still reside in the mountains is, of course, a determinant of the number of letters that are exchanged; migrants from high-class families have fewer kinsfolk back in eastern Kentucky.

Furthermore, the fact that no relationships are observed between class origin and visiting in eastern Kentucky (or visiting exchanges) suggests that the concept and meaning of "family homestead" differs among the various social classes. Migrants from high-class families, as we noted during field work, often view their visits to eastern Kentucky as holiday outings rather than family reinforcement ritual; migrants from intermediate-class families, on the other hand, think of such visits more as an obligation dictated by familistic norms. Though the pattern of frequency is similar in these cases, we believe the content or meaning attached to such visits differs. We would also entertain a comparable argument as to why branch-family interaction does not vary with class origin; though the kin network is not any less important for high-class migrants, the meaning of kin interaction may be quite different.

Predictably, however, the higher the social class, the more friendship ties have been established with persons "outside" of the mountain migrant community. Yet it is significant that a larger proportion of intermediate-class migrants report "very little" contact with urban natives as compared with high- and lower-class migrants (who have greater contact). An intervening variable, the ecological situation of intermediate-class families, must be taken into account. Intermediate-class families, in general, are more isolated socioculturally; they tend to reside in one or the other of the small "eastern Kentucky" settlements that have sprung up in the countryside around the great cities and industrial zones of southern Ohio. High- and lower-class migrant families, on the other hand, are more dispersed residentially and more likely to be located in the larger metropolitan centers of southern Ohio—the former in the suburbs and the latter often in urban slums; in either of these cases, for example, female migrants have greater opportunity to "make friends" with urban natives than do their intermediate-class counterparts.

In terms of the psychology of adjustment, our findings (Table 9.2) show that migrants from higher-class families are less nostalgic for "home," tend to express their feelings of happiness more positively, and are more likely to possess a sense of involvement with the larger society—an optimism about their place in the world—than migrants from lower-class families. It appears that by severing or modifying certain ties with family homestead and mountain society, higher-class migrants have made or are making a relatively smoother or less stress-producing adjustment to the realities of their situation in the urban industrial setting.

Now let us examine the patterns of relationships between various aspects of interactional and psychological adjustment in the case of each of the social-class groupings of migrants (Table 9.4). Our aim is to interpret the meaning of these observed patterns in the light of what we know about Beech Creekers and the Beech Creek migration system.

Among high- and intermediate-class migrants we find a negative relationship between extent of worry and frequency of visiting nearby kin; this relationship does not exist among lower-class migrants. High-class migrants also show greater anxiety if they are not actively involved with a close-knit kin group. Why these patterns do not hold for lower-class migrants is unclear; perhaps an aggressive confrontation with urban life (a characteristic of the high-class families) tends to generate tensions as well as to erode familistic norms. It may also be that high-class migrants view the branch-family network more as a problem-solving unit and, for that reason, those who sense they are somewhat "alone" in the area of destination tend to worry a great deal more about various difficulties they perceive or have encountered.

Only in the case of intermediate-class migrants does a strong association appear between expressed happiness and frequency of visiting nearby kin. This suggests the presence of situational or attitudinal factors which are more or less unique to them and which, in effect, are necessary conditions for the relationship to become manifest. Compared with other migrants, they tend to be more familistic; the familistic orientation of the mountain subculture is *reinforced* by situational circumstances in the area of destination which typify the settlement pattern of the intermediate-class family groups from Beech Creek. Therefore, kin interaction is and remains an important determinant of happiness for intermediate-class Beech Creek migrants in particular.

**Table 9.4.** Relationships between various aspects of migrants' psychological and interactional adjustment, by social class origins.*

| | Interactional Adjustment Variables | | | | | | |
| | Branch-family | | Urban ties | | Stem-family | | |
| Psychological Adjustment Variables | Size of kin group | Freq. of visiting kin | Social contacts | Friendship ties | Visiting E. Ky. | Visiting exchanges | Letter exchanges |
|---|---|---|---|---|---|---|---|
| **Higher Class (N = 36)** | | | | | | | |
| Residential stability: | | | | | | | |
| Nostalgia: | | | | | | | |
| Happiness: | | | | | | | |
| Worry: | −.32 | −.44 | | | | | |
| Anomia: | | | | | | | |
| Anxiety: | | −.49 | | | | | |
| **Intermediate Class (N = 63)** | | | | | | | |
| Residential stability: | | | | + | − | − | − |
| Nostalgia: | | −.51 | | | +.38 | +.34 | |
| Happiness: | | +.47 | | | | | −.34 |
| Worry: | | −.36 | | | | | |
| Anomia: | | | − | | | | |
| Anxiety: | | | −.47 | − | | | + |
| **Lower Class (N = 45)** | | | | | | | |
| Residential stability: | | | | | −.38 | | |
| Nostalgia: | | | | | | | |
| Happiness: | + | | | | | + | |
| Worry: | + | | | | | | |
| Anomia: | | | | − | | −.40 | −.48 |
| Anxiety: | | | | | −.39 | | |

* NOTE: The social class origin of 17 migrants was not ascertainable.

With respect to the pattern of relationships between indicators of involvements with non-eastern Kentuckians and various aspects of psychological adjustment, only one relationship is noted when we control on social-class origin. Intermediate-class migrants who feel they have very little contact with urban natives are more likely to show symptoms of psychological anxiety. This fact can be understood more clearly in the light of related findings. Female migrants generally express greater anxiety than male migrants and, in their case, the fewer social contacts with urban natives, the greater the level of anxiety. Furthermore, though intermediate-class migrants as a category express only slightly lower levels of anxiety, their level of social contacts with urban natives is considerably less than that of other migrants. By making inferences from these patterns of interrelationships, we again arrive at the conclusion that the ecological situation, i.e., the relative cultural isolation of intermediate-class Beech Creek migrants, is an important factor to consider in explaining the phenomenon in question. Female migrants from these families are the more culturally isolated, and for that reason a larger proportion of them manifest symptoms of psychological stress. In other words, anxiety is more characteristic of female than of male migrants, and it is simply a situational fact resulting from the familistically organized migration system that intermediate-class female migrants in this case do not have as much opportunity for informal social contact with people from "outside" the mountain society.

It is especially interesting that no other relationships are noted (of reliable strength) between the indicators of urban social ties and psychological adjustment when social class is taken into account. This aspect of interactional adjustment may be a phenomenon that has little bearing upon other aspects of migration-adjustment; the independent effect of urban social ties appears to be negligible. To the extent that these indicators measure the migrants' assimilation into the informal structure of urban life, the observations made here are noteworthy for future research.

Considering the relationships between indicators of involvement with stem-family and psychological adjustment, we find that intermediate- and lower-class migrants tend to conform more to the expected pattern than higher-class migrants. Though high-class migrants, on the average, visit as much in eastern Kentucky as other migrants, such visiting behavior is not associated with any of the psychological adjustment indicators. And despite the fact that high-class migrants exchange letters with people in eastern Kentucky less frequently, on the average, than lower-class migrants, those who correspond frequently with kinsfolk and friends in the mountains are not likely to be either more or less adjusted psychologically than those who do not. In short, migrants from high-class Beech Creek families, whether because of situational realities or orientational adjustments to situational realities, do not turn to the mountains and their family homesteads in time of stress nor in their search for identity and stability; they do, however, rely to some degree upon the branch-family network as a stabilizing structure and problem-solving unit.

Stem-family ties, on the other hand, play some part in the psychological adjustment of migrants from low-class families in Beech Creek. Feelings of anomia, for example, which vary inversely with social-class origin, are negatively associated with both visiting and letter exchanges by them with persons in eastern Kentucky. The greater prevalence of anomia among low-class migrants, then, may be explained by the severance or modification of interactional ties with family and friends in the mountains—a consequence of migration—coupled with an apparently strong need for such interactional ties. But we also find that those low-class migrants who have severed or modified ties with family and friends in the mountains—who visit less often in eastern Kentucky—are inclined to be more stable residentially in the urban community, yet show symptoms of greater anxiety. This is not surprising if we consider that anxiety may be fostered by urban involvement, that these two aspects of adjustment (anxiety and residential stability) tend to go hand-in-hand, and that residential instability may be reinforced by interaction with stem-family. Low-class migrants were "rootless" in many respects even in the Beech Creek neighborhood situation. In their encounter with urban industrial society, the insecurity of not having a place—a homestead—back in the mountains to which they can return in time of stress and to which they can cling as a symbolic refuge and source of identity undoubtedly contributes to their feelings of despair and hopelessness. Because they thereby assume (or must assume) an attitude of permanency in the host community, the processes generating alienation may have been encouraged.

In the case of intermediate-class migrants, we observe the "cushioning" effect of the stem *and* branch family network. The familistic orientation of these migrants, as pointed out earlier, tends to be reinforced by their characteristic pattern of settlement in the area of destination, which itself is a consequence of the stem-family form of migration. They are happiest when actively involved with a close-knit family group; they are also less inclined to worry about things and not as likely to experience extreme nostalgia for home and the mountain way of life.

Intermediate-class migrants, however, who for one reason or another encounter some difficulty in adapting to the new situation and who cling to an identification with their mountain "homestead," can and do return to the mountains for "visits" and presumably for familistic and cultural reinforcement. This may be a transitional phase of the adjustment process. In any event, the stem-family structure seems to provide a "haven of safety" for those who have not been able to satisfy their interactional needs through the branch-family network. Cohesive family structures at both ends of the migration stream serve to complement each other in the reduction or alleviation of tensions resulting from the process of adjustment.

Nevertheless, the level of anxiety of intermediate-class migrants varies inversely with the amount of social contact they experience with persons native to the urban area. This phenomenon, we believe, is a manifestation of the fact that these migrants (especially the women) tend to be more isolated socially by reason of their pattern of residential location. Because of generally high social interactional needs (Kentuckians like to "socialize") and the need to feel accepted by others outside of the immediate family circle, frustration of such needs undoubtedly generates some tensions and anxieties. In other words, we believe that anxiety and feelings of social ostracism are aspects of the same syndrome and that the syndrome occurs in cases, such as these intermediate-class migrants (and especially the women), in which a high need for social acceptance encounters either real, socially structured, or self-imposed barriers to social interaction.

We are aware that further verification and elaboration, both theoretical and empirical, are necessary before an explanatory model will emerge, before a developmental sequence can be posited, and before the relative importance of social class origin in the process of an individual's adjustment to situational circumstances associated with rural-to-urban migration can be understood. Nevertheless, let us review what we have learned from the Beech Creek case.

The branch-family network, it appears, performs a supportive role for migrants from high-class families in Beech Creek by providing them with an intimate group to which they can turn for help and advice about problems before such problems become internalized in the form of psychological tensions. High-class migrants, who in many ways even prior to migration had been more committed to the value standards of middle-class America than other Beech Creekers, utilize their kinship group for much the same purposes and in much the same manner as we might expect among a "normal" American population. The notion of "family homestead" and its supportive functions seems to be inapplicable in this case. It is also plausible, of course, that those high-class migrants who are more fully committed to middle-class American norms and values and hence experience a greater degree of tension have modified their earlier close relationships with the branch-family network as a consequence of the urban encounter. In any event, if generalizations can be drawn from these observations, we must consider that interaction with family and friends *in the mountains* is *not* an important factor in the psychological adjustment of migrants from high-class Beech Creek families. These migrants and their adjustment patterns, for one reason or the other, appear to represent a later phase in the migration of Beech Creek family groups.

The branch-family network, in the case of migrants from intermediate-class Beech Creek families, similarly performs an important integrative and supportive function. Unlike the pattern for high-class migrants, involvement with persons in eastern Kentucky also shows evidence of being a stabilizing influence. Our data suggest the presence in this system of a "haven of safety"; i.e., a place with kin and friends in the mountains to which the migrant feels he can return, and indeed does, if adjustment problems are encountered in the area of destination. Furthermore, there is reason to believe that the pattern of residential location of intermediate-class migrants affects the patterns of adjustment; familistic bonds are reinforced by social and cultural isolation from the urban context.

The complementary interplay between stem- and branch-family networks, which, in the case of intermediate-class migrants, serves as a supportive framework providing stability at both or either ends of the migration stream, does not seem to exist in the case of migrants from lower-class families in Beech Creek. The psychological adjustment of lower-class migrants appears little affected by branch-family involvements; feelings of despair and insecurity may be a normative condition among these families, and the family group, as an entity, may be unable to provide the necessary aid (economic, social, psychological) to help its members satisfy their changing needs. A "cushioning" bond with stem-family homestead such as exists for intermediate-class migrants serves as a stabilizing factor only in a limited sense in the case of lower-class migrants. This has serious implications because of their great need for social, psychological, and economic support. Among lower-class migrants, the transitional pattern (stabilizing functions performed by the branch-family network) appears to be absent; hence, seeking stability from an unstable situation in the mountains without complementary support from a cohesive branch-family network can and probably does delay the transitional adjustment process.

In many ways and for a variety of reasons, then, when compared with migrants from high- and lower-class Beech Creek families, the pattern of adjustment of migrants from intermediate-class families appears to be modeled more along the lines of a stem- *and* branch-family system of rural to urban migration. Nevertheless, there is little doubt that the kinship factor—whether in the form of a cohesive stem-family, branch-family, or complementary stem- *and* branch-family network—enters into and affects various aspects of adjustment among all classes of migrants.

## LEVEL OF SCHOOLING: Less Educated Migrants Are More Dependent Upon Stem-Family Support in the Process of Adjustment

In years past, when Beech Creek was a more or less self-sufficient locality (and even today as mountain neighborhoods have become the targets of economic development and educational reform programs), it was exceedingly difficult for a Beech Creek youngster to seek out, arrange for, and pursue a high school education. If he were blessed with considerable encouragement and support from his parental family, there was still the physical barrier of Beech Creek's geographical isolation to overcome. The more fortunate youngsters, whose parents were willing and able to allocate a portion of their meager family incomes toward their schooling, could "board out" in town or in the dormitory of the area high school, which had been established and organized for that purpose. Going to school often meant a long hike to the road in the cold, predawn hours of a winter day and, in the grey evening, a wearysome trek back home to confront "chores." Jesse Stuart's descriptions of these hardships are apropos to the Beech Creek case.[5]

Many Beech Creekers, nevertheless, did enter high school, and some earned diplomas. Among the migrants, about 14 percent had started high school but had dropped out prior to completion, about 22 percent had completed high school, and a few of the latter had gone on to college (a number became school teachers and one man, who had migrated out before 1942, earned a Ph.D. and became Professor of Education at a large western university). The majority of Beech Creek migrants, however, are on the other end of the education continuum; 64 percent had completed only eight grades or less of formal schooling.

For study purposes, we regard those who attained more than eight grades of schooling as the "more educated." By including the high school dropout in this upper grouping (aside from the analytic necessity of having a sufficient number of cases for reliable statements) we make that category more inclusive of individuals who possess orientations favorable toward learning which, over the years, they may have exercised by pursuing various informal means of self-education. One should bear in mind that the distribution of educational attainment is skewed; we are dealing with a population that is characterized by a very low median level of schooling even among the "more educated."

Level of schooling, we find, is not associated with any of the indicators of interactional ties with stem- and branch-family networks (Table 9.1). In that sense at least, education does not seem to effect an erosion, or a reinforcement, of the familistic value-orientations characteristic of the Beech Creek sociocultural system. It is, however, associated with the extent to which migrants have been absorbed into the informal social life of the host community. The more educated are likely to have more social contacts and friendship ties with urban natives, which suggests that "schooling" facilitates the process of integration. That such integration can be effected without at the same time eroding familistic interactional patterns is a paradox meriting further contemplation and future research attention.

Only one significant relationship is noted between level of schooling and the various aspects of psychological adjustment (Table 9.2). Consistent with many previous studies, anomia and educational attainment are negatively associated;[6] the less schooled migrants are more likely to express feelings of hopelessness and despair. That migration is a "condition" accentuating this relationship can only be suggested, not demonstrated, in the present context.

Among the less educated migrants (Table 9.5), happiness seems to be determined by frequent interaction with a close-knit kin group in the area of destination. Indeed these individuals, as we observed in the field, tend to equate "happiness" with familistic activity. Furthermore, they are in some ways dependent upon the stem-family for support in the process of adjustment. If they maintain a pattern of frequent face-to-face interaction with kinsfolk and friends back in the mountains, they are less likely to manifest feelings of hopelessness and despair, i.e., to be anomic. In that sense, the stem-family structure performs an integrative function. Also, if we interpret these data correctly, the stem-family offers the less educated migrant a "haven of safety" in time of stress; those who are inclined to worry a great deal, for example, visit "home" more often. (One might argue that greater involvement with kinsfolk in the mountains adds to the migrant's catalog of worries; but we would ultimately arrive at the same conclusion, namely, that the

**Table 9.5.** Relationships between various aspects of migrants' psychological and interactional adjustment, by level of schooling.

| | Interactional Adjustment Variables | | | | | | |
| | Branch-family | | Urban ties | | Stem-family | | |
| Psychological adjustment variables | Size of kin group | Freq. of visiting kin | Social contacts | Friendship ties | Visiting E. Ky. | Visiting exchanges | Letter exchanges |
|---|---|---|---|---|---|---|---|
| **Higher, More Than Eighth Grade (N = 58)** | | | | | | | |
| Residential stability: | | | | | | | |
| Nostalgia: | | | | | | | |
| Happiness: | | | | | | + | |
| Worry: | | − .52 | | | | | |
| Anomia: | | | | | | | |
| Anxiety: | | − .40 | | | | | + |
| **Lower, Eighth Grade or Less (N = 103)** | | | | | | | |
| Residential Stability: | | | | + | − .41 | − | |
| Nostalgia: | | | | − .29 | + | + .29 | |
| Happiness: | | + .54 | | | | | |
| Worry: | | | | | + .27 | | |
| Anomia: | | | | | − .29 | − .32 | |
| Anxiety: | | | | − | | | |

stem-family structure provides the Beech Creekers with a *raison d'etre.*) Similarly, those less educated migrants who are in some ways dissatisfied with the urban way of life, who feel nostalgic for home and mountains—perhaps because they have acquired few friendship ties among urban natives in the host community—visit home more often. That is, they have access to a "supportive cushion" provided by the stem-family homestead, and this support, whether actualized or normatively "promised," is extremely important during the transitional phase of adjustment. Frequent visits home, of course, may reinforce feelings of nostalgia and residential instability; but the alternatives may be extreme despair, apathy, alienation, and behavioral deviance.

For more educated migrants, the pattern of findings resembles that of "high-class" migrants (compare Tables 9.4 and 9.5). The branch-family network, we note, is in some ways involved in the adjustment process; the stem-family network plays a lesser role, and social contacts and friendship ties with urban natives seem to have no effect. Symptoms of anxiety and worry are associated with a pattern of infrequent face-to-face interaction with nearby kinsfolk. Anxiety and worry are probably also by-products of the increasingly heavy demands of urban involvements and economic aspirations. But the branch-family network serves as a problem-solving unit helping to alleviate tensions before they become internalized as anxieties, and helping to rationalize difficulties before they become plaguing worries. That no other relationships emerge in the case of more educated migrants is noteworthy; it suggests that the educated migrants are more adaptable to circumstances encountered through migration and not as dependent upon the stem-family structure as their less educated counterparts. Education may be an important "bridge" in the acculturation process;[7] the stem-family form of migration, however, provides an important avenue of access to existing opportunities elsewhere—with transitional stability—for those who must still confront "the new and strange."

# LEVEL OF LIVING: Material Affluence Affects the Migrants' Dependency Upon Stem-Family System

An individual or family's material level of living is one factor in the complex, multidimensional phenomenon, socioeconomic status. Evidence can be readily drawn, from a more or less normal population, demonstrating the linkage between this and such other dimensions of socioeconomic status as educational attainment and occupational prestige. Beech Creek migrants are a somewhat atypical population; it is difficult to distinguish meaningful occupational or educational status differences among them. We know, however, that they vary considerably in their material achievements, i.e., in their economic success over the years after migration, and we are quite certain that Beech Creekers subscribe to the goal of material affluence and value it as a sign of social position. Because we wanted an indication of the socioeconomic status *achieved* by migrants in the area of destination, and because we wanted this indicator to be based upon relatively objective external criteria of social rank (hence in juxtaposition to the more particularistic criteria used in the original delination of social class in the Beech Creek neighborhoods), we focused on "level of living" and adopted a nine-item scale as our instrument of observation.[8]

Beech Creekers, as we know, moved away from the mountain neighborhoods to areas of greater economic opportunity elsewhere in order to improve their material lot in life. The extent to which their expectations were fulfilled, we reasoned, would enter into the adjustment process as an important condition affecting not only changes in familistic interactional patterns, but also changes in the need-dispositions of the migrants.

We find, however, that level of living is not, at least by itself, an important determinant of the Beech Creek migrants' interactional situation (Table 9.1) or state of mind (Table 9.2). Those who enjoy a relatively high level of affluence are apt to be more socially involved with urban natives as well as with kinsfolk in the area and, quite understandably, less inclined to reflect back upon the mountain way of life in nostalgic terms. Indeed, they appear to be more integrated into the host community. Of greater theoretical interest, however, is the failure of these data to show direct linkages between level of living and other dimensions of psychological and interactional adjustment. This suggests the possibility that countless earlier migration studies that have defined "adjustment" in socioeconomic terms (e.g., as level of living, socioeconomic status, money income) may have little relevance or explanatory power in helping us to understand the complex processes by which and through which rural migrants adjust, in a social psychological sense, to social circumstances they encounter in the urban areas of destination.[9]

Among more affluent migrants, symptoms of anxiety and anomia vary inversely with the degree to which urban social ties have been established (Table 9.6). These individuals not only maintain a generally higher level of such involvements than their less "successful" counterparts (we infer that affluence reinforces the need for extra-familial social contacts), but such involvements appear to have functional consequence in terms of the migrant's state of mind. On the other hand, interaction with kinsfolk seems to have little bearing on the more affluent migrants' psychological condition. If they have many kinsfolk living nearby, they are more inclined toward an attitude of permanency in the host community; family ties *are* important, but affluence seems to foster a mode of adaptation that counters reliance upon, and perhaps even transcends, the kin network.

Among less affluent migrants, we find greater convergence between

Table 9.6. Relationships between various aspects of migrants' psychological and interactional adjustment, by level of living.

| | Interactional Adjustment Variables | | | | | | |
| | Branch-family | | Urban ties | | Stem-family | | |
| Psychological adjustment variables | Size of kin group | Freq. of visiting kin | Social contacts | Friendship ties | Visiting E. Ky. | Visiting exchanges | Letter exchanges |
|---|---|---|---|---|---|---|---|
| **Higher Level of Living (N = 66)** | | | | | | | |
| Residential stability: | +.34 | | | | −.32 | | |
| Nostalgia: | | | | | | | |
| Happiness: | | | | | | | |
| Worry: | — | | | | | | |
| Anomia: | | + | −.36 | −.39 | | | |
| Anxiety: | | | −.32 | | | | |
| **Lower Level of Living (N = 95)** | | | | | | | |
| Residential stability: | | | | | −.28 | | |
| Nostalgia: | | | | | +.31 | | — |
| Happiness: | | | | | | | |
| Worry: | | | | | | + | +.29 |
| Anomia: | −.29 | | | | −.28 | — | |
| Anxiety: | −.33 | | | −.28 | | | |

various dimensions of psychological adjustment and familistic interactional patterns. These Beech Creekers tend to be oriented toward the stem-family, through which they seek, and undoubtedly find, stability and social significance (such involvements probably also generate certain kinds of worries). If many kinsfolk reside nearby in the host community, which happens in the latter stages of stem-family migration, the branch-family network tends to perform a similar stabilizing function, namely of assuring the migrant that he is not alone in the world. This sense of assurance gives the less affluent migrant greater confidence in coping with problems; anxieties are allayed, and he is freed to reach out from the kin network into the urban social world. Nevertheless, because his situation and needs are somewhat different from those of more affluent migrants, he is more dependent upon integrative functions performed by the stem-family system in the process of adjustment.

# CHURCH MEMBERSHIP: Involvement in Religious Groups Fosters Social Integration

Southern Appalachian migrants in northern cities, as numerous observers have noted,[10] characteristically turn to sect and church groups as legitimate outlets for their pent-up frustrations and as a means of anchoring themselves against the impersonal forces of urban life. Many sociologists, as well as theologians, would argue that in times of stress —whether individual, familial, or societal—churches and sect groups can and do perform leading roles in the restabilization process. In the Beech Creek case, therefore, we would expect that migrants who are involved in church activities will exhibit patterns of adjustment different from those of migrants who are not church goers.

Beech Creekers, as we observed them in the mountain neighborhoods, were a religious people but not necessarily church joiners. Even today, Beech Creekers tend to shy away from participation in any kind of formal organizations. Hence, it is significant that over two-thirds (65 percent) of the migrants "belong to" an organized church or sect group in the area of destination.[11]

Migrants who are church members, compared with those who are not affiliated with any church group, tend to have a pattern of adjustment indicative of greater involvement in and sense of belonging to the urban community (Tables 9.1 and 9.2). They have wider social contacts and more numerous friendship ties with urban natives, do less visiting with people back in eastern Kentucky, are less inclined to feel nostalgic for home, and are more likely to express sentiments of residential stability. Though they worry more than those who don't belong to a church group, and though symptoms of anxiety are more common among them, this probably indicates a greater involvement and commitment to confront and cope with the problems of day-to-day living in the urban environment.

Among church members (Table 9.7), anxiety symptoms and anomia vary inversely with degree of urban social contacts; this is clearly a pattern also among older migrants, more recent migrants, and those who

Table 9.7. Relationships between various aspects of migrants' psychological and interactional adjustment, by church membership.

| | Interactional Adjustment Variables | | | | | | |
| | Branch-family | | Urban ties | | | Stem-family | |
| Psychological adjustment variables | Size of kin group | Freq. of visiting kin | Social contacts | Friendship ties | Visiting E. Ky. | Visiting exchanges | Letter exchanges |
|---|---|---|---|---|---|---|---|
| **Church Member (N = 105)** | | | | | | | |
| Residential stability: | | | | | | | |
| Nostalgia: | | | | | | + | |
| Happiness: | | | | | | | |
| Worry: | − | | | | | +.30 | |
| Anomia: | − | + | −.32 | | − | | |
| Anxiety: | | | −.32 | −.27 | | + | −.30 |
| **Not Church Member (N = 56)** | | | | | | | |
| Residential stability: | | +.46 | | | − | | |
| Nostalgia: | | | | | + | | |
| Happiness: | | | | | | + | |
| Worry: | | | | | + | | |
| Anomia: | | | | −.27 | −.25 | | |
| Anxiety: | | −.37 | | | | | |

have attained higher levels of affluence. One of the important factors affecting that pattern may be the migrant's need for interpersonal contact with others which, in turn, affects his church or sect group affiliation. Through subsequent religious activity, the need for interpersonal contact may be reinforced, and if that need cannot be satisfied (because of situational, economic or social reasons) anxieties and feelings of despair may be generated. In any event, it is evident that extra-familial involvements are bound into the adjustment pattern of church-going migrants. The more contact these migrants have with family and friends in the mountains, the more they tend to show evidences of worry; but, in their case, variations in degree of interaction with kinsfolk seem to have less consequence upon psychological adjustment than the factor of social ties with urban natives.

Beech Creek migrants who are not affiliated with a church or sect group, on the other hand, seem to be more dependent upon the kin network in the process of adjustment. That they have not felt the need or availed themselves of opportunities to join a church group lends credence to this interpretation. These Beech Creekers are not "loners"; they seek intimate response from significant others, but their orientation is toward the kin group. The presence of a large number of kinsfolk nearby, for example, is concomitant with a feeling of permanence, i.e., residential stability in the host community, and if the kin network is a close-knit, cohesive group, the migrant is less likely to manifest anxiety. Visits back to the mountains, moreover, appear to complement friendship ties with urban natives as a factor fostering attitudes of hope, social worth, and human dignity; anomia, in this case, may be a result of having been situationally isolated from stem-family homestead as well as socially isolated from urban friendship groups.

Unlike other conditions taken into account during the course of our inquiry, church membership is a social attribute that has its origins in a deliberate, voluntary act prompted by the migrant's own need-dispositions at a particular time and place in his life. Indeed, affiliation with a religious organization may be viewed, in certain respects, as an indicator of adjustment. Migrants who participate more in the on-going social life of the host community are less dependent upon the kinship structure for integrative support and transitional stability. Church and sect groups may serve as a means to stimulate these involvements among such a migrant population as the Beech Creekers. In other words, religious organizations function as "compensatory structures" complementing or supplementing functions normally performed by the kin network in the process of adjustment.

# AGE: Older Migrants Are More Isolated from Kinsfolk; Their Frustrated Need-Dispositions Produce Certain Kinds of Stress

Older and younger persons, it is reasonable to suppose, will manifest different patterns of adjustment to situational circumstances associated with migration. Age is indicative of an individual's status in the family group, for example, and this status in turn affects his basic need-dispositions and role-expectations. If these role-expectations and the needs associated with age status have been learned or acquired within the context of a familistically-oriented sociocultural system, such as the mountain neighborhoods of Beech Creek, then they may be somewhat out of context in the more urbanized sociocultural situation at the place of destination, such as City A in Ohio. Tensions may be generated within the migration system and certain kinds of stress may be produced within the personality system of older migrants in particular. Hence, we should regard the age variable as a possible factor affecting the adjustment process.

Individuals in the Beech Creek migrant population are twenty years of age and older. Reducing the age variable to a dichotomy, we divided the population at forty years of age. Migrants forty or over constitute 22 percent of the total. All of these "older" migrants had been adults in 1942; they, in effect, are "older generation" Beech Creekers. Though many of the "younger" migrants also had migrated as adults, a considerable proportion had accompanied their migrating parents as children or teen-agers. The older migrants are a more homogeneous category of persons whose formative socialization was effected, by and large, within the mountain subculture; whereas the younger migrants are a more heterogeneous category of persons who were more directly, and at an earlier age, exposed to the influences of urban America.

Older migrants are somewhat more socially isolated (i.e., disengaged) from the kin network than younger migrants (Table 9.1). They interact less frequently with members of their kin group nearby or in eastern Kentucky and they are more inclined to be residentially stable and to think of the urban area as "home" (Table 9.2). Such orientational and behavioral differences associated with age are to be expected;[12] in one sense, they are a function of an individual's position in the family life cycle. Older migrants, for example, often represent *the* stem-family—the uprooted and transplanted leaders of a family group. But a redefinition and reorganization of family group boundaries is a normal phase of the family-life cycle, and older persons have undoubtedly become more involved with their children's families and less involved with the family affairs of well-established siblings. The disruptive influence of residential relocation through migration, however, would exaggerate this process of family group reorganization, and the uncertainties that accrue may offer a partial explanation of why older migrants tend to be more anomic.

Among older migrants the statistical relationships between interactional and psychological dimensions of adjustment are relatively strong

(Table 9.8). This suggests that age is an important condition affecting the adjustment process and that older migrants are in some ways less adaptable to changing interactional patterns and situational circumstances than younger migrants.

The extent to which older migrants are burdened with worries of one kind or another appears to be a function of the degree to which they are involved with a large, cohesive branch-family group. If they have many kinsfolk living nearby—whether married children or siblings—and experience frequent interaction with them, they are less inclined to worry. Older migrants, too, are less likely to evidence symptoms of anxiety if they are able to maintain a pattern of familial interaction with the branch-family network and a pattern of social interaction with

---

**Table 9.8.** Relationships between various aspects of migrants' psychological and interactional adjustment, by age.

| Psychological adjustment variables | Branch-family | | Urban ties | | Stem-family | | |
| | Size of kin group | Freq. of visit-ing kin | Social contacts | Friend-ship ties | Visit-ing E. Ky. | Visit-ing ex-changes | Letter ex-changes |
| --- | --- | --- | --- | --- | --- | --- | --- |
| *Younger, Under Forty (N = 125)* | | | | | | | |
| Residential stability: | | | | + | − .30 | | |
| Nostalgia: | | | | − .28 | + .25 | | |
| Happiness: | | + | | | | | |
| Worry: | | | | | | | |
| Anomia: | − | | − .32 | | | | |
| Anxiety: | | | | | | | + .27 |
| *Older, Forty or Over (N = 36)* | | | | | | | |
| Residential stability: | + | | | + | | | |
| Nostalgia: | | | | | + .25 | | |
| Happiness: | | + | | | | | |
| Worry: | − .77 | − .45 | | | | + .45 | |
| Anomia: | | | | − | − .69 | − .53 | |
| Anxiety: | | − .44 | − .62 | − .32 | | | |

urban natives which suggest that they are honored with a stable, useful, and respected position in the kin structure and in the host community. Their need for social interaction with significant others seems to be very strong; their ability to tolerate any measures of social rejection or familial avoidance seems to be very weak. Older migrants, we infer, are much involved (psychologically) with their branch-family group, and if interactional patterns are modified or familial communication channels disturbed, for whatever reasons, frustrated need-dispositions not compensated for by extra-familial social ties with urban neighbors and friends will generate certain kinds of stress, such as those indicated by our measures of anxiety and extent of worry.

On the other hand, older migrants look back toward the mountains in their quest for meaning and a sense of social worth. If they do not or cannot maintain a regular pattern of visiting with kinsfolk and friends in the mountains, perhaps because they have become so heavily involved with the problems of their immediate family and children, they are more likely to be anomic. It is as though interaction with people back home performs a major integrative function in the process of adjustment, providing the older migrant with a stable identity and reference point in society's larger scheme of things. The greater incidence of anomia among older migrants, it seems, can be explained by the modification of social bonds with their homestead in eastern Kentucky. To be sure, involvements with stem-family also reinforce a nostalgia for home and perhaps add to a catalog of worries; but those same involvements undoubtedly foster stability and allay those feelings of hopelessness that so often accompany the aging process.

Among younger migrants, who in certain respects are more oriented toward and bound into the larger kin network than older migrants, we find a weaker pattern of interrelationships between the social and psychological dimensions of adjustment. Degree of interaction with branch-family network is not connected with any of the aspects of psychological adjustment. However, younger migrants who feel nostalgic about home and who are not fully settled into or satisfied with the urban situation visit back in the mountains more often. Feelings of anxiety too, it seems, prompt them to write home more frequently. In other words, the kin group is sensitive to their needs; the stem- and branch-family network stands ready to provide necessary support and assistance. Of course, one may also interpret these data to mean that younger migrants are more adaptable to interactional changes concomitant with migration; aspects of psychological adjustment are not directly linked with differences in familistic behavior patterns.

Among younger migrants factors extraneous to familial involvements have greater consequence than the kinship factor in determining the migrant's frame of mind and orientation toward the world around him. We note, for example, that anomia varies inversely with degree of urban social contacts. Likewise, younger migrants are less likely to feel nostalgic for home if they have numerous friendship ties with urban natives. Although we are unable to document our supposition, we are quite certain nevertheless that a younger migrant's interpersonal relations in the work situation (in the case of men) or in the urban neighborhood (in the case of women) have much to do with his social and psychological stability.

In short, the kinship structure serves to "cushion" the transitional adjustment of younger migrants; but many needs of younger migrants extend outward and beyond the boundaries of the family group and cannot be "satisfied" by a cohesive kin network. The needs of older migrants, on the other hand, who in some ways have attained greater stability in the host community, are directed inward and toward the family group; but modifications in the network of interaction with kinsfolk—whether because of situational circumstances or changing role definitions—tend to frustrate those needs, generating tensions and psychological strains.

# LENGTH OF URBAN RESIDENCE: The Recent Migrant Finds Stability and Social Meaningfulness within the Context of the Kin Network

The adjustment of migrants is a process. For a proper understanding of this or any other sociological process, the temporal factor must be taken into account.

In the Beech Creek case, designed as a longitudinal study dealing with a total population of migrants, the temporal base is 1942. Since then and over a period of two decades, the Beech Creek neighborhoods, the Beech Creek sociocultural system, and the Beech Creekers themselves—in the area of origin as well as in the areas of destination—were exposed to a wide variety of change-producing influences and circumstances in addition to the more or less natural phenomena of individual aging and maturation. Beech Creekers did not leave the neighborhoods all at once as a group; migration from the neighborhoods resembled a steady stream during these twenty years. Furthermore, though most were young adults when they migrated, the selective processes probably differed at different points in time. We are aware, for example, that social class position in Beech Creek had much to do with the strategy of migration.

For a number of reasons we can expect that Beech Creekers who had migrated earlier would have patterns of adjustment different from those who had migrated more recently. Recent migrants tend to be younger and somewhat more representative of the lower than of the higher social class groupings in Beech Creek. And they are undoubtedly different from earlier migrants in many other ways, for they were drawn from a more contemporary mountain neighborhood situation—a socio-cultural environment which itself had changed considerably from the one earlier migrants had left. Then too, earlier migrants had probably experienced a longer period of more direct exposure to urbanizing influences in the cultural contact situation outside of the mountains and, of course, had been favored with more time for initial difficulties to be reconciled within the urban setting.

We must necessarily deal with this complicated temporal dimension and its various implications in a simplified, exploratory fashion. Beech Creekers who have resided outside of the eastern Kentucky area for at least ten years are regarded as "earlier" migrants (they constitute 53 percent of the total); some were youngsters accompanying their parents. "Recent" migrants, on the other hand, are those who have resided outside of eastern Kentucky for less than ten years; they were at least ten years old when they left.

Earlier migrants interact less frequently on the average with kinsfolk and friends in eastern Kentucky, are less inclined to nostalgia about home and the mountains, and are more likely to have a large number of kinsfolk nearby as well as a large circle of urban friends; they are also more likely to manifest symptoms of psychological anxiety (Tables 9.1 and 9.2) than are recent migrants. Yet differences between early and recent migrants are not as striking as differences between older and younger migrants.

Earlier migrants may appear to be less closely attached to the stem-family network for the simple reason that so many members of their family group had joined them, over the years, in the area of destination. The stem of the family, around which branch-families cluster, may itself have been transplanted. This would explain why they have a similar level of involvement with the branch-family network as recent migrants.

It is surprising that aspects of psychological adjustment are not more directly linked with length of residence outside eastern Kentucky. It is difficult to understand, for example, why feelings of residential stability are not associated with length of urban residence, although nostalgia for home and mountains is. Perhaps the familial structure itself is adaptable in a functional sense to the changing needs of its members, even though the form of extended family relationships tends to be maintained over a long period of time. This was Leplay's insistent theme in his discussions about the relative social merits of a stem-family pattern of familial organization over other forms he had observed through his studies of worker and peasant families in 19th Century Europe.

Among earlier migrants, who appear to be less attached to the stem-family homestead than recent migrants, we find that a large amount of visiting back in the mountains is concomitant with greater nostalgia and, conversely, lesser urban residential stability (Table 9.9). If these

**Table 9.9.** Relationships between various aspects of migrants' psychological and interactional adjustment, by length of urban residence.

| Psychological adjustment variables | Interactional Adjustment Variables | | | | | | |
|---|---|---|---|---|---|---|---|
| | Branch-family | | Urban ties | | Stem-family | | |
| | Size of kin group | Freq. of visiting kin | Social contacts | Friendship ties | Visiting E. Ky. | Visiting ex-changes | Letter ex-changes |
| Recent Arrival, Less Than Ten Years Out (N = 75) | | | | | | | |
| Residential stability: | | − | | + | − | | |
| Nostalgia: | | + | | | | | |
| Happiness: | | | + | | | | |
| Worry: | − .35 | − .52 | | | | | |
| Anomia: | − .46 | | | − .44 | − .34 | | |
| Anxiety: | − .35 | | − .35 | − .31 | − | | |
| Earlier Arrival, Ten or More Years Out (N = 86) | | | | | | | |
| Residential stability: | + | | + | | − .29 | | |
| Nostalgia: | | | | | + .29 | | |
| Happiness: | | + .31 | | | | | |
| Worry: | | | − | | + .40 | + .39 | + |
| Anomia: | + | | | | | | |
| Anxiety: | | − .30 | | | + | + | + |

migrants maintain close ties with the family homestead, they are also more inclined to worry (presumably because they are more involved with family problems or, perhaps, because they turn to the stem-family in time of stress). It seems, then, that a differentiation has occurred among earlier migrants: some, over the years, have made a clear "break" with family and friends in the area of origin and have attained a relative degree of residential stability in the host community; some have not.

Among the earlier arrivals, frequency of branch-family interaction is linked positively with degree of happiness (as is also the case among male, intermediate-class, and less educated migrants) and inversely with symptoms of anxiety (as is also the case among high-class, more educated, and older migrants). Earlier migrants, we know, are more inclined toward anxiety than recent migrants. Here, then, we infer that the branch-family network performs some tension-relieving functions. Earlier migrants not only find great happiness through familial interaction but turn to, and indeed are dependent upon, their kin group for psychological reassurance. Although, on the average, they can count more urban natives among their circles of friends, that fact alone appears to have little relevance in explaining their psychological adjustment or orientation toward the urban social world.

Among recent migrants who, categorically, are somewhat more closely tied to the family homestead, those who visit "home" frequently, for whatever reasons, are not as likely to be anomic as those who visit eastern Kentucky infrequently. Yet these Beech Creekers are also not as likely to be anomic if they are part of a large, effective kin group in the area of destination, and/or if they experience numerous social contacts with urban natives. Similarly, we observe that newcomers who are involved with (i.e., who have "joined") relatively large kin groups are less likely to manifest symptoms of anxiety and worry; anxiety, too, is inversely associated with degree of urban social contacts. Obversely, newcomers who are more "on their own" are more likely to show signs of concern and stress. Recent migrants have a strong need for social interaction with significant others; frustration of that need, which may happen because of situational circumstances encountered in the area of destination, can and does foster feelings of hopelessness, despair, and anxiety. For the recent migrant from Beech Creek then, the stem and branch-family network performs an integrative function; through it he seeks and generally finds some measure of stability and social meaningfulness.

However, it is not so much the frequency of interaction with kinsfolk that makes a difference in the psychological adjustment of the newcomer as it is the sheer presence of numerous kinsfolk nearby. To be sure, frequency of visiting nearby kin varies inversely with extent of worry; the branch-family network is utilized as a problem-solving group during the early stages of migration. For psychological stability and social identity the recent migrant needs to feel that he is part of a large kin group; kin visiting may be an activity that is "adjustable" depending upon needs of the moment. In other words, by its sheer presence a large kin group offers the migrant a sense of security that comes from knowing that "someone close is nearby;" the branch-family network functions as a "haven of safety."

Non-kin friendship groups also play a compensatory role in the adjustment of recent migrants; the more social contacts with urban natives, the less anomia and anxiety. A migrant's degree of extra-familial involvements is probably indicative of the degree of "openness" of his family group to modernizing influences, as well as of his own general need for close, personal interaction with other people. From either point of view, it seems clear that the degree to which the newcomer's interpersonal involvements extend beyond the boundaries of kinsfolk and culturally-similar friends is, at least, concomitant with certain important dimensions of adjustment. In that sense non-kin friendship groups can and do perform integrative functions which in some ways complement functions performed by the branch-family network during the early stages of urban transition.

# 10 BEECH CREEK MIGRANTS AND MIGRATION: Summary and Conclusions

One of our main objectives for initiating this project was to further the study of migration *within a sociological framework*. We also wanted to uncover and explore additional facts that would lead to a fuller, more comprehensive understanding of Appalachian migration. These efforts, we felt, would eventually prove useful in formulating appropriate policy decisions at local, state, and federal levels that are designed to make the entire process of migration and the urban relocation and adjustment of rural populations more beneficial to society as a whole.

The sociological objective was pursued in two ways. First, on the basis of a systematic review and analysis of the current literature on migration and aided by the thought-inputs of an interdisciplinary group of advisers, we developed a theoretical perspective for the sociological study of migration. From this frame of reference, and in light of available facts about Appalachian society, culture, and migration streams, a guiding hypothesis and conceptual approach were derived for the Beech Creek research. Second, we designed the longitudinal study, incorporating both survey and quasi-participant observation methods. To note the convergence of findings from two or more basically different methodological approaches organized within the same general study context and utilizing the same general interpretative scheme can be a useful strategy for assessing the validity of research conclusions. This is especially important when the degree of predictive validity of generalizations couched in strictly quantitative terms is not very high, as is often the case in the social sciences. Moreover, our scientific aim was neither to test an hypothesis in the formal sense, to explain the phenomenon of migration in a total sense, nor to achieve a high degree of statistical prediction in the statements derived from our findings. We see this research mainly as theoretically explorative. Through the process of exploring we have "tested" the utility of the guiding hypothesis, interpreted its meaning within the context of this particular case, explained some of the major behavioral determinants and factors associated with the various phases of Appalachian migration, and achieved a modest degree of prediction, especially in the adjustmental phase. Some lines of future theoretical development relevant to a sociology of migration have been suggested.

With respect to the secondary objective, namely to discover facts about Appalachian migration that might prove useful in policy decisions, we have attempted to bring to bear upon the findings our knowledge of the study population acquired over two decades. This longitudinal dimension has enabled us to understand in depth, and to be in a position to communicate the intricate problems involved in the processes of migration and post-migration adjustment which are not usually revealed through cross-sectional surveys and not often possible in migration studies. Our statements of fact about the Beech Creek case have been distilled from statistical analyses of quantitative data *and* a long period of direct observation of, and personal interaction with, our subjects. Furthermore, because of the nature of our research design, the emphasis has been upon people rather than places. This orientation, we submit, should be the heart and soul of any sensible and just policy formulations with respect to rural-to-urban migration streams, whether from the mountains of Kentucky or from other economically depressed regions of the world.

# CONCEPTUAL FRAMEWORK: Recapitulation

Migration, as we conceive it, is a system-maintaining process. The system is constituted by the social organization at the place of origin of the migrants (the donor subsystem), the social organization at the place of destination of the migrants (the recipient subsystem), and the social organization of the migrants themselves. By saying that migration is a system-maintaining process, we mean that the structural strains in either the donor subsystem, or the recipient subsystem, or both, as they arise under the complex conditions of their day-to-day functioning, can reach points beyond which they will begin to act in a way to destroy the subsystems (and, by definition, the system as a whole). One such strain, for example, might be due to a lack of sufficient resources to be allocated to the satisfaction of the legitimate needs of the actors in a subsystem. When such strains occur in one sector of the migration system, their management is effected by withdrawal of a sufficient number of actors from the subsystem where the strain is most acute. Conceived in these terms, migration is one means of maintaining the stability of the system as a whole.

From this point of view migration may be regarded as a two-way process between the donor and recipient subsystems; structural strains can occur in both subsystems at different times, thus giving rise to a flow of migrants in one direction or the other. This whole process can be illustrated by analogy with two streams of fluids connected by a series of small channels or capillaries. The big stream, urban American society, and the small stream, rural Appalachian society, have many things in common, yet they are quite distinct in other respects. They are moving toward a junction or confluence, at which point the composition of the two streams would become more or less the same. This merging is brought about or helped by an interchange of the content of the two streams at many points (in space and in time). The interchanges themselves are effected by differences in pressures at the two ends of any given capillary. Thus, the almost constant movement of migrants between urban-industrial Ohio and Appalachian Kentucky may be regarded as one of these capillaries; some people are migrating and some are returning. In either case an interchange of the elements of social organization of urban American society and rural Appalachia is occurring to the degree to which these elements are not the same. This interchange tends to make the two social organizations more and more similar as time goes by.

We also see migration as a collectivity or group process, and not simply as the result of a few individuals at random picking up, moving, and relocating elsewhere. In other words, from a sociological point of view, migration is the movement of persons from one interactional system to another, preceded by considerable deliberation among those who are leaving and those who are staying behind. As in most human behavior, a decision to migrate is guided by value considerations.

Our main theoretical concern, after conceptualizing migration as a system-maintaining, interactional (group-oriented) process, was to explore the part played by the stem-family, a theoretical construct employed by LePlay, in the social adjustment of migrants in the area of destination. We view "social adjustment" as a dynamic state in which the individual actors are able to satisfy or fulfill the responsibilities of their major roles but without compromising their integrity and identity.

The two sets of roles we have been most concerned with are in the sectors of kinship and occupation. The migrants originated in a rural familistic cultural situation, and the most obvious determinant for their migration was occupational in the economic sense.

From the above theoretical considerations we derived an overall guiding hypothesis, namely that the greater the functional adequacy of the stem-family (modified to include the network of "branch-families") of the Beech Creek sociocultural system in responding to the changing needs of the Beech Creekers, the more adjusted the migrants will be both as individuals and families. In exploring the functional adequacy of the Beech Creek family we broadened our perspective to include the "branch-families" because we were thinking of the social adjustment of the migrants within the total migration system, namely the Kentucky-Ohio system, and not just in Ohio. Whereas the Beech Creek family is an abstraction from the Beech Creek sociocultural system, Beech Creekers are found at both ends of the migration system, and the migrants' social adjustment cannot be understood without taking into account the total kinship network.

# BEECH CREEK YESTERDAY

Let us recall briefly the locale where our story began and the social context from which the migrants were drawn.

Beech Creek, in 1942, consisted of three more or less contiguous mountain neighborhoods, each of which was composed of a scattering of houses along a creek or on the flats near the river, as is typical of the highland settlements. Rugged topography, poor roads and primitive means of transportation and communication isolated the neighborhoods from much of the outside world. To a visitor, the natural surroundings were scenic, but one's vision was limited by the sharply rising hills, and this seemed to make the Beech Creek people prisoners of their circumstances.

For the mountaineer it was a continuous struggle to wrest a living from those hills. Most Beech Creekers were descendants of the early settlers who had taken possession of the available bottomland along with the valuable stands of virgin timber. As time went on, continuous logging all but depleted the forest resources, and the flat land available to each family had dwindled by the practice of parcelling among succeeding generations. Still, each family had a small farm and some wooded hill land, though neither was commercially valuable. Farm and home formed the "place" around which almost the whole of a Beech Creeker's life revolved.

Some men added to the family income by doing odd jobs, such as logging, during certain seasons of the year, or by going to work in the coal mines in neighboring counties. Some families grew tobacco as a cash crop, and some sold their surplus eggs and livestock. This income never amounted to much; almost 90 percent of all farm products were consumed at home. Beech Creekers, in those days, basically depended on their farms and families for economic survival.

The family, as in many traditional societies, was a working and consuming unit made strongly cohesive through the interdependencies of age and sex roles. Children were under the direct supervision of their parents. The women were responsible for the household duties and for the garden and chickens. When they worked outside the house, as during corn-hoeing or tobacco-cutting seasons, it was almost always on the "place" and in the company of husbands or sons. There was not much variation in the women's work except, perhaps, when they canned vegetables and prepared pork for storage. In all these activities, the daughters helped their mothers as apprentices for job-roles they would assume in their late teens.

The men worked mostly outdoors, doing the heavier farming tasks such as plowing and planting, clearing land, looking after the livestock, and "raising coal." Their sons were expected to help.

In this subsistence agricultural setting, the collective welfare of the conjugal family and of the kin group as a whole was of prime importance. Individual needs were subordinated to the needs of the family.

Familism also characterized other aspects of the Beech Creek way of life, but the familism of Beech Creek was in certain respects different from that found in many parts of the non-Western world. The primary orientational emphasis was upon the conjugal family and secondarily upon a network of mutual aid relationships among conjugal families within a kin system. Furthermore, rather than excluding either conjugal or consanguine bonds the kin network included both, differentiating only in terms of the strength of social interactional ties. Because the conjugal bond received primary attention, the Beech Creek family was basically not unlike that of the modal American family. This similarity may perhaps be traceable to a common source, namely, the Judaeo-Christian ethic, which ascribes special importance to the conjugal family, a union brought about by God's mediation. Nevertheless, the emphasis on familism and its associated network of kinship ties points to the degree to which Beech Creek had remained outside the mainstream of life in American society, which, especially in the urban areas, had experienced institutional differentiation in the wake of modernization and industrialization. Traditional societies and fragmented "communities," such as those of rural Appalachia, have few formal institutional arrangements to meet the various needs of their population. They invariably depend upon the extended family to fulfill many of the needs that cannot be met through the conjugal family. In other words, the familism of Beech Creek, as it pertains to the system of kin orientations and obligations, represented a combination of the American conjugal family structure and a variation of traditional extended family relationships. (The variation was a bilineal extension of kinship relations among a group of conjugal families.)

The norms associated with marriage reflected this combination of patterns. Choice of a marriage partner, for example, was not only limited by geographic isolation but also through the influence of familism. Young people had to act with deference to the wishes of their extended family for, after all, their spouses would become a part of the larger kin network. However, the marriage ceremony itself was very informal and simple, without any ritualistic trappings; the Puritan ethic dominated the situation.

Customarily, a newly married couple lived with one of their parental families until they had their first child. This was not looked upon as any infringement on the new conjugal pair, but rather as a practical solution to the problem of limited resources. Dwelling units were difficult to arrange. Beech Creek was not a place that offered many choices.

Most Beech Creek couples had five or six children within ten to fifteen years of their marriage, and the older children helped in bringing up the younger ones. While the father was generally regarded as the patriarch who held ultimate authority for all matters pertaining to the family and homestead, the mother was head of the household, supervising the housekeeping and child-rearing chores. The children both feared and respected their father, whereas they sought affection from their mother, who generally served as their confidant throughout their lives. Older married children usually settled close-by and visited the parental homestead daily. It was only natural that their earlier relationships with parents and siblings were maintained and extended into adulthood. In other words, most normal activities of Beech Creek families carried the imprint of a familistic social organization.

Beech Creek familism had two characterizing qualities, both emerging from the primacy of the conjugal family. First, the boundary of the conjugal family was sharply drawn so that extended family relations and obligations would not erode or weaken the functioning of the conjugal family. For example, the father, and never the grandfather, was the patriarch with ultimate authority in the family. Again, no one person outside the conjugal unit exercised disciplinary control over the members. Second, because of the independence of the conjugal family, wider extended kinship relations did not emphasize either the paternal or maternal side of the family. The extended kinship unit was a *family group,* not formed solely on the basis of blood ties, but composed rather as a functional entity which included both sides. (The actual representation, in interactional terms, of each side was determined by such factors as personal rapport, patterns of mutual aid, and, to some degree, social class. Inter-class marriages, for example, tended to weaken the kin unit.)

The myth of extreme simplicity and homogeneity of small, traditional, and isolated communities has long ago been exploded by the findings from anthropological field studies. Beech Creek is not unique in that respect. Whereas these mountain neighborhoods were characterized by the qualities of a "gemeinschaft" type of social organization with its emphasis on primary groups and informal channels of communication, they were by no means a homogeneous locality grouping (or clustering of locality groupings) in which there was no social class differentiation. On the basis both of objective evidence (observation of social interactional patterns and socioeconomic style of life) and the subjective evaluation of the people themselves, a social class hierarchy was easily discernible. These class distinctions were reflected throughout Beech Creek life in a variety of ways.

Higher-class families placed a great value upon hard work and material achievements. Their children were better educated, better clothed, and better nourished than the children of other families. They participated more faithfully in church activities, and they severely disapproved of drinking, dancing, and card playing (as individuals they were actually less likely to indulge in these fundamental "sins"). Sexual promiscuity, of course, was frowned upon.

Since the lower-class families were generally at the other end of the continuum in these behaviors and attitudes, it is easy to see why inter-class marriages might have tended to weaken the solidarity of family groups. Marriages and close interactional ties almost never crossed class lines.

The characteristic puritanism of Beech Creek, perhaps a cultural holdover from earlier times, manifested itself in a number of ways and played a considerable part in the rationalization of the class structure. There was an almost morbid preoccupation with the threat of evil. Behavior was invariably seen as either "right" or "wrong," with no tolerance justified. "Right" was clearly self-discipline, hard work, keeping away from sensual pleasures, marital fidelity, thrift, and making sacrifices for future goals. The opposites were "wrong." Higher-class families praised and practiced the "right" qualities. They regarded the relative wealth that had accumulated in their hands as a sign that God's blessings had been bestowed upon them because of the good life they were leading. This is not unlike the rationalization for material achievements found throughout many segments of American society.

Individualism, an obvious characteristic of the Beech Creek personality, appeared to have been derived from the basic tenets of puritanism coupled with a firm belief in the ultimate rightness of democracy. It provided the Beech Creeker with an unsettling, but driving strength. "Every man is a child of God and equal before Him." Whereas the inheritance practices in Beech Creek were in accordance with this belief, social class behavior did not follow the same pattern. The conflict between what was ideally cherished and what was actually practiced resulted in many Beech Creekers verbally denying the existence of any social class distinctions in their midst. In that respect, and in others, individualism produced an element of tension within the social organization of these mountain neighborhoods.

This, then, briefly summarizes some of the main features of the Beech Creek way of life as it was: an economy based upon subsistence agriculture, a kinship-dominated social organization differentiated along class lines, and a traditionalistic value system that emphasized familism, puritanism, and individualism. These very characteristics, which enabled Beech Creekers to cope with the problems of existence under unfavorable external circumstances, eventually gave rise to conditions that resulted in a mass exodus from the mountains.

# STREAM OF OUT-MIGRATION

Though the rough terrain and poor transportation facilities posed formidable barriers to effective communication with the outside world, Beech Creekers were never completely isolated from the currents of change in American society. During the Civil War, for example, Confederate soldiers foraged around the neighborhoods for livestock and horses and, since most families in that area were sympathetic to the Union cause, some Beech Creek men served with the Union armies.

After the War, the veterans returned home with new perspectives of the outside world. Then too, during the period of intensive logging of the Cumberland Plateau, lumber companies brought newcomers to the area and provided many Beech Creekers with seasonal off-farm employment, cash income, and a variety of social contacts with persons from other parts of the United States. When the demand for unskilled industrial labor reached a peak during World War I, numerous Beech Creek families were already cognizant of their relative economic deprivation and, as a consequence, were willing to avail themselves of the opportunity to seek out an easier life through migration. That population movement, which had started as a trickle from the mountain hollows and out of the region, soon swelled to the proportions of a mighty stream.

Migration was not merely a contemporary phenomenon, but an integral part of Beech Creek's history. Indeed, even some of the original settlers eventually moved on to other places. In time, as the established families multiplied and land and forest resources became scarcer (in absolute terms and also relative to other areas of the country), migration became an increasingly attractive alternative to chronic economic deprivation. Yet the population of the neighborhoods held at a fairly stable level (from 1920–40) because the increase through births compensated for the loss through deaths and migration. World War II and the "pull" of jobs in the industrial centers of Ohio, however, brought dramatic changes. During the two decades 1942–61, a little more than three quarters of the residents of Beech Creek moved away. Only about one quarter of those who migrated settled in other parts of Appalachia (mainly close by Beech Creek), whereas over half relocated in southern Ohio and the remainder in areas of central Kentucky, Indiana, and other states.

At the time of migration from eastern Kentucky most migrants were young, in their late teens or early twenties. Few, only a tenth of the total, were over forty. About half the men but only a quarter of the women were unmarried when they left. Although some eventually returned (about 10 percent were "temporary" migrants), the majority of migrating Beech Creekers remained as permanent members of the host communities, with little or no inclination to move back to the mountains.

Temporary or permanent, migration from Beech Creek was a group phenomenon. The majority migrated as parts of families and joined existing households (kinsfolk) at the place of destination. Those who moved "alone" were mostly unmarried persons, and the rest were joining their spouses. A few unmarried men established themselves in rented rooms in the general vicinity of kinsfolk. All unmarried women initially resided with some kin; they were never "alone." In short, Beech Creek migration was *not* random in any sense and not merely an individual matter. Indeed, most Beech Creekers moved from a cohesive family setting, with family members, to a cohesive family setting at the place of destination.

Another characteristic of Beech Creek migration worthy of note is the relationship between an individual's position in the social class hierarchy of Beech Creek and the period when he moved out of the region. In general, persons from higher-class families dominated the first wave of migration, while persons from lower-class families made up the bulk of the more recent wave. This was an understandable pattern in the sense that those from higher-class families had more formal education, higher aspirations, greater financial resources, and were more sensitive to the relative advantages of work opportunities outside the region.

Although the desire for economic betterment was one of the primary motivations for migration, it would be incorrect to conclude that this was all that was involved. Migration is much too complex a phenomenon to be explained by any one factor. Many migrants were also concerned about their children's future, for example, or wanted to live near other members of their kin group who had migrated earlier, or to have access to better shopping, medical, and educational services. Like the role of vitamins in good nutrition, these noneconomic factors contributed to the final decision to migrate.

We found that most of the Beech Creekers who left the Appalachian Region relocated in certain industrial centers in, essentially, the same general area of the Ohio Valley. These centers, for the most part, are within weekend commuting distance from Beech Creek. Why they settled in these particular places, rather than elsewhere in the southern Ohio area, is perhaps due to a combination of factors including historical accident and kinship ties. In the very early days of Beech Creek migration, for example, members of some Beech Creek families found work in Ohio and settled in certain towns or in sections of the metropolitan area near the factories. They became the established links for further chain-migration over the years, and from that time on the kin network began to channel the flow of migration. This phenomenon is in line with an important behavioral principle in the sociology of migration. Beech Creekers, like most other people, preferred to relocate in areas where they could find a social organization as similar (as comfortable) as possible to that which they were leaving, provided the deficiency they were seeking to overcome (e.g., low income) could be satisfied in the area of destination. No other aspect of their social organization was more significant to Beech Creekers than kinship ties and family.

Another factor associated with the migrants' choice of destination was their social class origin. Migrants from "high" and "intermediate" class families tended to relocate near other migrants from similar class backgrounds; i.e., the Beech Creek social classes tended to "cluster" residentially in the area of destination. This is understandable if we recall that kinship, social class, and social interaction were closely interlinked within the social organization of Beech Creek. The fact that "lower" class migrants manifested a more dispersed pattern of relocation may be explained by the extreme poverty of these families, which permitted them little control over the situation, and by the relative weakness of kin ties, a characteristic of their life style.

# MOUNTAIN FAMILIES IN TRANSITION

In dealing with the problem of rural to urban migration one of the major concerns of policy-makers and planners, and to a large extent also of social science researchers, is with the effects or social aftermath phase of migration. Whether framed in evaluative terms by policy-makers or in normative terms by researchers, the issues involved can perhaps be best understood (and/or resolved) by viewing this aspect of the phenomenon, as most other aspects, from the theoretical perspective of a total migration system. Such a conceptualization demands that we take into account the social consequences of physical relocation upon both the donor and recipient subsystems as well as upon the migrants, and that we examine the interrelationships of those consequences. In short, we are led to consider the system as a whole and the transitional changes occurring in each of its parts. (Let it be understood, however, that the focus of the present study has been primarily upon the social organization of the migrants, and that changes in the social organizations of the recipient and donor subsystems coming about as a result of large scale in- or out-migration have entered into our exploration only insofar as they throw some light upon the main target of inquiry.)

When rural migrants move to urban settings they inevitably confront some obvious contrasts between the old and new ways of life. Beech Creekers were no exception. In the work world of the factory, for example, they were expected to perform tasks for which they were not adequately trained and to maintain a steady routine during rigidly specified hours under the direct supervision of a foreman. This was in sharp contrast to the less formal and relatively independent pattern of work which characterized subsistence farming in Beech Creek. Similarly, the tone and rhythm of life was different in the host community of the urban area from that in the mountain neighborhoods of Applachia.

That these potentially stressful contrasts did not become more disturbing to the migrants and disruptive of their pattern of living was due, perhaps, to two or three mediating conditions. First, the monetary rewards and financial security associated with work in the urban industrial area were far more satisfactory for these families to maintain their desired material style of life than they had been or could have been back in the mountains of Kentucky. Second, most Beech Creekers resided in close proximity to, and often in the same neighborhood with, some of their kinsfolk and many fellow Kentuckians. Even though the tempo of community life was rather "urban," the social interactional situation tended to be fairly comfortable and in many ways "rural familistic" because the participants—neighbors, friends, and kin—shared a common cultural heritage. Of course, there was always the possibility of visiting back in the mountains on a weekend, for a summer vacation, or during an extended lay-off. Indeed, visits back to the family homestead provided Beech Creek migrants with a convenient *and institutionalized* escape valve for the frustrations they inevitably encountered on the job or in the host community. As a collectivity, Beech Creekers looked toward the hills for renewal of their strength.

Because of the pattern of visiting back and forth, youngsters in Beech Creek had the opportunity of becoming acquainted with kinsfolk, family friends, and conditions in southern Ohio. This experience was an integral part of their socialization during the process of growing up. Their subsequent migration was a natural outcome of that experience and represented the continuation of the family pattern and neighborhood tradition. Upon arrival in the urban area, the newcomer was warmly received into the established branch-family network. He and his immediate family found a "haven of safety" to bolster their individual initiative and to sustain them through the transitional period. Furthermore, if the urban situation or their own frustrations became unmanageable, it was always possible to return to the family homestead in the mountains.

As individuals and families, then, the Beech Creek people were channeled into areas of greater economic opportunity and, through a system of migration structured in terms of stem- and branch-families, they were extended the necessary social support to cope with the difficult problems of transition. The stem-family form of migration, in other words, provided the migrant and his immediate family with social moorings at both ends of the migration system. That such moorings existed can be seen from the steadiness and persistence of out-migration over the years and from the settlement of branches of each family group near one another in the urban area. Despite the spatial distance separating stem- and branch-families, it is clear that their social worlds were intertwined. (Consider, for example, the degree of visiting interchanges, the rapidity of communication, the strength of mutual aid, and the feelings of identity, nostalgia, and concern for one another.) On both ends of the migration system, family and kin were ready to help the individual migrant. In coping with transitional difficulties, the Beech Creeker and his immediate family were not alone.

In economic terms, the migrants have done very well over the years. For the most part they have attained a reasonably adequate, though relatively modest, level of living, and their incomes compare favorably with those of the American working class in general. A few have done even better, achieving supervisory roles in industry or professional status as school teachers. On the other hand, to be sure, a few continue to struggle to eke out even a meager livelihood in the urban area; for them, the inadequacies and injustices of the past linger as an ever present reality.

Beech Creekers generally had acquired their initial jobs from information supplied through the informal network of communication among kin and friends in both the areas of origin and destination. As time went on, they became more skilled at their work and more familiar with the demands of the industrial job market. Their self-confidence increased and their desire for material improvement was markedly bolstered. The more skilled and ambitious among them sought out and found, without the direct help of family and kin, better paying and higher-status jobs. For some, in other words, upward social mobility did not cease after the event of migration from Appalachia.

Concomitantly, and as the result of a number of interrelated factors, the familistic orientation of Beech Creekers, at least in its traditional form and emphases, was somewhat weakened. In the urban environment and in the work situation of the factory, for example, some interaction, both formal and informal, with persons representing a variety of cultural traditions was inevitable. Contractual relationships and obligations had to be observed, and it was often necessary to relegate relationships with kin to a secondary concern. This erosion of strong reliance upon family and kin had a parallel effect of reinforcing the individualism and personal ambitions of Beech Creekers. Such changes in attitude were manifested in a number of ways: seeking better housing, even though it meant moving away from kinsfolk in the "little Kentucky" community; gradually decreasing the frequency of visits to eastern Kentucky over the years; gradually increasing the degree of social intercourse with local people and urbanites; utilizing and learning to enjoy the recreational facilities of the city; looking to banks and stores for credit, rather than to kin; and so on.

Industrial employers in the Ohio Valley generally welcomed Kentucky mountain migrants as a relatively cheap source of labor. "Briarhoppers" were willing to work hard and, furthermore, were not especially eager to join and support union activities. Since the Kentuckians tended to arrive in the host community as members of established family groups, factory owners were somewhat assured that the workers' social situations outside the plant were fairly stable and not too likely to interfere with job efficiency within the plant. Their workers could cope better with long lay-off periods because they were not alone in the host community. Then too, if employers wanted to recruit additional workers they could quickly draw upon the unemployed and underemployed pool of Appalachian manpower by simply passing the word out through the informal communication network, i.e., the kin system, which was connected directly into the factories of Ohio through earlier migrants.

This large and consistent influx of Appalachian migrants into the receiving communities over the years of course generated some social difficulties. Although tensions between newcomers and natives were occasionally evidenced, they were kept by and large within manageable bounds and were usually manifested covertly, as verbal barbs rather than open conflict. But rates of delinquency, truancy and crimes of passion were said to have increased as a result of this influx. Beech Creekers and other Appalachian people are accustomed to a rather independent life and are not fully cognizant of the prevailing mores and legal norms when they arrive as newcomers in the city. Moreover, their children often experience great difficulty in adapting to the more rigorous educational standards of the urban schools and in adjusting to the expectations of their new peer groups. Numerous other community problems attributable to this massive Kentucky-Ohio migration stream could be mentioned (e.g., the strain on various institutions and on the supply of adequate housing), but their delineation was not our intent in this study. It is clear, however that the absorption of Beech Creekers and other Appalachian migrants produced changes and social tensions within the host communities. From the points of view of urban natives and of government officials, welfare workers and educators in the urban area, the migrants, particularly the newcomers, represent a configuration of very complex problems.

On the other side of the ledger, the massive stream of out-migration also effected great changes and some difficulties in the areas of origin. The migrants, for example, were mainly young people who were leaving the area at the beginning of their work careers; until then, they had been solely "consumers." Even so, out-migration undoubtedly stimulated the economy of Appalachia and generated the flow of more cash money (through internal economic adjustments and because migrants often sent portions of their income and savings back home). The draining of population from Beech Creek, for instance, facilitated a rearrangement of land ownership and a redistribution of job opportunities. Levels of aspiration rose and channels of communication with the outside world became more efficient and effective. Indeed, continued migration stimulated further migration. Because of this, the economic well being of the people who remained behind was in some respects enhanced and, although significant structural changes were inevitable, the social continuity of their way of life, for better or worse, was assured.

From an overall perspective, migration from Beech Creek and rural Appalachia has functioned as a system-maintaining process. It has provided a continuing stream of socially stable new recruits for the industrial expansion of southern Ohio and urban America. It has provided the Beech Creek people with a legitimate means to become masters of their own destinies and to protect their cultural heritage and social organization from those forces of change that could only have led to social chaos and human misery.

# EPILOGUE

# 11 THE BEECH CREEK NEIGHBORHOODS TODAY

Our interest throughout this volume has focused primarily upon the migrants from Beech Creek who are residing in areas outside of Appalachia. We wanted to record their story and to explore how they have fared over the years and how they have adjusted or accommodated their lives to the circumstances associated with relocation. These people had moved away from their family homesteads in the Beech Creek neighborhoods and away from the personalistic, puritanistic, familistically-oriented cultural setting, within which and for which they were reared, and into the more impersonal and unfamiliar environs of an urban industrialized area, where they were confronted with many complex and often unanticipated social demands. Through the process of migration their social world had been changed and the course of their lives had been altered from that which it might have been had they remained at the place of origin.

There is yet another side to the story of the Beech Creek people. Those who remained behind—who chose to make their homes, raise their families and, eke out their existences in the mountain area—have also experienced a change in the pattern of their lives over the years. Indeed, the impact of change elements diffused from the urban, industrial centers of America (in this case, mainly from urban Ohio) may have been as influential or almost as influential in disturbing the sociocultural world of persons in the Beech Creek neighborhoods as it was at the more obvious point of contact between these two worlds, i.e., in Ohio. Phrased another way, the intrusion of change elements into the Beech Creek sociocultural system as it exists in and is maintained by kinship and neighborhood groups in the Appalachian enclaves of southern Ohio may have been less rapid and more selective than in certain situations in the mountains of eastern Kentucky.

It is important, therefore, lest we draw practical conclusions and action-oriented recommendations from an incomplete account of the Beech Creek people, to consider what has happened over the years to the way of life of those who have remained in the Beech Creek neighborhoods. The sociological study of migration, as we view it, is sociological and relevant to theories of social change only insofar as it concerns itself with the boundaries and changing dimensions of a given sociocultural system. Since the locus of that system is at the place of origin as well as at the place of destination of migrants, an examination of the social situation on the sending-end is useful for understanding the character of this migration stream and, possibly, its effects upon the donor system. Moreover, because we are also interested in providing a valid perspective on the people of and from this mountain locality, which is not unlike many other rural neighborhoods in Appalachia, we regard it as a fitting and appropriate concluding note to come full circle in our study by revisiting, briefly, the Beech Creek neighborhoods a quarter of a century after our initial field work.

# LONESOME COUNTRY

Like much of the rural hinterland of Appalachia, Beech Creek is lonesome country these days, and one is impressed at once by the return to nature, so to speak, of the area. Bottomlands which used to be cultivated and intensively cropped are now in grass or weeds. In the early spring, if his eyes are sharp, one can discern the various stages through which cultivation of the hillsides has retreated; because the higher elevations were deserted first, the taller trees are at the top. Trees and bushes appear to be creeping down the steep mountainsides. Briars are everywhere and seem to clutch at the clothing as you wander the old paths.

Walking up along one of the creeks one soon becomes aware of the large number of seemingly empty stretches between occupied homes; occasionally an abandoned house with sagging rooftop and vines growing across the windows breaks the monotony. The general scarcity of people is obvious, especially to a visitor from town or city. Indeed, fewer than half as many people reside in the Beech Creek neighborhoods now as in 1942, when the population numbered about four hundred persons. Today there are fewer than forty households. Flat Rock, which is over the ridge from the creek basin and the most isolated of the three neighborhoods, has virtually disappeared, having dwindled to about three remaining families.

Visitors who are inclined to nostalgia may be saddened by the realization that, while the roads into this mountain locality are much better than they were in the days when muleback was the practical form of transportation, many of the people who might have used these roads have long since moved out. Paradoxically, the families still living in the area are now in some ways more isolated from meaningful social contacts with other people than they ever were, in spite of the fact that it is easier for them to get out and visit families who live some distance away.

Over the years, a great amount of inter- and intra-neighborhood residential movement has taken place. This was fostered, in part, by the large scale out-migration, which facilitated a rearrangement of land ownership patterns and a redistribution of economic opportunities within the region. Thus, many Beech Creek families who had chosen to remain in the mountain area had been able to upgrade their living standards by moving on to better farms, or to places closer to the main roads and the nearby towns. As a consequence, the narrower valleys and the hollows leading off from the main creeks have become depopulated, and "rural" residences in the mountain counties have become concentrated as string settlements mostly along the principal highways which, as a rule, follow the big creeks or the river. At first glance it is easy to be deceived by the seeming residential prosperity and populousness along these mountain highways; this is what most visitors and tourists see as they drive through an Appalachian county. When one gets off the main road and into the rural hinterland, as one must still do to visit the Beech Creek neighborhoods, the picture changes, and the meaning of published reports about the region's poverty and demographic trends becomes clearer. Beech Creek is lonesome country nowadays, and calling it "lonesome country" is, from a Kentuckian's perspective, a damning thing—it suggests a social condition that the personalistically-oriented mountaineer would prefer to avoid.

# EXPANDING HORIZONS

With depopulation of the area, neighborhood institutions and facilities have been weakened, church support and attendance have declined, and the local one-room schools have been forced to close. Beech Creek children are now bused to a large, new consolidated grade school that serves this end of the county and brings together children from neighborhoods that formerly had almost no contact with each other. Also, most teenage youngsters now are able to get out to the main highway during the winter months, where a bus will take them to the consolidated high school at the county seat town twenty miles away; hardly any local children board in at the private high school in Schooltown, which was once the only feasible alternative for those wishing to go beyond the eighth grade.

Many families now own or have access to the use of an automobile or pick-up truck and, as a result, they are able to take advantage of a far wider range of community services. The numerous small neighborhood stores of the "storage-bin" variety (which were opened only and whenever a customer appeared), where Beech Creek people did most of their shopping and where they often gathered to talk, visit, and quarrel, have virtually disappeared. One such store still exists, however, perhaps because it is located on the highway and is easily accessible to several neighborhoods; it serves mainly as a clearing-house for local gossip and only incidentally as a retail outlet for goods and commodities.

Beech Creek people will generally go to Schooltown for automobile repair shops, gasoline stations, a drive-in movie, restaurants, and medical attention (a small, church-supported hospital clinic is located there). But even Schooltown is losing its former importance as a shopping center. Several of the larger stores, which used to enjoy a bustling business not many years ago and were often crowded with shoppers, now have a woebegone, uncared-for look. People are driving farther, to the larger county seat town to do their shopping; the range of services there is greater and the stores are in many ways more attractive. Although shopping is still an important event in the lives of Beech Creek people, it has become less personalized, less a group-centered affair, as the territorial boundaries of the Beech Creekers' field of activities have expanded beyond the narrow confines of their immediate neighborhoods.

# RURAL POVERTY

Farming on a commercial scale is not, and never was, an important economic enterprise in this mountain area. Even part-time commercial farming does not seem to offer adequate returns for the amount of capital and labor inputs required to make a go of it on and around these steep hillsides. Of course, most Beech Creek families live on places that would be classified technically as farms. Some cling to and continue to manage a small tobacco base (usually about a half-acre allotment which, if they are lucky and burley prices are high, may produce a gross income of approximately $500 per year). We can still see fields of corn here and there, occasionally an improved pasture, some steers, a few cows, maybe a pen of pigs, and often a large garden near most houses. These marginal farming activities, which have declined rapidly in recent years, are essentially noncommercial, aimed at producing foodstuffs for home consumption; they yield very little cash money and, perhaps because the attitudinal basis for subsistence agriculture is being eroded by the forces of modernization, increasingly less produce for the family dinner table.

Nowadays an impressively large proportion of the income flowing into the Beech Creek neighborhoods comes from transfer payments of one kind or another. Over half of the families receive welfare payments, and about a third participate in the so-called "donated foods" program, i.e., they receive "surplus commodities." Some get a bit of income from retirement pensions, veterans' pensions, survivors' benefits, aid to dependent children, allotments from sons in military service, and/or various other governmental aid programs. Indeed, almost all families in the Beech Creek locality derive much or most of their income from such sources. The remarkable thing is how little money income comes into the neighborhoods as wages or salaries. The few men who are employed work on road construction projects for the county, in a local sawmill, in a small coal mine nearby, and at various odd jobs often on a non-regular basis; their wages are low.

Houses in this area lack many of the modern conveniences we tend to associate with the "good life" in contemporary urban America. They are small, typically have about four rooms, are often in need of major repairs, and rarely have inside toilets. All the homes have electricity now, almost all have refrigerators, and many have washing machines of the wringer-type; but none have telephones, only a few have T.V. sets, and many families must still pump their water from an outside well.

Clearly this is a rural poverty area. Nearly all of the families can be called "poor" by national standards. Although none of the Beech Creekers is starving, there is evidence of a great deal of malnutrition. Their folk diet, modified by modern consumption habits (symbolized by the "pop" bottle, the hot dog, white bread, and the candy bar), is certainly not adequate for good health. Nevertheless, if measured in strictly monetary terms, Beech Creek families are undoubtedly better off now than ever before in their history. They have more cash income per capita, even though much of it comes from welfare and governmental assistance programs. In human terms, however, this increasing cash income has stimulated all kinds of new wants and new ways, which, paradoxically, may have contributed to the present state of affairs, namely, that Beech Creekers are far less independent than they once were.

## UNCERTAIN FUTURE

Beech Creekers are themselves aware of the many important changes that have occurred in these neighborhoods in recent years. They recognize that depopulation of the area, improvement of the roads, and the coming of electricity have had profound effects upon their lives. They appreciate that their standard of living has markedly improved and that they now enjoy more conveniences than ever before. In spite of the fact that they are obviously deprived of many material advantages that have accrued to kinsfolk and friends who live in urban Ohio, they will invariably say they are "satisfied" with the way things are and content with their lot in life. This is their home, the neighborhood they have known all their lives, the place where they reared their children, the family homestead to which their kinsfolk in Ohio return.

Indeed, Beech Creek men see their present life as much more satisfying than it was in the past. Economic conditions are better, farming is no longer the only means for survival, and a man's life has become easier. The women, however, have experienced greater difficulty in adjusting to the circumstances that change has wrought, and many find the contemporary situation in this relatively isolated mountain locality less satisfying than it ever was. They feel more deeply than the men the loss of family members, children, neighbors and friends through out-migration. They are more affected by and concerned with changes in the social interactional patterns—and these patterns have changed enormously over the years.

In looking to the future, most Beech Creekers focus their attention on such things as further improvement of the roads and better job opportunities in the mountain area. A spirit of cautious optimism seems to prevail—a curious mixture of fatalism and hope. They appear resigned to the situation as it is—content within the framework of difficult but existing social circumstances. Yet they worry; the future is quite uncertain. What will they do, for instance, if and when the proposed dam is built that will eventually create a lake covering this entire locality?

Many of the Beech Creekers still harbor aspirations to live in Ohio or elsewhere, closer to their children or kinsfolk who had migrated earlier. If economic conditions become strained in the mountains relative to opportunities in the Ohio Valley, and if governmental assistance programs fail to provide an adequate cushion for the transitional difficulties inevitably associated with regional development, there is little doubt that many of the remaining families in Beech Creek will pull up stakes and move out. Most Beech Creekers are psychologically prepared for this eventuality, and some would welcome it. For out-migration is an integral part of the history of Beech Creek, firmly embedded in the social fabric of mountain life.

One thing is clear: whether fostered by a continuation of the normal trend for individuals and families to seek better lives for themselves elsewhere, by a mass exodus generated by an economic crisis, or by a forced evacuation resulting from the construction of a dam, the process of the final disintegration of the Beech Creek neighborhoods as a viable social entity is irreversible.

# APPENDIXES

## Appendix A

### ORGANIZATION OF THE RESEARCH PROJECT

The following materials and discussion are appended to this volume on the assumption that research findings can be understood and interpreted more meaningfully if the mode of inquiry, methodological strategies, field work circumstances, and practical difficulties of a study are fully comprehended. It is also our hope that future research projects encountering similar situational and procedural problems to those reported here (in longitudinal studies of social change, for example) can benefit from and build upon the Beech Creek experience.

### THE RESEARCH PROGRAM

The general objective of this project was to study the social adjustment and personal stability of all persons still living who were residents of the Beech Creek neighborhoods in 1942. The original Beech Creek population was viewed as a total migration system encompassing both the donor sub-system (abstracted from the sociocultural context at the place of origin) and the recipient sub-system (abstracted from both the sociocultural milieu at the place of destination and the social characteristics of American urban life in general). Although primary concern was with migrants in their new communities, it was also necessary to focus some research interest on individuals and families who continue to reside in the mountain area.

From the beginning, this was envisioned as an exploratory study aimed at making some contributions to what might be called the "sociology of migration." We wanted to organize a study in depth of the rural-to-urban migration process (specifically, Appalachian migration), drawing upon insights from various disciplines and combining case study methods with survey techniques.

#### Systematic Utilization of Information from Original Beech Creek Study

A major justification for initiating a re-study of the Beech Creek population was the quantity and quality of background information available about these people.[1] We had access to materials which described, or from which we could reconstruct, the essential characteristics of the sociocultural context from whence the migrants were drawn. Specific data were on hand about each individual's position in the social structure of the Beech Creek neighborhoods in 1942 (e.g., family group affiliation, social class origin). Insofar as this background information could be systematically utilized at various stages of the research process, the study could command a dimension of depth not otherwise possible. The following strategies were employed:

(a) In the form of impressionistic information about the study population, the earlier work provided a base-line for building a useful conceptual/theoretical framework and for developing a research design and research instruments in line with the experience world of these people. For example, knowledge about the Beech Creek kinship system derived from the original study was instrumental in formulating the guiding hypothesis for the re-study.

(b) Similarly, as impressionistic information, the earlier work yielded rich insights for the interpretation of findings from the follow-up study. For example, knowledge of the expected role behavior of men and women in the Beech Creek neighborhoods of 1942 provided important clues for interpreting differences observed in the patterns of adjustment of male and female migrants in the areas of destination.

(c) In the form of specific data about individuals, some information from the earlier study was incorporated directly into the survey design and analysis. For example, social class origin was used as an independent variable in analyzing the migration and adjustment processes.

(d) Background knowledge about specific individuals and their neighborhood-of-origin was useful in helping field interviewers gain entrée and establish rapport. For example, the interviewer's ability to mention a respondent's kinsfolk by name and to discuss Beech Creek in knowledgeable terms often made the difference between a truly warm reception and covert suspicion.

(e) Information about specific individuals, as recorded in the earlier (1942) field notes or in notes made from continued observation of the Beech Creek population over the years, was used as a check on the reliability of certain portions of the survey data. For example, in coding data on migration, the out-migration records accumulated from periodic censuses of the neighborhoods were compared with individual migration histories obtained from interviews with migrants; in the event of discrepancies, additional information was obtained from informants in the field.

## Phases of Activity

The research program was organized into four distinct, but interrelated, phases of activity.

(a) *Exploration of the problem and formulation of theoretical perspectives.* This phase of the program included a detailed review of the contemporary literature on migration[2] as well as numerous field trips to both Beech Creek and Ohio by members of the research staff for sensitizing discussions with key informants. Moreover, an attempt was made to gain a measure of conceptual depth by pursuing various aspects of the problem through an interdisciplinary staff seminar organized for that purpose.

(b) *Follow-up survey.* A survey of the entire study population, i.e., a total migration universe, gathered the necessary framework of information for assessing the general situation and for exploring specific hypotheses about the process of adjustment within a migration system.

(c) *Case studies.* Intensive field interviewing and quasi-participant observation of selected individuals and families were conducted by the professional staff in order to obtain greater understanding about the migration/adjustment process and to explore the systemic linkages between the donor and recipient sub-systems.

(d) *Focused interviews on occupational adjustment.* The important problem of the rural male migrant's adjustment to the industrial situation could not be dealt with adequately within the survey or case-study designs. For that reason, this was organized as a separate phase of activity under the general research program.

## ADVISORY COMMITTEE: THE EXPLORATORY PHASE

A "Professional Advisory Committee" was organized on a topical seminar basis for the purpose of exploring the research problem in a holistic manner. This interdisciplinary group included representatives from anthropology, economics, clinical psychology, home economics, agriculture, extension education, and sociology. All were acquainted with one or more aspects of the problems associated with migration from Appalachia. There were specialists in demography, intergroup relations, mental health problems, community medicine, medical sociology, sociology of education (school dropout studies), agricultural development, and family life.

The Committee met every two weeks during the fall semester of 1960–61. A complete picture of the ensuing intellectual exchange and its by-products among a group of a dozen or more people meeting informally in a semi-structured situation to discuss a complex research problem cannot be expressed adequately in words. We can only summarize categorically the tangible results of those encounters.

First, as the sessions progressed, the project's scope and meaning and its implications for studies of migration in the U.S.A. and abroad became clearer. The specific problem was placed in a more general context of problems associated with change and development in many areas of the contemporary world. This resulted in the research staff's attempt to build a conceptual framework with utility for studying migration and the adjustment of migrants as sociological phenomena in both developed and developing countries. Fresh insights from a variety of perspectives were cast upon such fundamental but difficult questions as: "What is meant by migration?"; "What is the content of adjustment?"; "What is the difference between migration as a demographic phenomenon and migration as a sociological phenomenon?"; and "How do such notions as social system, social integration, and social differentiation enter into the study of migration?" In short, the group encouraged and pressured the research staff to struggle to develop and sharpen its conceptual approach to the specific problem on hand.

Second, discussion of the developing research design in the presence of behavioral scientists from a number of disciplines alerted the research staff to the dangers of superficially utilizing certain techniques and methodological procedures available from those disciplines. It was made clear, for example, that within the given framework of financial resources and technical competencies it would not be wise to attempt an elaborate psychological testing program for any significant number of migrants; that had been considered in the early planning. It is one thing to learn about these risks from readings of the professional literature, but it is quite another to be impressed about the complexity of these problems through personal discussions with scholars who had employed such techniques in research involving people from the study area.

Third, the Committee encouraged the staff to do everything possible to lift the data that were to be collected out of the usual statistical verbalizations to a level of meaningful interpretation of events affecting a group of individuals interacting in daily life. The development of a case study phase is evidence that the Committee's point of view was accepted.

Fourth, the Committee functioned as a sounding board for the research staff's ideas in formulating the study design, both theoretically and methodologically. This was accomplished in the open sessions as well as in private consultations with individual members who served as understanding critics in helping to "zero in" on all possibilities that the study offered for research. For example, "thrown in and kicked around" during seminar discussions were the possibilities of studying family structure and intergenerational aspects of migration, the relationship of socialization processes to migration, the usefulness of building some aspects of reference group theory into the theoretical framework, the way that migration can be conceptualized as an integral part of the social structure itself, how a theory of value reinforcement can be used to understand the class differences in adjustment, and so on. Although the final design was the responsibility entirely of the research staff, it is no exaggeration to say that this design was influenced in no small measure by open and critical discussions during these Professional Advisory Committee meetings.

## Frame of Reference

The theoretical framework for an exploratory study need not be elaborate and firmly systematized. It is precisely because useful middle-range theories and findings from previous research are not available, or only loosely connected to the immediate concerns, that an exploratory study is initiated. Even so, to facilitate the orderly collection of information relevant to a specific problem, conceptual guidelines must be established; if, in addition, such a scheme contributes greater insight into the phenomena under investigation, then the process of theory building has been advanced.

The frame of reference guiding the Beech Creek Project was developed as an attempt systematically to link kinship structure with migration process. It is not our purpose here to explain the bases for this formulation, nor to pursue the various concepts in detail. Suffice it to note that our frame of reference and guiding hypothesis are founded upon much information about the socio-cultural origins of the Beech Creek population, an exhaustive review of the contemporary literature on migration, and an intensive interdisciplinary exploration of the problem. Subsequently, through the interaction of factual knowledge, theoretical perspectives, and intuition, we hope to have derived from the Beech Creek experience a useful approach—and perhaps also to have suggested some useful sociological dimensions—for future research on the problem of rural-to-urban migration.

## THE SURVEY PHASE

The survey phase was designed to collect data on *all* those persons still living (1961) who were residents of the Beech Creek neighborhoods in 1942. We wanted to find out what had happened to them during the intervening years and how they were getting along. Many had moved from eastern Kentucky and were living elsewhere; their adjustments to the circumstances associated with migration were of central concern.

The survey was organized in terms of a "total migration universe," i.e., migrants and nonmigrants. This enabled us to collect the necessary information to explore how the Beech Creek-Ohio situations operate as a single migration system, the nature of the linkages between the two ends of the migration stream, and how the boundaries of this system are maintained. Construction of the survey instruments was guided by the major hypothesis. Since this was an exploratory project, some peripheral interests, e.g., social change in the original neighborhoods, were incorporated into the design.

## Construction of the Interview Schedules

For research convenience, the original Beech Creek population was divided into three segments on the basis of residence location in 1961.

(1) *Original neighborhoods:* all those individuals who were living in the Beech Creek neighborhoods.

(2) *Nearby neighborhoods:* all former Beech Creekers who were living in eastern Kentucky (State Economic Areas 8 and 9) but not in the original Beech Creek neighborhoods as delineated in 1942. For the most part, these people reside nearby in adjacent neighborhoods or towns "closer to the road."

(3) *Migrants:* all persons residing outside the specified boundaries of eastern Kentucky who had been residents of Beech Creek in 1942.

Because each of these segments of the Beech Creek population represents different situations with respect to external circumstances as well as "ties with the old neighborhoods," three sets of interview schedules were developed. This was for administrative convenience (wording changes and the like had to be made in light of situational differences) and does not indicate a conceptual differentiation of the migration system.

Field work strategy called for two separate schedules in each instance: one for individuals, both men and women, and the other for family-households. Information about the family-household was obtained from either one of a conjugal pair regardless of his or her Beech Creek origin. In many cases, for example, the spouse of a former Beech Creek resident was not a Beech Creeker but could supply, nevertheless, the necessary information about the household situation, family composition, and visiting patterns. This possibility, then, allowed for a certain amount of flexibility, which is desirable in a field interviewing situation.

For the most part, questions were structured or semi-structured. Structured questions were usually followed by open-ended probes in order to tap the nuances of response content and to assess the respondent's frame of reference. An effort was made to hold down the individual interview to about one and one-half hours, and the family-household interview to about one-half hour. The final schedule was pre-tested in both a rural Appalachian and an urban setting.

## Foci of Inquiry

The survey instrument was designed to yield data on patterns of migration, nature of individual and family adjustments, supportive functions of the family-kinship system, and individual and family interactional patterns. A brief, very general description of the kinds of information solicited from each respondent may help to suggest the foci of inquiry:

(1) Residential history since 1942, and pattern of migration in each instance.

(2) Detailed description of first move from eastern Kentucky, situation before and after moving, and problems encountered.

(3) Work history since 1942, and details about present job.

(4) Biographical data, including age, sex, and marital status.

(5) Indicators of adjustment, such as feelings of nostalgia for the old neighborhoods, satisfaction and identification with the new community, feelings of residential stability, state and sources of happiness and worry in the past and at present, symptoms of psychological anxiety, anomia and related attitudes, and so forth.

(6) Sentiment structure, in terms of moral ideologies, religious beliefs, political attitudes, familistic orientations, normative expectations in times of crises, and perception of changes in way of life.

(7) Leisure-time activities, including individual visiting relationships, formal participation in church and other organizations, and informal activities.

(8) Family-household composition and biographical data on each individual in the household.

(9) Interaction with close kin and ecological distribution of members of extended family.

(10) Inter-area visiting patterns, as, for example, between Ohio and the Beech Creek neighborhoods, and between the Beech Creek neighborhoods and nearby neighborhoods.

(11) Intra-area visiting patterns between families within the original Beech Creek neighborhoods.

(12) Non-familial visiting patterns and, in the case of migrants, contacts with non-Kentuckians.

(13) Level of living, income, and housing conditions.

## Preparation for Field Work

In preparing for a follow-up survey of this kind, one of the first tasks is to locate the residence of each individual in the study population. Specific addresses are required and, fortunately, this was not a major problem for us. Although almost twenty years had elapsed since the earlier study of Beech Creek, up to date records had been kept on the whereabouts of most of these people. Informants in Beech Creek or Ohio were usually able to supply supplementary information. Only a few individuals were not located.

About a month before field work commenced, letters were sent to key persons in Ohio and Kentucky introducing the interviewers by name and explaining the general purpose of the survey. Members of the research staff personally visited some of these people in order to "set the stage" for the interviewers and to help allay any natural suspicions that might be aroused. "The word got around" through informal communication among members of the various family groups.

In addition to the research staff and a graduate assistant who functioned in the dual role of field director and interviewer, three husband-wife interviewer teams were employed during the summer months of 1961. One team was assigned the task of interviewing in eastern Kentucky, and the other two teams were charged with locating and interviewing the migrants in Ohio and elsewhere. For this field situation, and with the kinds of interviewing problems that would be encountered, a husband-wife team seemed to be the most efficient operational unit; moreover, it also helped in alleviating the very serious and almost inevitable problem of interviewer morale.

## Interviewer Training

During the course of a full-week training school, interviewers were made ready for their mission. The survey's purpose was explained, field work strategies and tactics were discussed, and the interviewer's role and responsibilities were delineated.

The survey instruments were systematically reviewed so that the interviewers would grasp the logical (i.e., psychological) flow of information gathering and understand the researchers' intent vis-a-vis each question. A manual of instructions was employed to facilitate this learning process and to serve as a reference in field editing.

Interviewers were shown pictures, taken in the field specifically for training purposes, to acquaint them with the Beech Creek neighborhoods and with the people they would be interviewing. Case histories of selected Beech Creek families were used as illustrations. Actual interviews, recorded on tape by staff members in the field, provided "live" examples of interview situations and excellent material for critical discussion. Mock interviews (role-playing) helped to set a pattern of behavior which, in turn, helped to build the interviewer's confidence in his ability to control the interview situation. To sensitize the interviewers to the complexity of an interview situation, "homework" was assigned from various textbooks dealing with the subject, and speakers were brought in to elaborate in semi-technical terms on field work tactics and how these influence the interview situation.

The very important problem of how to establish a working rapport with respondents was dealt with at length, and suggestions were offered on how to cope with the mountaineers' characteristic trait of shyness with strangers. To aid in the initial entrée, each interviewer was supplied with a set of about twenty photographs of people and places in the Beech Creek neighborhoods. These were used as discussion starters to help "break the ice" with respondents prior to launching the formal interview. The interviewers were encouraged to "identify" with Kentucky and to "use" the image of "Jim Brown" in the process of establishing rapport.

In short, the training program was designed as a learning experience through which the interviewers would come to understand, as fully as possible, (1) the general nature of the survey, (2) the specific kinds of information they would be seeking, (3) the cultural "peculiarities" of the study population, and (4) the approaches they could use to establish rapport and to get a successful interview. No less important, the training program also attempted to generate an esprit de corps within the survey organization that could carry the members through the tedious job of locating and interviewing, often under difficult situational conditions, such a widely dispersed population. In retrospect, the research staff and interviewers (the latter were interviewed systematically by the staff after field work was completed) felt that these aims were accomplished and that the interviewers had entered the field situation reasonably well prepared.

## The Field Situation

Interviewer teams worked out from the central office at the University in areas at least one hundred miles, and often as much as two hundred miles away. Travel was a major expense and a major difficulty. Because of the geographical dispersion of the study population, each team was assigned a particular area, such as a city, and thereafter operated much on its own, reporting weekly to the field director or central office. Schedules were edited in the field and again at the central office.

In this kind of field situation, where respondents are widely scattered with considerable driving distance between locations, and often through highly congested traffic conditions in urban Ohio, or over very rough country roads with frequent hikes up "hollows" in rural eastern Kentucky, maintaining interviewer morale and adequate control over the field situation are critical problems. Each interviewer must make judgments of strategy as the field situation unfolds and is evaluated. Flexibility of operation is a practical necessity, and it is precisely this need for flexibility that compounds the problems of "control" and "morale."

If a respondent, for example, is not at home for one reason or the other when the interviewer calls, it is exceedingly frustrating for the interviewer; a "call back" requires a great deal of time, travel, and planning. Often a number of call backs are required before contact is made, and many interviews have to be planned for the evening hours, particularly if the individual is employed in a manufacturing industry. In the latter case, "shift" work further complicates the interviewer's ability to plan ahead for a day's activity. Although the nature of the field situation in eastern Kentucky is different, in many ways, from that of urban Ohio, the problems are no less complicated.

For surveys of this kind, a field worker must be highly disciplined, with a strong sense of responsibility, an adequate understanding of the task at hand, and a personality Gestalt that remains calm, cool, and collected in the course of locating the respondent's place of residence and getting the necessary interview Most important, it demands that the interviewer be able to maintain a high level of interest in the person being interviewed, even though he may have experienced a great deal of difficulty in tracing him down and in establishing the initial contact.

In this as in most other surveys, very little is known about the performance of the interviewer within the interview situation; we can only report that the interviewers were selected carefully, that they experienced a full week of intensive training prior to entering the field, that the work was organized to provide continuing supervision, that schedules were edited promptly, and that the information collected was reliable insofar as could be determined by spot checks.

## Field Work Closure

We attempted to leave the situation as relatively undisturbed as possible; this is a professional obligation and, we might add, an ethical responsibility. Maintaining a receptive climate was also a practical necessity, because a second phase of field work, case studies of selected family groups, was planned for the following year.

The interviewers were informed about the importance of assuring future rapport, instructed as to desirable practices to follow in closing an interview, and charged with the responsibility of maintaining a favorable image in the field.

Their efforts were reinforced by sending "thank-you" letters and "Certificates of Cooperation" to all respondents.

## The Study Population: A Summary

The survey phase was designed to collect data on all those individuals, still living, who were residents of the Beech Creek neighborhoods in 1942.

Of the three hundred ninety-nine persons enumerated in the original 1942 census of the neighborhoods, forty-two had died by July 1, 1961. Furthermore, thirty-eight persons were designated as "transients" at the time of the original study. These "transients," for one reason or the other, were temporary residents in the Beech Creek area, not well known to the more permanent members of the neighborhoods or to the investigator, not really a part of the on-going social life in the area, and, therefore, not "included" as a source of data for the original study. Most of them had moved away during the period of initial field work in 1942 or shortly thereafter; sixteen of them now live in Ohio, eight in Indiana, and fourteen in other parts of eastern Kentucky. These people were excluded by design from the follow-up phase. Thus, the base population for the survey is three hundred nineteen persons.

Of this base population, forty-eight persons were not interviewed for various reasons: eight live in states too distant to be contacted by interviewers (two in Florida, one each in Minnesota, California, Kansas, Virginia, Texas, and Oklahoma); three were incarcerated or hospitalized (two in penitentiaries, one in a mental hospital); four were in the military service; four were senile; five were too ill, physically or mentally, to be interviewed; thirteen were unavailable (address unknown, on extended vacations, repeated call-backs, shift work interfered, etc.); and eleven refused to cooperate (flat refusals or obvious avoidance behavior). In total, two hundred seventy-one interviews were completed, and these constitute the study population. In two cases in which the individual was not available, household information was obtained from the spouse.

Table A.1 shows the residence location of individuals included in the base population, the number who were interviewed and are included in the study population, and the percent that the latter is of the former (percent interviewed).

## Note on Coding

It is not necessary to detail the procedures we followed in converting raw survey information into symbolic terms for analysis. For the most part, they are fairly routine operations. A few general points about the coding process, however, may provide a basis for better understanding the nature of the data from which our findings emerge.

Prior to construction of a code key, all responses to open-ended or unstructured questions were categorized from hand-tabulated listings of an appropriate sample or, in some instances, of the total response universe. We attempted to formulate as many categories as possible from the actual responses. In no case were responses "forced" into preconceived categories; the empirical categories, however, were ordered vis-a-vis theoretical concerns. Verbatim response listings were kept on file so that they could be used to interpret and illustrate findings at a later stage of analysis and writing.

During the fall and winter of 1961–62, five women were employed as coders. The work was supervised at all times by a member of the research staff whose

**Table A.1.** Base population, study population, and percent interviewed, by residence area, 1961.

| Residence area 1961 | Base population number | Study population number | Percent interviewed |
|---|---|---|---|
| Beech Creek neighborhoods, total: | 80 | 68 | 85.0% |
| Beech Creek basin: | (39) | (31) | |
| Laurel: | (32) | (28) | |
| Flat Rock: | (9) | (9) | |
| Other eastern Kentucky, total: (nearby neighborhoods) | 54 | 42 | 77.8% |
| Institutional situations, total: (military, penal, asylum) | 7 | 0 | 0% |
| Migrants, outside eastern Kentucky, total: | 178 | 161 | 90.4% |
| Other Kentucky: | (22) | (21) | |
| Ohio: | (129) | (122) | |
| Indiana: | (17) | (16) | |
| Tennessee: | (2) | (2) | |
| Other States: | (8) | (0) | |
| Total, all areas: | 319 | 271 | 85.0% |

responsibility was to manage the development of an appropriate code key, train the coders for their various assignments, check the work in process, and make final judgments in all cases where the coder was uncertain as to the correct classification of a particular response. Accuracy, insofar as possible, was important, because the survey dealt with a relatively small number of cases, and even random coding errors might confound observed relationships. Migration histories caused the most difficulty, and, wherever possible, the migration histories of individual members of the same family were compared as a reliability check on the respondent's recall. For key items, such as identification numbers, age, sex, education, social class origin, scale scores, and the like, a 100 percent coding reliability check was made by recoding and comparison. In addition, a number of items were recoded, as a check on accuracy, by a member of the research staff, particularly where the item summarized a whole pattern of events, e.g., migration history of the individual since 1942. For other items requiring a great deal of coder judgment, a 50 or 35 percent reliability check was made, depending on its importance to the general analytical scheme; where coding errors greater than 3 percent were discovered, the item was recoded. Finally, coding reliability checks were also made by machine cross-tabulations after the data had been punched on cards.

## THE CASE STUDY PHASE

The case study phase was planned as an integral part of the larger research project. Its primary objective was to add greater depth of understanding by supplementing data collected during the earlier survey phase.

Although the case studies are to be published as a separate volume, some of the information gathered during this phase of field work was utilized in the present work as a basis for the interpretation of findings and by way of illustration. Moreover, the insights gained from our "total immersion" in the migrant culture are inextricably bound into the entire fabric of this study. It is important, therefore, particularly for those who are concerned with the methodological problems of combining case study and survey techniques into an integrated approach, to note the organization of this phase of the Beech Creek project.

As in the survey phase, we focused on the structure and function of the extended family and kinship system in relation to the process of migration and the transitional adjustments of migrants and their families within the Beech Creek migration system. It was implicitly assumed that, all other things being equal, individuals moving from a rural familistic folk culture to an urban industrial community will experience certain strain-producing situations to which they must adapt. The stem-family structure, we hypothesized, performs a supportive function in facilitating this transition, in helping to alleviate tensions generated by initial frustrations, and in helping the migrants become integrated socially into the urban community.

The foci of inquiry, therefore, were like those of the survey phase. But here we also wanted to observe their empirical referents "in depth" within the context of a total interactional system.

Our aim, in other words, was to view the Beech Creek and Ohio sociocultural worlds through the eyes and minds, so to speak, of the Beech Creekers—to see and to understand how these people perceive the respective situations. This research orientation is based on the premise that reality, in terms of social relationships, has its locus in the individual personality system. Of course, one may argue very properly that such things as culture, values, and the like are social realities which exist quite distinct from individual personalities, in the sense that they are valid components of any system of human interaction. Nevertheless, a relatively unstructured approach which probes at subjective experiences is useful for exploratory purposes. By "knowing" how Beech Creekers view their world, concepts and patterns can be abstracted that may lead to meaningful insights and hypotheses. If these hypotheses offer promise for extending the boundaries of knowledge about the migration process and about human interaction in general, if they help to modify or elaborate a body of theory, then verification can be pursued in future, more structured research.

Inference, then, plays a leading role in field work of this kind. We attempted to learn, for example, all that we could about structural strains generated within the migration system by the spatial dispersion of its members. Such strains were manifested in what our subjects said, felt, and did. As empirical referents converged, a pattern emerged which had to be verified not only by drawing logical and theoretically meaningful conclusions from the available evidence, but by further systematic observation through continued field work. Lest erroneous conclusions be formulated from flimsy, ill-perceived data, "doubt," an ever-present element, had to be arbitrated by reason and by checking information from numerous angles, in numerous situations, through numerous informants. When a fact was established, its relevance to other facts was pursued. Deviations from an emerging pattern had to be explained in full. In other words, the more evidence we accumulated that relationships existed between unit-events observed in the field and that these relationships were not spurious, the more certitude we had that our conclusions were correct. The primary objective was "depth of understanding" within the context of a total interactional system (the case studies), and this could only be achieved if observed facts, intuition, and inference were maintained in proper balance.

A secondary objective was to provide the research team with an opportunity to acquaint itself first-hand with situational factors affecting the transitional adjustment process in communities receiving large influxes of Beech Creek and other Appalachian migrants. Intimate knowledge about these situations would enable us to interpret the survey data more meaningfully.

This objective was achieved almost automatically as a result of living in the Ohio communities where Beech Creekers reside, becoming acquainted with many Beech Creek families, discussing the situation with professional persons and other key informants in the area, shopping in local stores, reading local newspapers, and so on. In other words, sensitivity and understanding were generated through our exposure to the experience world of the migrant in the recipient subsystem.

The nature and scope of this phase of activity (as with the survey phase) was delimited by the availability of financial resources, personnel time, and professional competencies and interests. To assure a parsimonious treatment of the problem within a framework of feasibility, it was necessary to develop a unified conceptual approach and to specify, prior to entering the field, those areas of information we would initially pursue. It was essential that the families drawn into this phase of the study—the targets of inquiry—be selected carefully and with considerable forethought as to the probability of obtaining information in depth about the total interactional systems in which they are involved.

## Selection of the Family Groups

The earlier study of Beech Creek (1942) established the existence of "family groups." These family groups consisted mainly of families of old parents and their adult children or of adult siblings and their grown children's families. The group composition was determined, however, not merely by kin relationships, but also by social relationships among kin. Thus, a conjugal family related by blood to a number of other families in the neighborhood was considered to belong to that family group with which it, as a family, had the strongest social bonds.

To gain some measure of representativeness while keeping the task of field work within reasonable bounds, three Beech Creek family groups were chosen on the basis of: (1) social class position in Beech Creek, 1942; (2) area of residence where migrants are concentrated, 1961; (3) number of individuals and nuclear family units included in the group; and (4) probability of establishing rapport. An attempt was made to select groups that had direct kinship ties with families still residing in the Beech Creek or nearby neighborhoods.

Initial emphasis was on the recipient end of the migration system. Preliminary observations of the respective situations revealed that a "splitting-off" of the original family groups had occurred over the years. In effect, new patterns of family groups were emerging from the old patterns delineated in 1942. Since field work resources were limited, the decision was made to begin developing these case studies with members of the original family groups who appeared to form interactional units in the areas of destination. Closeness of kin ties and residential propinquity of its members determined which segment of an original family group was drawn into this phase of the study.

To facilitate further explanation, let us describe the pertinent structural characteristics of each "emergent" family group that formed a nucleus for a case study.

*Family Group A* (The Andrews Family). This was a very large, "high-class" family group in Beech Creek. The emergent sub-group included a core of eight nuclear families, seven of whom reside in and around a small city in southern Ohio; one family lives back in the old Laurel neighborhood. Sibling ties joined all but one of these families; the parents had been dead for more than ten years. The other family is a sibling's daughter and her conjugal family living in Ohio. Additional members of the original family group were drawn into the study as field work progressed and as the kinship/interactional network was established.

*Family Group B* (The Barnett Family). This was an "intermediate-class" family group in Beech Creek. Its nucleus was an aged mother (who died in 1961), her older sons and daughters, and their married children and families. A "division" was in process, and two sub-groups were emerging. One sub-group, residing in and around a small town in southern Ohio, was composed of an older son and his spouse, and his three married daughters and their families. The other sub-group was composed of an older daughter (of the aged mother) and her spouse living in Beech Creek, their younger son and his nuclear family living in Beech Creek, and five older married sons and daughters and their families living in Ohio. Except for one of the migrant daughters who had married into the Andrews Family and was living in a small city in Ohio, the migrants (all siblings) resided in the same small town along with members of the other sub-group. Two other nuclear families, joined by sibling ties to these sub-groups, were also included, and peripheral members of the larger family group were drawn into the study as field work progressed.

*Family Group C* (The Carter Family). This was a "low-class" family group in Beech Creek that had divided into two distinct sub-groups. The emergent sub-group selected for study was composed of an older man, who is "head" of the family, his wife, and their five married children and their families. With the exception of a son and his family living in a small town nearby, the entire family group reside in a low income situation in a very large city in southern Ohio. The older man's sister and her husband, who had reared him after their parents had died, live in a rural eastern Kentucky county and are the closest kin representing the Beech Creek end of this system. Only distant kin relationships tie the family group directly to the original Beech Creek neighborhoods.

These three family groups "best fit" the criteria advanced and offered the best possibility for successful data-collection within the framework of available resources. A good working rapport could be established with a minimum expenditure of time and energy. The plan was to learn a great deal about these people and their relationships with other members of their family in a relatively short summer of intensive field work. Since there were about twenty-three separate households included on the Ohio end of the migration system, we were confronted with a prodigious field work task if "depth of understanding" was to be achieved.

## Organization of Field Work

Concerning each of these family groups, we wanted to know: (a) how kin relationships facilitated and entered into the process of migration and the transitional adjustments of migrants and nonmigrants on both ends of the migration system; (b) how and to what extent the family group preserves the old Beech Creek cultural system in the context of a mass, complex industrial order; and (c) something of the nature of the family group, i.e., the nature of the bonds that unite family group members and the social meaning of these relationships. An appropriate study guide was developed which elaborated these themes in terms of researchable questions, and a division of responsibility was agreed upon among the research staff members.

Field work was organized as a team effort that involved the research staff and included our wives and children. A field station was established in a small town in southern Ohio where many of the Beech Creek migrants lived and which was centrally located also with respect to other families that were to be contacted. The "field station" consisted of two small three-room apartments in two separate duplex houses. One room was converted into an office; the others were used as living quarters.

Time in the field was limited. Preliminary contacts with a number of families were made long before intensive field work was initiated, but even so, two months appeared insufficient for the task on hand. As an experienced anthropologist would be quick to note, this limitation represented a serious weakness in the study design. To make effective use of what time was available, field work procedures were organized as efficiently as possible.

Prior to entering the field, a background information file was prepared on each individual in each of the family groups. Any pertinent information that could be gleaned from the survey schedules and from the old field notes were recorded. Furthermore, all the information available on children in these families, other members of their households, family visiting patterns, and individuals closely connected by kinship, marriage, or visiting relationships to individuals in the original family groups was included. This background information file served as a handy reference which was kept up to date during the course of field work.

All observations were systematically recorded *on tape* (i.e., verbally), rather than by the more traditional but energy-consuming process of writing up field notes late into the night. The use of battery-operated portable tape recorders made it possible to do this almost immediately after an interview was completed. An attempt was made to tape verbatim interviews directly with respondents, but this produced too many rapport problems and was ruled out as a useful procedure.

To assure a reasonable uniformity in data-collecting activities and a continuing degree of conceptual unity in developing the case studies, members of the research team met together periodically for focused discussion. These taped discussions provide a record of comparative observations and insights as they emerged from field work experiences.

Information was obtained from family group members mainly through informal discussion and, occasionally, via more formalized interviews. By focusing on an individual's "life history" it was possible to probe with a minimum of difficulty; this approach "made sense" to most Beech Creekers. A great deal of "visiting" had to be done, however, before an individual's "record" was completed. Whenever possible, information about specific individuals or families was obtained indirectly from key informants who volunteered the information during the course of casual discussion. Semi-participant observation also provided additional data.

In general, all of the families contacted were cooperative. Initial suspicions, of course, were encountered; initial shyness, a cultural trait, was even more of a problem during the early stages. But, with patience, a working rapport was established with each family after numerous "ice-breaker" visits that included the younger members of our research team (i.e., the children), and after various inter-family activities that included "showing slides" of the Beech Creek neighborhoods and of other areas of the world, "breadmaking parties" supervised by the staff wives, and "lawn picnics." Most Beech Creekers associated our information-collecting activities with "writing a history of the Beech Creek people;" a few understood that it represented something more than this, e.g., "studying our family." In almost all cases, research entrée and successful field rapport were directly attributable to the comfortable image these people retained about similar activities in Beech Creek twenty years prior.

## THE FOCUSED INTERVIEW PHASE

The focused interview phase was planned and executed by a graduate assistant in collaboration with the research staff.[3] It deals with male migrants selected from the survey population and focuses more specifically upon the patterns of reaction and adaptation to the industrial work situation that are concomitants of the transitional adjustment process within this Appalachian migration system (see Chapter 7).

An attempt was made to explore such questions as: "What are the patterns of reaction and adaptation to occupational circumstances associated with a stem-family form of migration?"; "What personality and situational factors facilitate the process of adjustment, and what factors cause the most disturbance?"; "Do lingering cultural orientations frustrate the Appalachian worker's adaptation to the industrial work role?"; "How does the kinship structure affect job recruitment, job stability, and the occupational aspirations of rural-to-urban migrants?" Such questions as these, which could not be dealt with adequately within the survey or case study phases, became foci of inquiry in this third phase of the Beech Creek project.

A major purpose of the inquiry was to formulate and develop meaningful hypotheses about the occupational adjustment of rural to urban migrants through the systematic amalgamation of empirical knowledge and sensitized insight gained from intensive field work experience. The research objective was *not* to test hypotheses, but rather to synthesize statements that have validity and theoretical significance about the phenomenon under observation within this specific situational context. Future research, utilizing a more structured approach to the problem, is requisite before generalizations can be drawn that apply to rural migrant populations beyond the immediate scope of the Beech Creek case; future research, however, will be more parsimonious if the Beech Creek situational context is understood.

Enumerative data form the skeletal frame in this kind of study; "depth," which can be thought of as the qualitative "filler," comes from careful consideration of each case, the total field work experience, and the theoretically significant insights that can be abstracted from these materials. The final form and meaning of the resultant contribution is dependent as much upon the creative ability (i.e., sociological imagination) and total experience of the investigator as on the empirical findings themselves; synthesis, in other words, is more important than analysis, provided analysis is based upon systematic observation that is both probing and objective.

## Procedures and Interview Guide

In addition to information obtained through face to face interviews with a selected number of Beech Creek male migrants, data were also collected from various other sources. A great deal of pertinent material was gleaned from both the original 1942 study files and from the 1961 survey phase. Furthermore, to assess the general work situation in the area of destination, a number of industrial leaders—personnel managers, foremen, union officials—in southern Ohio were interviewed. The variety of unanticipated observations one makes in field work of this kind, when systematically recorded, provides an unusually rich source of sensitizing information.

A depth-interview guide was developed for use in a partially-structured interview situation with respondents. Some degree of flexibility in the process of getting valid information from an informant was considered essential for a number of reasons. Mountain people, for instance, are not inclined to elaborate on their responses when the interviewer poses his query in a formal, structured manner. A focused interview seemed the appropriate strategy that would be most productive and yield the kind of information sought.

Interviewing of this kind takes various forms and goes under various names, e.g., the "focused" interview, the "clinical" interview, the "depth" interview, the "nondirective" interview. Commonly, these interviewing strategies are used for intensive study of perceptions, attitudes, motivations, and so forth. Here, of course, a depth interview guide was used in order to delve more deeply into the area of occupational adjustment in the case of workers, each of whom had been exposed to a similar experience, migration from a rural farm to an urban industrial work situation. We recognized that the strategy employed differs somewhat from that described by Merton, Fiske, and Kendall[4] in that their procedure demands a great deal more knowledge of the total structure of a situation and also calls for the use of a specific hypothesis. Nevertheless, we refer to the procedure actually followed as a "focused interview," because this is the best single descriptive label of the interviewing strategy.

The interview guide was organized so as to focus upon three meaningful periods of time in the process of migration and transitional adjustment. *First,* the interviewer attempted to probe the respondent's situation prior to migration from eastern Kentucky. What kind of work had the respondent been doing before he migrated? What were his feelings about this kind of work (usually farming)? What was the work routine, pay, and the like? *Second,* the interviewer probed the situation immediately after migration. How did the respondent secure his first job? How did he learn the new work role? Was he prepared in any way? What were his feelings about this job, about the work conditions, about his co-workers, and the like? Why did he leave this job, if he did? *Third,* the respondent's present job situation was explored in depth. How did he secure this job? What are his present working conditions, duties, salary, and so on? Is he satisfied with his work, and what does he like or dislike about it? What are his job aspirations? What are his attitudes toward union activities? How does he perceive the effect of his rural background upon his present occupational status?

Similarly, a depth-interview guide was developed for use in getting pertinent information from industrial leaders (key informants). The format covered four main topics: (1) general information about Kentuckian workers, including an assessment of their collective qualifications, problems, company loyalties, and the like; (2) characteristics of Kentuckian workers on the job, including problems of training, co-worker relationships, attitudes toward discipline, absenteeism, job turnover, etc.; (3) characteristics of Kentuckian workers off the job, which was an attempt to tap the industrial leaders' perceptions of the rural migrants' subculture and how this influences job performance; and (4) union activities of Kentuckian workers, and how management and union officials feel about the Kentuckians' attitudes toward unions.

## The Study Population and Key Informants

The study population was limited to male Beech Creek migrants residing (1962) in or near a large metropolitan center in southern Ohio (City A). The fifty-seven men who are included represent over 83 percent of the male Beech Creek migrants to Ohio. Complete interviews were obtained from thirty of these men. Five persons refused to be interviewed; partial interviews were obtained from four; and the balance (eighteen) were not available for a variety of reasons (not at home on several occasions of call-back, on extended vacations, unable to be located for one reason or the other).

As mentioned, depth interviews were also obtained from a number of key informants representing, as spokesmen, the industrial leadership of southern Ohio. These included industrial relations managers, employment supervisors, general foremen, labor pool foremen, shop stewards, and the like. They represented such diverse concerns as paper making companies, steel producing companies, manufacturing companies, and industrial labor unions.

## The Field Situation

As with the survey phase, the field situation was difficult in that the interviewer encountered many problems of locating, contacting, and establishing a relaxed climate for the interview with subjects who were widely dispersed residentially, and whose work schedules were varied.

Nearly all of the interviews were secured during the months of July and August of 1962. Interviews with the industrial representatives were conducted during another period of field work, in early 1963.

In general, after locating the residence of a potential respondent (which in some cases was not a mere formality, because several had moved during the ensuing year since the survey), the first contact with a subject was for the purpose of establishing rapport or renewing acquaintanceships. Each respondent, therefore, was contacted at least twice by the interviewer and, in most cases, more often.

A major problem in the field was with the specific time of day for scheduling an interview. Most respondents worked shifts. The "day shift" is from 7:00 A.M to 3:00 P.M.; the "swing shift" is from 3:00 P.M. to 11:00 P.M.; and the "graveyard shift" is from 11:00 P.M. to 7:00 A.M. Arranging an appropriate time for interviewing those men working the third shift and, to a lesser extent, those working the second shift, was not an easy task. The fact that many workers rotated work shifts (on one shift for a number of days, then on another, etc.) also complicated the arranging of interviews. These conditions, though making field work tactics frustrating, were by themselves not responsible for the relatively large number of "unavailables"; in all cases, regardless of when a respondent was available, an attempt was made to get an interview.

In general, the more structured portion of an interview ran about two hours in length; to this, however, one must add a considerable amount of time for "visiting," informal discussion, and the like, depending upon specific circumstances. "Probe" questions were pursued during the more informal atmosphere after factual material had been recorded; in no case were the respondent's replies to these probes recorded in his presence. A verbatim account was made, from memory, outside of the interview situation. Often, further clarification of this "informally obtained" information was made in the course of one or more "follow up" visits, again in a very informal atmosphere.

Field notes were organized each night, and the focused interview schedules completed and edited as soon as possible after terminating an interview. Revision of and additions to the interview schedule proceeded throughout the course of this field work operation. The goal was to obtain valid information from which one could formulate meaningful hypotheses and build a useful theory focused on the phenomenon of the occupational adjustment of rural-to-urban migrants.

# Appendix B

## FAMILY SITUATION AND THE MIGRATION EVENT

The following report is a supplement to Chapter 5. It summarizes in tabular form the results of a detailed case-by-case analysis of certain aspects of the migration event. This analysis was undertaken to explore how the migration of Beech Creekers from Appalachian Kentucky was structured and channeled along kinship lines.

Individual cards noting the appropriate information about each Beech Creeker included in the study population, as well as any information that might aid in the interpretation of his or her pattern of migration, were sorted by hand. At this point, efficiency was sacrificed for the sake of greater validity: we wanted to be certain that any additional knowledge we had about an individual case was brought to bear in describing that individual's pattern.

Our attention focuses upon three structural aspects of the migration event: (1) whom the migrant lived with prior to moving from the mountains, (2) whom the migrant moved with, i.e., the composition of the migration unit, and (3) whom the migrant joined at the place of destination. Thus, the family-household structures at both ends of the migration stream are taken into account.

In studying these tables one should note that the analysis was organized in terms of the migrant's marital status and sex. The numbers in parentheses refer to the number of individual cases, and the categories at the right represent a breakdown of the categories at the left. Joining a "new household" means that the migration unit—whether the individual Beech Creeker alone or accompanied by parents, siblings, or friends—did not move into an existing household situation but, rather, formed a "new household" at the place of destination. It should also be noted that if a Beech Creeker lived with or migrated with his parents, other members of the parental household may have been present (a unit designated "sib" simply means that siblings were the closest kin present).

**Table B.1.** Male migrants, unmarried (N = 46).

| Family of origin situation (living with whom?) | Migration unit (migrated with whom?) | Family-household at destination (joined whom?) |
|---|---|---|
| Both parents (37) | parents (3) | sib (2)<br>new household (1) |
| | sib (1) | new household (1) |
| | friends (6) | close kin (5)<br>new household (1) |
| | alone (27) | sib (15)<br>close kin (3)<br>new household (9) |
| One parent (7) | parent (2) | parent (2) |
| | sib (1) | sib (1) |
| | friend (1) | sib (1) |
| | alone (3) | sib (1)<br>close kin (1)<br>new household (1) |
| Sib (2) | alone (2) | sib (1)<br>close kin (1) |

**Table B.2.** Female migrants, unmarried (N = 21).

| Family of origin | Migration unit | Family at destination |
|---|---|---|
| Both parents (16) | parents (1) | new household (1) |
| | sib (2) | close kin (1)<br>new household (1) |
| | alone (13) | sib (5)<br>close kin (4)<br>nonclose kin (4) |
| One parent (2) | alone (2) | sib (1)<br>nonclose kin (1) |
| Sib (1) | alone (1) | sib (1) |
| Close kin (2) | alone (2) | close kin (2) |

**Table B.3.** Female migrants, just married (N = 10).

| Family of origin | Migration unit | Family at destination |
|---|---|---|
| Both parents (8) | spouse (8) | close kin (2) new household (6) |
| One parent (1) | spouse (1) | new household (1) |
| Sib (1) | spouse (1) | new household (1) |

**Table B.4.** Male migrants, married, no children (N = 6).

| Family of origin | Migration unit | Family at destination |
|---|---|---|
| Spouse and both parents (3) | spouse (3) | parents-in-law (1) sib (1) new household (1) |
| Spouse and one parent (1) | alone (1) | new household (1) |
| Spouse only (2) | spouse (1) | new household (1) |
|  | alone (1) | sib (1) |

**Table B.5.** Female migrants, married, no children (N = 10).

| Family of origin | Migration unit | Family at destination |
|---|---|---|
| Spouse and parents or parents-in-law (6) | spouse (5) | parents (1) sib (1) new household (3) |
|  | alone (1) | sib (1) |
| Spouse only (4) | spouse (4) | sib-in-law (1) new household (3) |

**Table B.6.** Male migrants, married with children (N = 29).

| Family of origin | Migration unit | Family at destination |
|---|---|---|
|  | spouse and children (2) | new household (2) |
| Nuclear family and parents or parents-in-law (5) | spouse, children and parents-in-law (1) | new household (1) |
|  | alone (2) | sib-in-law (1) new household (1) |

**Table B.6.** Male migrants, married with children (N = 29). (*Continued*)

| Family of origin | Migration unit | Family at destination |
|---|---|---|
| Nuclear family only (22) | spouse and children (10) | older child (3)<br>sib (1)<br>new household (6) |
| | alone (12) | parents-in-law (1)<br>older child (1)<br>sib (3)<br>close kin (1)<br>new household (6) |
| Spouse only,<br>children absent (2) | spouse (2) | older child (2) |

**Table B.7.** Female migrants, married with children (N = 38).

| Family of origin | Migration unit | Family of destination |
|---|---|---|
| Nuclear family and parents<br>or parents-in-law (2) | spouse and children (2) | new household (2) |
| Nuclear family only (17) | spouse and children (14) | older child (3)<br>sib (1)<br>new household (10) |
| | spouse only (1) | new household (1) |
| | children only (1) | older child (1) |
| | alone (1) | sib (1) |
| Children only, no spouse,<br>with parents (6) | children only (4) | spouse (4) |
| | child and sib (1) | sib (1) |
| | alone (1) | nonclose kin (1) |
| Children only,<br>no spouse (10) | children only (9) | spouse (9) |
| | alone (1) | spouse (1) |
| Spouse only, no children,<br>with parents (1) | spouse (1) | older child (1) |
| Spouse only (1) | spouse (1) | older child (1) |
| Alone (1) | alone (1) | older child (1) |

# Appendix C

## ADJUSTMENT PATTERNS:

## Social and Psychological Dimensions (Methods and Approach)

This is a supplement to Chapter 9. Our aim is to delineate the methods and approach that were used to explore selected dimensions of the complex phenomenon of adjustment which, in the Beech Creek case, are relevant to migration and meaningful within the social context of the changed and changing situation in the area of destination. Attention focuses on the manner by which the theoretical frame of reference is interpreted in researchable terms and on such technical details as the development of appropriate measuring instruments and the logical formalities of three-variable analysis.

## INTERACTIONAL ADJUSTMENT AND THE KIN NETWORK

After moving from one residential locale to another the migrant, because of spatial distance between the area of origin and area of destination, must modify to some extent his patterns of relationship with kinsfolk, friends, and former neighbors in the area of origin. For example, he can not expect to maintain day to day, face to face visiting with people who live, let us say, over one hundred miles away. In time he also comes into contact with and, unless he chooses to become a social isolate, involved with such other people as neighbors, work group members, and kinsfolk in the area of destination. We refer to these changes in pattern of interaction as "interactional adjustment." Some migrants, of course, for one reason or the other, adopt new patterns or adapt to situationally induced changes more readily or more completely than other migrants. That, for research purposes, becomes a measurement problem and, for the sociological study of migration, an interesting and significant phenomenon to pursue.

### Involvement with Kinsfolk in Area of Destination (Branch-Family Ties)

In most cases, the Beech Creek migrant was not a "loner" when he arrived in the area of destination.[1] To the contrary, he often joined kinsfolk who had migrated before him and, almost invariably, his initial residence was in the general vicinity of a number of other close kin families whom he could visit and call upon for assistance in time of need. Similarly, he in turn was often joined by other kin from Beech Creek whom he assisted.

We would expect, however, that with the passage of time, and for many reasons, the migrant's need and feelings of obligation to maintain close ties with kinsfolk would become less strong, more diffuse. As the Beech Creek socio-cultural system is modified or absorbed by the sociocultural system of the larger society and as the Beech Creekers' needs change in the context of a more urban interactional system to which Beech Creekers are exposed, the interactional bonds which hold branch-families together undoubtedly change and, in one or the other sense, weaken. Furthermore, various segments of the Beech Creek population probably have greater or lesser need for maintaining strong interactional ties with kinsfolk (this is, demographically and in other ways, a heterogeneous population) and in situations where such individual need-dispositions are not in accord with normative pressures or cannot be expressed in concrete behavioral activity, tensions may be generated.

The ideas outlined above, drawn from our theoretical frame of reference, are consistent with impressions formulated from continued observations of Beech Creekers over the years. In order to explore some of these notions, two indicators of the migrant's degree of involvement with kinsfolk in the area of destination were constructed.

Our focus of concern was the migrant's effective kinship group in the area of destination. "Effective kinship group" implies those persons related to him by blood or through marriage on whom (in keeping with the normative standards of the Beech Creek sociocultural system) he can count for assistance and support of one kind or another in time of crisis.[2] Operationally, this group was defined as the migrant's "close kin," inclusive of parents, parents-in-law, siblings, siblings-in-law, and, if they resided outside his immediate household, his adult children. "Area of destination" implies the migrant's normal visiting community, the territory within which he can maintain a pattern of frequent visits with kinsfolk without extraordinary expenditure of time, money, or energy. This area was defined, arbitrarily, as a 50-mile radius from the migrant's place of residence.

Analysis of the results of this arbitrary definition vis-a-vis the migrant's total kin group shows, because of the residential clustering effect of chain-migration, that almost all kinsmen who had migrated were captured by the definition. In cases where kin-group members resided outside the delineated area they were, more often than not, very far removed from the migrant's circle of visiting (e.g., in California, Tennessee, etc.).[3]

The first indicator is simply a count of the number of close kin the migrant has within the area of destination. That "score" was dichotomized at just below the median. If a migrant has six or more close kin nearby, he was assigned to the "high involvement" category, as being involved with a large, effective kinship group in the area of destination. At best, the measure is a crude attempt to reduce a complex reality into simple terms. Nevertheless, if size of branch-family network has anything to do with the adjustment of Beech Creekers, then this indicator is a useful tool for exploratory purposes.

The second indicator, a more meaningful measure in many ways, is based upon the first. Frequency of visiting with each close kin in the area, as reported by the migrant, was converted to a yearly count. The sum of this total amount of visiting divided by the total number of close kin yielded an average visiting frequency. Average visiting frequency is interpreted as an indicator of the degree of interaction the migrant maintains with kinsfolk in the area of destination and, indirectly, of the strength of familial bonds within the kinship circle. Of course, duration, intensity, and content of interaction are not taken into account. However, the simple fact of "seeing" kinsfolk—in many ways a reinforcement ritual—is a valid indication that some degree of familistic sentiment or cohesion, some form of attachment to extended family group, exists. It is this dimension, a migrant's degree of attachment to the branch-family network in the area of destination, that is the focus of inquiry. The "score" was dichotomized at about the median point so that those who visit with close kin on the average of more than once a week were included in the "high" category.

The two indicators, though positively associated $(\bar{C} = +.42)$,[4] are not simply measures of precisely the same phenomenon, as we shall demonstrate.

## Involvement with Natives in Area of Destination (Urban Ties)

The possible strain-producing situations which might confront the Beech Creek migrant during the transitional adjustment process and perhaps cause difficult disturbances and tension-management problems within the migration system are, we believe, allayed by and through the kinship group. That is, in a stem-family system of migration, the kin group helps the individual migrant solve certain initial problems and assists him in becoming a functional member of the urban community.

With the passage of time, however, as the migrant comes into repeated and prolonged contact with persons native to the host community—in the neighborhood, at work, in church—such non-kin, non-mountain people may in more and more meaningful ways become incorporated into his pattern of interaction and frame of reference. The migrant's orientation toward his family and his reliance upon kinsfolk for guidance and help in crisis situations, for example, may be replaced by an orientation toward and reliance upon friendship groups composed of non-kin. If the non-kin persons with whom the migrant strikes up friendship and perhaps visiting relationships are persons from a similar socio-cultural background, e.g., eastern Kentucky, then the effects of such contacts upon the migrant's personality and behavior may be negligible. Indeed, the orientations the migrant brings with him into these encounters may be reinforced by the interaction that ensues. But, if the non-kin persons with whom the migrant comes into repeated contact are persons indigenous to the urban community, then the likelihood is greater that a truly cross-cultural confrontation is, and has been, taking place.

Two indicators of the Beech Creeker's degree of involvement with persons native to the area of destination were formulated in order to explore these ideas.[5]

Our first indicator focuses on "contacts with non-eastern Kentuckians." It is based upon the following question: "In your daily life, how much contact do you have with people who are natives of this area? I mean Ohio, Indiana, etc., people who were born and raised in this area—not eastern Kentuckians." Response categories were: none at all, very little, some, a great deal. In effect, we were asking the migrant to make a qualitative judgment about his degree of contact with non-eastern Kentuckians. And he undoubtedly made that judgment not only in terms of facts perceived and knowledge about what is "normal," but also in line with his own personal needs and predispositions about such intergroup relationships; i.e., the question called forth subjective criteria. The variable was handled as a dichotomy with "none at all" and "very little" constituting the "low contact" grouping (40 percent of the Beech Creek migrants).

As noted earlier, only a few Beech Creekers (11 percent) feel that in their daily lives they do not have any contact at all with non-eastern Kentuckians. These persons are not necessarily social isolates; it is clear, however, that they manifest a pattern of cultural isolation vis-a-vis the larger society into which the Beech Creek sociocultural system has been transplanted.

Our second indicator focuses on "number of non-eastern Kentucky friends." It is based upon the following question: "About how many of these people (natives of this area) would you say were close enough friends so that you meet in one another's homes?" As with the previous question, we were asking the migrant to make a qualitative judgment (who were his close friends?). That judgment, however, was expressed in quantitative terms; hence, responses were less an expression of the migrant's own predispositions and needs, and more an assessment of situational facts. This variable also was handled as a dichotomy; those reporting four or more noneastern Kentucky "close friends" constituted the "high" category (56 percent of the total).

Let it be noted that 21 percent of the Beech Creekers (13 percent of the males and 29 percent of the females) reported that they do not have any close friends who are natives of the area of destination. These "isolates" generally reside in one or the other of the "little Kentucky" cultural islands in or around the industrial centers of the Ohio Valley.

The two indicators of social assimilation are positively associated ($\overline{C} = +.62$).

## Interactional Ties with Kin and Friends in Area of Origin (Stem-Family Ties)

By moving from one area to another, the Beech Creeker, like other rural-to-urban migrants, is spatially separated from kinsfolk and friends with whom he had been intimately associated prior to moving. Those interactional ties, however, are not necessarily severed abruptly in the process of migration, although the frequency of face to face contact is, and must be, reduced to a considerable degree. Sentiments, i.e., normative expectations about person to person relationships, which are deeply imbedded in the migrant's personality through countless earlier socialization experiences, cannot be ejected from his system, figuratively speaking, in one day. To the contrary, the personality system and the normative system which tends to support it strain toward maintaining the form of interaction, i.e., the boundaries of the interactional system as it was prior to the migrant's departure from the family group and homestead in the area of origin.

It is not surprising, then, that Beech Creekers and other Appalachian migrants like to avail themselves of every opportunity to visit relatives and friends back in the mountains. This visiting phenomenon, so characteristic of the Appalachian migrant, is, we believe, a manifestation of the familistically-oriented personality system straining to maintain bonds with the interactional system with which it is in accord (i.e., with persons in the area of origin).

In time, however, as the migrant experiences more and more of the urban world and as his needs and interests change, his interactional ties with persons in the area of origin will become less tenacious and visiting and other forms of communication less frequent and less meaningful. It is also quite likely that various segments of a rural migrant population respond differently to circumstances associated with migration. For whatever reasons, the reduction of face to face interaction between persons in the area of origin and persons in the area of destination, and the modification in form and content of such interactional bonds between these two sub-systems, would be indicative of changes and modifications in the form of the family system itself.

Three indicators, two of which differ mainly in methodological terms, were employed to tap this dimension of the interactional adjustment process.

We asked: "How many times during the past year did you visit eastern Kentucky?" Assuming that longer visits provide greater opportunity for cultural and familial reinforcement and also suggest stronger attachment to and dependence upon the donor system by the individual migrant, the temporal duration of each visit was taken into account. Response categories were in terms of number of visits made for periods of (1) one day, (2) only overnight, (3) a few days, (4) more than a few days, and (5) longer than two weeks. The simple five-point scale, when multiplied by the number of visits per category, yielded a summated visiting score.

In much the same manner, a simple summated scale of visits received from eastern Kentucky was constructed. We asked: "How often during the past year did you have visitors from eastern Kentucky in your home?" Responses were in terms of visiting units, i.e., groups of visitors, rather than individual visits.

The median score for both scales was about 6 points. A score of 6 may mean two long weekend visits, or three overnight visits, or some other equivalent combination. A lesser score indicates that visiting, if at all, was of relatively short temporal duration and, therefore, that interactional ties between branch-family and family homestead are relatively weak.

There is, of course, a direct correlation between visiting *in* eastern Kentucky and visits received *from* eastern Kentucky. For purposes of analysis, we utilize the former, *the visiting in eastern Kentucky* score, dichotomized at just below the median, as an indicator of the migrant's need for cultural reinforcement and of his degree of attachment to and involvement with the donor system.

Our second indicator, which parallels the first, was obtained by combining the score of visiting *in* eastern Kentucky with the weighted score of visits received *from* eastern Kentucky. The "high" category includes migrants who scored "high" on the first indicator *plus* those who scored very high, above 10 points, on visits received. This second indicator of *visiting exchanges with people in eastern Kentucky* takes into account the possibility that some migrants may be considerably involved with kinsfolk and homestead in the mountains but, because of situational, health, or other reasons are themselves unable to make the long, difficult journey.

Visiting is only one, albeit an important, form of communication between the migrant and his relatives and friends back in the mountains. Letter writing, for example, is another kind of communication linkage that in same cases, depending upon level of literacy and other factors, helps to maintain a degree of cohesion between the branch-family and its homestead in eastern Kentucky.

We asked migrants: "About how often do you (and/or your spouse) write to relatives in eastern Kentucky?" and, "About how often do you get letters from relatives in eastern Kentucky?"

In both cases the median frequency was about two letters per month, with about a third of the migrants writing and receiving letters at least once a week, and with only about 10 percent never communicating by mail at all. Of course, there is an almost straight-line correlation between frequency of writing and receiving letters, but only a moderately high relationship between letter writing and visiting in eastern Kentucky ($\overline{C} = +.42$).

A composite indicator, dichotomized, was used for analysis purposes. Migrants writing their relatives in eastern Kentucky at least once a month and, likewise, also receiving mail from them at least once a month, were included in the "high" category; all others were treated as "low" in terms of *letter exchanges with people in eastern Kentucky*.

## Summary: Interactional Adjustment Variables

Appropriate indicators were developed of three important aspects of the Beech Creek migrants' interactional adjustment. These indicators enable us to explore the "cushioning effect" of the stem-family system in the process of migration and to observe the functional adequacy of the kin structure vis-a-vis the particular needs of various segments of the Beech Creek migrant population.

Interrelationships between the three aspects of interactional adjustment should be noted. The degree of involvement of Beech Creekers with persons native to the area of destination, i.e., non-eastern Kentuckians, appears not to be associated with either of the other two aspects. This suggests that the integration of Beech Creekers into urban social groupings and social life is a phenomenon independent of the Beech Creekers' attachment to, and maintenance of ties with, kinsfolk, family homestead, and the mountain sub-culture.

A negative relationship is observed between the numerical size of the migrants' kin groups in the area of destination and the degree to which interactional ties are maintained with persons and family homestead in the area of origin. Beech Creekers with many close kin in the urban area tend to visit less in eastern Kentucky during a given year than Beech Creekers who are "supported" by smaller kin groups;[6] the negative relationship remains when we focus on visits received from eastern Kentucky. Likewise, migrants with many close kin nearby tend to communicate less often by mail with persons in eastern Kentucky.[7]

Average visiting frequency with close kin nearby, however, is not associated with the migrants' degree of interactional involvement with persons in the mountains. One should recall, in view of this apparent inconsistency, that the two indicators of involvement with kin in the area of destination were designed to measure somewhat different aspects of the phenomenon. It well may be that observed variations in the patterns of visiting in the mountains are more a function of the stage in the migration process of the Beech Creeker's family group than of the Beech Creeker's degree of identification with and loyalty to the family homestead. This interpretation is consistent with our conceptualization of the stem-family's role in facilitating migration.

## PSYCHOLOGICAL ADJUSTMENT: INDICATORS OF PERSONAL STABILITY AND STRESS

Six indicators of various aspects of the Beech Creek migrant's psychological adjustment were incorporated into our research design. We use the term "psychological" to imply that these attributes are indicative of certain facets of the migrant's personality structure—his state of mind, general orientation, sentiments, and the like.

## Identification with the Urban Locality ("Residential Stability")

One aspect of the migrant's psychological adjustment is his feeling of belonging to a locality group in the area of destination. Rural migrants who identify more with the urban locality than with the area of origin, who feel quite satisfied with their new way of life in the host community, and who tend to think of themselves as permanent residents rather than transients in the communities to which they have migrated have made, almost by definition, a certain kind of adjustment. A simple, six-item summated attitudinal scale was constructed to measure this feeling of permanency, this particular facet of adjustment.

The following items were selected, by analysis, from a battery of questions included for that purpose in the survey instrument:

(a) "How satisfied are you with your way of life in this community?"
(The term "satisfaction" is often used by the Kentucky mountaineer to sum up his feelings about a particular situation. When an eastern Kentuckian, for example, says "I'm satisfied," he invariably means that he has thought about the matter and has made up his mind to accept or, at least, to tolerate it. In much the same sense, we asked respondents to summarize their feelings about the host community.)

(b) "In general, how do you feel about living in this community—would you say it's a very good community, pretty good, not very good, or not at all good?"
(Like the previous question, this solicited a very general statement from the migrant about his assessment of the situation. A comparison with other communities is implied; to make the judgement called for, the migrant undoubtedly had some standard in mind which, in most cases, was the mountain locality in the area of origin.)

(c) "Suppose it were up to you alone and no one else, would you prefer to live somewhere else rather than in this community?"
(Here we tapped directly the migrant's residential restlessness, his feeling of residential stability. Slightly more than half said "no," they preferred "this community." Nevertheless, more than a fifth of the migrants said they would prefer to live in their old home neighborhood, Beech Creek. The remainder, for the most part, indicated preferences for other places nearby in the area of destination or for states such as Florida and California where climate and scenery are, in their opinion, more attractive than in the industrialized Ohio Valley.)

(d) "Where do you, yourself, feel is really your home?"
(To ask Beech Creekers this question, in effect, was to ask them where their hearts are, where their roots are, and whether or not they have cut themselves off, in sentimental terms, from the mountain neighborhoods and the mountain way of life. About half said that home was really "here, in this community," in the area of destination. Nearly all of the others, about half, said that Beech Creek, their old neighborhood in the mountains, was really home;

moreover, most of these people were quite sure that they would always feel that way about Beech Creek.)

(e) "If you could choose, where would you prefer to live when you get too old to work?"
(One of the more important reasons why these Beech Creekers, as family units, migrated away from the mountains was their need and desire to find work and economic opportunities not available to them in the area of origin. The need for work was ruled out in this question, by design; the focus was on retirement. Less than one-third expressed a preference to retire in the host community in the area of destination.)

(f) "If you could choose, where would you prefer to be buried?"
(This question was administered by the interviewer with a bit more tact than the rather blunt interview schedule phrasing suggests. Field observations, however, he had convinced us that the Beech Creekers had thought about the eventuality and had indeed made some plans. The question possessed strong discriminatory power in terms of the orientational attribute we wished to measure.)

The above six items were employed as indicators of the Beech Creek migrant's "residential stability." Response categories were dichotomized. On the one hand, an individual may have held a positive orientation toward the host community; on the other hand, an individual may have expressed a more negative attitude or, in some instances, a more positive inclination toward someplace else. Intercorrelation analysis revealed a high degree of linkage between the various items; a summated scale was justified. Because of the relatively small number of cases and the need to introduce control variables in the analysis program, scale scores were collapsed into a dichotomy; migrants scoring 4 points or more were classed as "high" in terms of residential stability (39 percent of total migrant population). Therefore, those who answered at least four of the six questions in a positive manner, i.e., as oriented toward the host community, were, for purposes of analysis, considered to be "residentially stable" and identifying to a high degree with the urban locality.

## Identification with the Mountain Region ("Nostalgia for Home")

Rural migrants are, symbolically speaking, caught up in and to some degree members of two sociocultural worlds. There is the social world in which they were reared—in this case Beech Creek, the mountain neighborhood, home. There is the other world—in this case Ohio, the great society, the urban community with which they and the Beech Creek sociocultural system have come into prolonged contact. It is the latter, the migrant's sense of belonging to or accommodation with the host community, that we attempted to measure by means of a "residential stability" scale. It is the former, the migrant's feeling of attachment to and longing for the old home neighborhood and an earlier way of life, that we attempted to measure here. We wanted to identify those migrants who, in terms of their orientational set, were more a part of the Beech Creek world than of the outside world into which they and the Beech Creek system had been transplanted.

Four questions were selected from the previous battery of items on the basis of content and discriminatory power (items c, d, e, and f). Though response patterns were handled somewhat differently, the two scales are to some extent polar opposites. Response categories were dichotomized so that expressed preferences for eastern Kentucky, which almost always referred to Beech Creek or one or the other neighborhoods nearby, were construed as positive responses. All other expressed orientations, as for example, for Ohio or central Kentucky, were handled as negative responses. The fact that these four items tended to be highly intercorrelated (tetrachoric r's range from +.59 to +.73) suggests that they were derived from a single attribute space and could be used to construct a four-item summated scale.

For analysis, the scale was dichotomized. Migrants who responded in terms of a "mountain orientation" on all four questions were placed in the "high" grouping (14 percent of all migrants). This decision focused our analysis on the extreme cases, i.e., the consistently nostalgic individual. One should note that almost all Beech Creek migrants express some degree, often a very high degree as measured by this scale, of nostalgia for home. But nostalgia, of course, is not necessarily symptomatic of a disturbed individual or of the presence of a disruptive element in one's pattern of behavior.[8] Since the study was exploratory, our strategy was to seek out those dimensions of psychological adjustment which *may be* symptomatic of dysfunctional stresses within the migrants' personality and the Beech Creek sociocultural system.

## Assessment of Life Situation ("Expressed Happiness")

Happiness is not only exceedingly difficult to know or attain, but also a very ambiguous concept to operationalize in research terms.

The migrant was asked to express his own pervasive feeling about his total life situation, his own assessment of how his existential gratifications add up. The interviewing form, leading to a summary statement, followed that of Gurin, *et. al.*[9] Expressed happiness, nevertheless, was measured by the migrant's response to a single question: "Taking things all together, how would you say things are these days—would you say you're very happy, pretty happy, or not too happy these days?" Those who said they are "very happy" were considered "high" on the happiness scale.

## Degree of Personalized Concerns ("Extent of Worry")

The extent to which an individual worries about things as well as the sources and objects of his worries are important and sensitive indicators of certain facets of his psychological adjustment. Like happiness, however, "worry" is difficult to research.

Questioning procedures were again borrowed from Gurin, *et. al.*[10] After being interviewed about sources of happiness and the like, the respondent was asked: "We're also interested in what people are worrying about these days. Everybody has some things he worries about more or less. What kinds of things do you worry about?" We also asked him to express the extent to which he felt concerned about each of the worries listed—was it "a lot," "somewhat," or "not very much?"

From this listing of worries and expressed degrees of concern, a crude "worry index" was constructed. The index was dichotomized so that migrants with scores of 9 or more out of the possible 15 points (23 percent of the population) were categorized as "high worriers." Sources of worry were not taken into account.

## Feelings of Normlessness and Despair ("Anomia")

Anomia refers to an individual's state of mind with respect to his own integration into a societal structure. In that sense, the more anomic individual manifests symptoms of normlessness, hopelessness, helplessness, and the like in the face of impersonal social forces he perceives as beyond his control. The anomic individual would have very little faith in the future and in his own ability to influence the course of events in a society and would be extremely pessimistic to the point of despair. A commonly employed measure of this personality orientation, the five-item Anomia Scale developed by Srole, was used as an indicator.[11]

The items included were as follows:

(1) In spite of what some people say, the lot of the average man is getting worse, not better.

(2) Nowadays, a person has to live pretty much for today and let tomorrow take care of itself.

(3) It's hardly fair to bring children into the world with the way things look for the future.

(4) These days a person doesn't really know whom he can count on.

(5) There's little use in writing to public officials because often they aren't really interested in the problems of the average man.

The resultant matrix from an inter-item correlation analysis revealed a satisfactory pattern of interlinkage; a summated scale was justified. Item responses were scored as: agree, 3 points; undecided, 2 points; disagree, 1 point. The final scale was collapsed into a dichotomy so that the "high" category focused upon extreme cases (32 percent of all migrants). Individuals classified as highly anomic agreed with at least three, and more often four, of the five items.

## Symptoms of Psychological Stress ("Anxiety")

As Gurin and associates explain, "Specific psychological, physical, or psychosomatic symptoms have often been used as critical diagnostic indices of psychological distress, both in research on mental disturbance and in actual clinical settings. Not only do symptoms have a certain amount of face validity as diagnostic criteria, but the use of a symptom list has the great advantage of administrative simplicity."[12] In using a symptom list as a measure of psychological disturbance, the present study leans heavily upon the work of Gurin et al. who, in turn, have built upon the works of Macmillan (Stirling County Study, 1957), Rennie (Middletown Study, 1953), and others.

As suggested from the earlier researches, a series of appropriate items was included in the interview instrument. From the results of a matrix analysis of these items (i.e., a crude factorial analysis), a six-item composite indicator was constructed which, referring back to Gurin's work, was loaded somewhat on the factor "psychosomatic disposition." The items are:

(1) Have you ever been bothered by nervousness, feeling fidgety or tense?

(2) Are you ever troubled by headaches or pains in your head?

(3) Have you ever had spells of dizziness?

(4) Do you ever have a loss of appetite?

(5) Do you ever have any trouble getting to sleep or staying asleep?

(6) Have there ever been times when you couldn't take care of things because you just couldn't get going?

Responses were considered "positive" if the respondent indicated that the symptom occurred "pretty often," "many times," or "nearly all the time." Summated scores were dichotomized so that a score of 2 or more was classed as "high" (34 percent of the migrants). Most Beech Creek migrants, in other words, scored rather low on this scale of anxiety; hence, one should bear in mind that we are *not* dealing with extreme cases, but rather with a category of people that show only a tendency toward the physical (i.e., psychosomatic) manifestations of psychological stress.

## Summary: Psychological Adjustment Variables

By classifying them under a common rubric, we suggest that the various indicators outlined above measure certain "psychological" aspects that should be considered in assessing the "adjustment" of Beech Creek migrants. If we observe the variability of these psychological attributes in relation to various aspects of the migrants' social interactional situation (as we have done in Chapter 9), we may delineate the nature and locus of basic disturbances or incongruities which, by inference, are consequents of rural-to-urban relocation and its aftermath, the processes of absorption of Beech Creekers and the Beech Creek migration system into the mainstream of urban America.

At this point, let us note the empirical interrelationships among these indicators of "psychological adjustment."

We find, of course, a markedly high negative association between the migrants' residential stability and nostalgia for home ($\bar{C} = -.49$).

We also observe that the expressed happiness of migrants is associated positively with residential stability ($\bar{C} = +.32$) and negatively with nostalgia for home ($\bar{C} = -.23$), but not at all with any of the other indicators. This implies that happiness, in the Beech Creek context, depends upon the reconciliation of migrants to situational changes brought about by a residential move from one locale (rural mountain) to another (urban industrial).

Finally, and more important, we noted that the migrants' psychological anxiety is linked positively with anomia ($\bar{C} = +.25$), extent of worry ($\bar{C} = +.27$),[13] and residential stability ($\bar{C} = +.24$). These empirical associations, to be sure, are of a low order. Nevertheless, they suggest that the "anxiety-anomia-worry syndrome" is concomitant with the migrants' greater involvement in and feeling of belonging to the urban milieu.

## SOCIAL AND PSYCHOLOGICAL DIMENSIONS:

### Configurations of Adjustment

In order to explore the meaning of adjustment and its empirical dimensions in the Beech Creek case, it is useful to examine the interrelationships which exist between the two sets of variables, namely, the psychological and social interactional. Findings are summarized in Table C-1.[14]

The degree of residential stability of Beech Creekers within the host community in, for example, southern Ohio, varies inversely with the amount of time they spend visiting in eastern Kentucky during the year. Knowledgeable informants, without doubt, would quickly testify to this fact. We find, moreover, that it is the extremely nostalgic migrant who is more likely to do a great deal of

**Table C.1.** Relationships between various aspects of migrants' psychological and interactional adjustment.

| Interactional adjustment variables | Psychological adjustment variables | | | | | |
| | Residential Stability | Nostalgia for Home | Expressed Happiness | Extent of Worry | Anomia | Anxiety |
| | Direction of Relationship and $\bar{c}$* | | | | | |
| Size of nearby kin group: | + | | | | | |
| Frequency of visiting nearby kin: | | | +.26 | −.23 | | −.24 |
| Social contacts with urban natives: | + | | | | −.30 | −.21 |
| Friendship ties with urban natives: | + | −.21 | | | | − |
| Visiting in eastern Kentucky: | −.29 | +.28 | | + | −.24 | |
| Visiting exchanges with people in eastern Kentucky: | − | +.21 | | + | − | |
| Letter exchanges with people in eastern Kentucky: | | | | | | |

* Note: In all cases, df = 1 and N = 161. Where $\bar{c}$, the corrected coefficient of contingency, is reported, P < .10. Where only direction of relationship is reported, P < .20 but >.10.

visiting back in the mountains. Of course, we have no way of knowing whether dissatisfaction with the urban locale prompts Beech Creekers to return often to the family homestead and to maintain strong attachments with kinsfolk in the mountains, or vice versa. Nevertheless, although nostalgia is negatively associated with the number of non-eastern Kentucky friends these migrants have made, residential stability is not. Since involvement with non-eastern Kentuckians and ties with family homestead are not related, these findings, if we consider them together, suggest that extremely nostalgic migrants tend to be less integrated socially into the heterogeneous informal groupings of the urban localities, and that this lack of integration is more a function of their extreme orientation toward the mountains than of their visiting patterns per se, i.e., of concrete behavior.

Anomia is connected with the interactional adjustment indicators in an interesting manner. Migrants who visit more often in eastern Kentucky tend to be less anomic. On the other hand, migrants who feel they don't have much contact with persons who are natives of the area tend to be more anomic. One might infer, though only tentatively at this point, that feelings of normlessness and despair (i.e., anomia) and feelings of being disengaged from the informal, more urbane groupings of city life, are very much part of the same general configuration in the Beech Creek case. Beech Creekers who manifest symptoms of anomia tend to look toward the family homestead and stem-family for support.

Happiness, in the Beech Creek case, seems to be linked positively with kin visiting in the area of destination. Migrants who claim to be "very happy" are more likely to exhibit a great deal of interaction with close kin nearby and to be part of a cohesive branch-family network. Those who interact with kin are also less likely to worry a great deal or to show symptoms of psychological anxiety.

Our data, moreover, reveal a tendency for anxiety to vary inversely with the Beech Creekers' assessment of their degree of social contacts with urban natives. It may be that extreme isolation from kinsfolk as well as isolation from the non-migrant segment of the host community are manifestations of or contribute to the anxiety condition.

It would be presumptuous to discuss these findings in anything but a very tentative and perhaps superficial manner. Many and sundry factors must be taken into account prior to drawing useful inferences about such a complex phenomenon as adjustment (see Chapter 9). Nevertheless, however tentative, a summary statement is in order.

Two, or perhaps three, discernible patterns seem to emerge from these interrelationships. The degree of interactional involvement of Beech Creekers within the branch-family network in the area of destination apparently affects their feelings of anxiety and tension; migrants who are active members of close-knit family groups are less prone to show symptoms of stress. Since none of the adjustment indicators vary significantly with size of the migrant's effective kin group, these findings suggest that *active* interaction with kin-group members, rather than simple, passive nearness to a potentially effective (supportive) kin group, has some effect, though weak, upon the social psychological adjustment of the migrants.

If we reduce these indicators into more general terms, it can be argued that active branch-family involvement is linked more with the migrant's state of mind vis-a-vis immediate concerns than with his feelings of identification with or sense of belonging to an ecological entity such as the urban locality in the area of destination, the neighborhood of origin in the mountains, or the larger society. On the other hand, the involvement of Beech Creekers with the stem-family and homestead in the area of origin has something to do with their general orientation toward the world, their sense of identity, their feeling of belonging. Finally, though a highly tenuous generalization, it appears that the migrants' involvement in the heterogeneous friendship groups, characteristic of the urban locality, is more a product than a factor which determines his sense of stability and personal adjustment.

Let us recall, however, that Beech Creek migrants, although stemming from a particular place of origin and sharing a common cultural heritage, are nevertheless a heterogeneous population with respect to a number of important behavior-influencing variables. These variables must be taken into account before we can learn from and build upon the Beech Creek experience (see Chapter 9).

# NOTES AND REFERENCES

## CHAPTER 1

1. For some background information on the settlement patterns and history of this area of the Southern Appalachian Region, see: Thomas D. Clark, *A History of Kentucky*, New York: Prentice-Hall, 1937; John C. Campbell, *The Southern Highlander and His Homeland*, New York: The Russell Sage Foundation, 1921; Virginia Clay McClure, *The Settlement of the Kentucky Appalachian Highlands*, unpublished dissertation, University of Kentucky, 1933; Elizabeth R. Hooker, *Religion in the Highlands*, New York: The Home Missions Council, 1933; Rupert Vance, "Frontier: Geographical and Social Aspects," *Encyclopedia of the Social Sciences*, Vol. 6, New York: The MacMillan Company, 1931.

2. See D. H. Davis, *The Geography of the Mountains of Eastern Kentucky*, Frankfort, Kentucky: Kentucky Geological Survey, Geologic Reports, Series 6, Vol. 18, 1924.

3. See U.S. Department of Agriculture, *Economic and Social Problems and Conditions of the Southern Appalachians*, Miscellaneous Publication Number 205, Washington, D.C.: U.S. Government Printing Office, 1935.

4. It was estimated, for example, that by 1910 in the Southern Appalachian Region the original hardwood stand of 45 billion feet had been reduced to 18 billion feet, and by 1922 to 5 billion. In 1935 it was estimated that the depletion of saw timber in the region was "approximately 3 billion board feet per year or about six times the growth of such material." See U.S.D.A., *op. cit.*, p. 35; Davis, *op. cit.*, p. 38; and also Harry M. Caudill, *Night Comes to the Cumberlands*, Boston: Little, Brown and Co., 1962, Chapter 6.

5. Coal had been found in the Kentucky River basin by Christopher Gist as early as 1750, and some coal had even been shipped on the Kentucky River as early as 1800. But coal mining did not become big business until after the railroads came, i.e., after 1900. By 1927, eastern Kentucky produced 48 million tons per year. See U.S. Bureau of Mines, *Mineral Resources of the United States 1927, Part II. Nonmetals*, Washington: U.S. Government Printing Office, 1930, p. 465. By 1944, coal production in eastern Kentucky reached a peak of nearly 52 million tons. See U.S. Bureau of Mines, *Minerals Yearbook: 1945*, Washington: U.S. Government Printing Office, 1947, p. 861. Nevertheless, coal beds in the Beech Creek area remained relatively inaccessible and uneconomic.

6. Bruce Poundstone and Walter J. Roth, *Types of Farming in Kentucky*, Lexington, Kentucky: Kentucky Agricultural Experiment Station Bulletin Number 357, June 1935.

7. The economic data presented here and in subsequent chapters were obtained through family-budget schedules. See James S. Brown, *Social Organization of an Isolated Kentucky Mountain Neighborhood,* unpublished Ph.D. thesis, Harvard University, 1950. The schedule used is shown in the appendix; it follows much the same form suggested by Carle C. Zimmerman and Merle E. Frampton, *Family and Society,* New York: D. Van Nostrand Co., 1935.

8. For more detailed data, see Brown, *ibid.,* pp. 107–109.

9. In general, the income levels of persons and families in the Beech Creek neighborhoods were far below the average for the eastern Kentucky mountain counties, and income levels in Appalachian Kentucky were far below the national average. For example, the per capita personal income for the years 1939 and 1947 was $556 and $1316 in the United States as a whole, $303 and $850 in Kentucky, and only $125 and $374 in the mountain county in which the Beech Creek neighborhoods are located. See George M. Nall, Carl R. Blankenship, and John L. Johnson, *Personal Income in Kentucky in 1955 and a Survey of Personal Income in Kentucky Since 1929,* Bureau of Business Research, University of Kentucky, May, 1957 (mimeographed).

10. McClure suggests that "up to the year 1850 the isolation of the Mountains cannot have been so great as it has generally been thought to have been, since numbers of people continued to come into the section from other states and . . . others who had left the State returned to their former homes." "It was not until improved methods of transportation turned traffic from the Mountain highways to less difficult channels, and improved farm implements that could not be used to advantage in the Mountains enabled the Blue Grass to push ahead of the eastern Highlands, that the terms *isolation* and *inaccessibility* began to be applied to the latter region." McClure, *op. cit.,* pp. 163 and 167. Isolation, in the sense used here, is a relative term.

11. In 1942 there was no organized church in Beech Creek, and most churches in the area had services only once a month. As a result, Beech Creek adults seldom went to church, and when they did go they went outside the neighborhood.

12. Some of the descriptive information about the social organization of Beech Creek presented here and in the next chapter was published earlier in somewhat different form. See James S. Brown, *The Farm Family in a Kentucky Mountain Neighborhood,* Kentucky Agricultural Experiment Station Bulletin 587, August 1952; James S. Brown, *The Family Group in a Kentucky Mountain Farming Community,* Kentucky Agricultural Experiment Station Bulletin 588, June 1952.

13. Occasionally, because of peculiar circumstances in the family, a youngster would specialize too exclusively in certain aspects of the work around the homestead, and this often led to unsatisfactory adult adjustment. One Beech Creek housewife, for example, was the oldest of thirteen children and the only girl in her family except for a baby sister. Her task in the family had been to take care of the younger children, and she was confined so exclusively to this task that she never learned to do anything else well. Her neighbors accounted for her inability to fulfill many of the functions of a successful housewife by her overspecialization in her parental family.

14. This was especially obvious in families that had only one son or only one daughter. In such cases marriage or outmigration created a role-vacancy within the family and, since replacements were not available, readjustment of the role content (i.e., work assignments) had to occur.

15. We are using the term "familistic society" in the sense suggested by Pitirim A. Sorokin, Carle C. Zimmerman, and Charles J. Galpin, *A Systematic Source Book in Rural Sociology*, Minneapolis: The University of Minnesota Press, 1931, Vol. I. Chapter 4, pp. 186–259.

16. By "neighborhood" we mean a "real social group—a group of individuals—bound by some ties or bonds—which unite them into one social group in life and not on paper only. These bonds make their lives and behavior closely interdependent, and infuse into their minds, in some form and some degree, feelings of oneness, solidarity, and community of interests." *Ibid.*, p. 307. Or, to put it another way, we mean by neighborhoods what Linton calls "bands," that is, "localized, socially integrated groups of fairly constant membership." Ralph Linton, *The Study of Man*, New York: D. Appleton-Century Company, 1937, p. 210. The importance of the neighborhood, or the band, is well emphasized by Linton's comment that if "we take society to mean a group of individuals who are mutually interdependent, mutually adapted in their attitudes and habitual behavior, and united by a feeling of solidarity," then ". . . the band *is* society as far as most of mankind are concerned." *Ibid.*, p. 219.

17. Sorokin, et. al., *op. cit.*, p. 308.

18. We should mention that there were observable differences in the degree of solidarity manifested by each of these three neighborhoods. The basin neighborhood, for example, was not a strongly integrated group in which people felt great loyalty to the neighborhood itself. As a matter of fact, there was little neighborhood pride, little cooperation in common tasks for the good of the whole group, and considerable conflict and bitterness among the people. Feuding and vicious gossip was not uncommon. A number of families refused to have anything to do with other families in the neighborhood. On the other hand the Laurel neighborhood was on the whole much more tightly integrated and a much more solidary group with "neighborhood spirit" and "neighborhood pride." The Flat Rock neighborhood, in this respect, tended to be more like the Laurel than the basin neighborhood.

How do we account for such differences? Compared with the Laurel neighborhood, the basin neighborhood was larger, both territorially and in population, households were more scattered, two school districts divided the neighborhood, the neighborhood had no church or regular church meetings where adults could come together to discuss neighborhood problems, kinship ties were less extensive and much more distinct, there were a larger number of relative "newcomers," and the social class composition was more diverse.

For further elaboration of these differences, see James S. Brown, *The Social Organization of an Isolated Kentucky Mountain Neighborhood*, unpublished Ph.D. thesis, Harvard University, 1950, pp. 162–170.

## CHAPTER 2

1. Talcott Parsons, "The Kinship System of the Contemporary United States," *American Anthropologist*, 45 (January–March, 1943), pp. 22–38.

2. *Ibid.,* p. 29.

3. Parsons writes that "the economic and social conditions of rural life place more of a premium on continuity of occupation and status from generation to generation than do urban conditions, and hence, especially perhaps among the more solidly established rural population, something approaching LePlay's *famille souche* is not unusual." *Ibid.,* p. 28.

4. "By household is meant all of the persons living together in a domicile who usually reside there; that is, who usually share the same table and sleep in the domicile." W. A. Anderson, *The Composition of Rural Households,* Ithaca, New York: Cornell University Agricultural Experiment Station Bulletin Number 713, 1939, p. 3.

5. For comparative data, see James S. Brown, *The Social Organization of an Isolated Kentucky Mountain Neighborhood,* unpublished Ph.D. thesis, Harvard University, 1950, Table 11, p. 468.

6. See Pitirim A. Sorokin, Carle C. Zimmerman and Charles J. Galpin, *A Systematic Source Book in Rural Sociology,* Minneapolis: The University of Minnesota Press, 1931, Vol. II, pp. 27–33; Horace Miner, *St. Denis: A French-Canadian Parish,* Chicago: The University of Chicago Press, 1939, Chapter 4; Charles P. Loomis, "The Study of the Life Cycle of Families," *Rural Sociology,* 1 (1936), pp. 180–199.

7. Conrad Arensberg and Solon Kimball, *Family and Community in Ireland,* Cambridge, Massachusetts: Harvard University Press, 1940, Chapter 7.

8. Miner, *op. cit.,* Chapter 10.

9. Ideally, marriage partners in this society were not to be related by blood. For a discussion of intermarriage or inbreeding in this area, see James S. Brown, "Social Class, Intermarriage, and Church Membership in a Kentucky Community," *American Journal of Sociology,* 17 (November, 1951), pp. 232–42.

10. For supportive data see Brown, *The Social Organization* ———, *op. cit.,* Table 17.

11. By "conjugal family" is meant the simple family consisting typically of husband, wife, and their unmarried children. It is "conjugal" because it is formed by marriage; this is in contrast to a "consanguine family," a family based on blood relationship. The term "conjugal family" is used here primarily to distinguish this group from the "extended family" or "family group" discussed later. See Ralph Linton, *The Study of Man,* New York: D. Appleton-Century Co., 1937, Chapter 10.

12. Of twenty-one families for which sufficient data were available for accurate judgment, the husband was dominant in fourteen, the wife in seven.

13. There were no instances of such deviation by a husband or wife in the area during the time this study was made, but there was much talk about past cases.

14. For further elaboration of this point see James S. Brown, *The Family Group in a Kentucky Mountain Farming Community,* Kentucky Agricultural Experiment Station Bulletin 588 (June, 1952), pp. 5–10.

15. *Op. cit.,* p. 68.

16. For examples of such instances see Brown, *The Social Organization* ———, *op. cit.,* pp. 228–234.

17. See Brown, "Social Class, Intermarriage, and Church Membership ————,"
*op. cit.*

18. The kinship terminology of Beech Creek was (and is) much the same as that of the United States at large. See Parsons, *op. cit.;* Brown, *The Family Group* ————, *op. cit.,* pp. 5–10. It should be pointed out, however, that in the Beech Creek case, apart from specific terms, such as "second cousin," which described relationships between individuals, there were several more general, inclusive terms which were applied to groups of any given individual's kin. "Generation" and "set" were two kinship terms often used; both referred to groups of people bearing the same family name. Thus, one might refer to the "Brown generation," the "Smith generation," or to different "sets" of Browns, or different "sets" of Smiths.

The term "generation" was used to designate whole groups of kinsfolk bearing the same name and was generally used to refer to all the descendants of one man. It was seldom used to distinguish different groups bearing the same surname.

The term "set" was used: (1) to distinguish different groups of people bearing the same name who were, so far as known, no blood kin at all, and (2) to distinguish different groups bearing the same surname who were known to be kin if relationships were traced back far enough, but whose relationships were not close. "Set," then, was ordinarily employed in referring to contemporaries, unlike the term "generation," which included people sharing a common ancestor but occupying different stages of descent.

Given the intricacies and specificities of kin terminology in Beech Creek, it is no wonder that "kin relationships were very extensive."

19. For a definition of these terms see Brown, *ibid.,* and Parsons, *op. cit.*

20. This suggests one reason for the lesser degree of solidarity among families in the basin neighborhood (noted earlier).

21. No information was available on the kin relationships of the Gamble family with seven other families living in the Beech Creek basin neighborhood.

22. For example, during the period of field work, a man about sixty-five years old, whose wife had died some years before, was forced to break up housekeeping when his daughter-housekeeper married. Since he had a fine farm, he tried to persuade his son-in-law to move onto his farm and live with him. Though he offered generous terms, and the farm was much bigger and better located than that of his son-in-law, the son-in-law refused to move, explaining that if he moved there his father-in-law would be "boss."

23. *Op. cit.,* p. 218.

# CHAPTER 3

1. "Stratification *in its valuational aspect* then is the ranking of units in a social system in accordance with the standards of the common value system." Talcott Parsons, "Revised Approach to Theory of Social Stratification," *Essays in Sociological Theory,* Glencoe, Illinois: The Free Press, 1954, p. 388.

2. For additional examples of informants' comments relating to the class status

of Beech Creek people, see James S. Brown, *Social Organization of an Isolated Kentucky Mountain Neighborhood,* unpublished Ph.D. thesis, Harvard University, 1950, Appendix III, pp. 502–517. Prior to field work, of course, the researcher had been sensitized to the implications of class phenomena and such statements as these by important sociological treatises published at that time. See, for example, Talcott Parsons, "An Analytical Approach to the Theory of Social Stratification," *American Journal of Sociology,* 45 (May, 1940), pp. 841–862; Allison Davis and John Dollard, *Children of Bondage,* Washington, D.C.: American Council of Education, 1940; Allison Davis, Burleigh B. Gardner and Mary R. Gardner, *Deep South,* Chicago: University of Chicago Press, 1941; John Dollard, *Caste and Class in a Southern Town,* New Haven: Yale University Press, 1937.

3. *Ibid.,* p. 850. Parsons goes on to say that "According to this definition the class structure of social systems may differ both in the composition or structure of the effective kinship unit or units which are units of class structure and in the criteria by which such units are differentiated from one another."

4. The membership of social classes according to one of these studies "can be identified empirically upon the basis of either of two types of information: (1) by records of common participation of individuals in non-economic groups, such as in churches, associations, and clubs and at large dances, teas, picnics, weddings, and funerals, and (2) by the verbal expression of individuals of their willingness to associate with other persons in these social relationships." Davis, Gardner, and Gardner, *op. cit.,* p. 238. Or, as Davis and Dollard have said: People are considered to be "of the same class when they normally (1) eat or drink together as a social ritual, (2) freely visit one another's family, (3) talk together intimately in a social clique, or (4) have cross-sexual access to one another, outside of the kinship group." *Op. cit.,* p. 261. See also W. Lloyd Warner and Paul S. Lunt, *The Social Life of a Modern Community,* New Haven: Yale University Press, 1941.

5. Informants, of course, often disagreed in their evaluations of individuals and families, and they varied from the more general rankings particularly when they were evaluating themselves, their kin, close friends, or enemies. But though there were differences, there was also much consensus in the evaluations.

6. The families did not fall into clear-cut groups, nor did the families fall into sharply divided groups when social participation was considered. Myrdal's description of class suits the Beech Creek situation admirably when he says that ". . . it is probably most correct to conceive the class order as a social continuum. In most communities, and certainly in the United States as a whole class differences between the nearest individuals at any point of the scale cannot be easily detected. It is only differences between individuals further away from each other that are easily observable. . . . There are no natural class boundaries." Gunnar Myrdal, *An American Dilemma,* New York: Harper and Brothers, 1944, p. 675.

7. For a more detailed analysis of intermarriage patterns in Beech Creek, see James S. Brown, "Social Class, Intermarriage, and Church Membership in a Kentucky Community," *American Journal of Sociology,* 17 (November, 1951), pp. 232–42.

8. Supporting data are reported by Brown, *Social Organization* ———, *op. cit.,* pp. 279–284, and Table 19, p. 477.

9. *Ibid.,* pp. 285–332.

10. Our intent here is to describe the "ideal types." Let it be understood, however, that as in the case of Davis, Gardner, and Gardner's "Old City," there was in Beech Creek "no strict uniformity in any specific type of behavior but rather a range and a 'modal average'." *Op. cit.,* p. 73.

11. Ralph Barton Perry, *Puritanism and Democracy,* New York: The Vanguard Press, 1944, p. 245.

12. We are using the term "moral" in a very limited sense.

13. Ralph Linton, *The Study of Man,* New York: D. Appleton-Century Company, 1937, p. 115.

14. Davis, Gardner and Gardner, *op. cit.,* pp. 75–76.

15. For a more extensive discussion of this topic, see James S. Brown, *The Family Group in a Kentucky Mountain Farming Community,* Lexington: Kentucky Agricultural Experiment Station, Bulletin 588, June, 1952.

16. Linton, *op. cit.,* p. 201.

17. This situation was similar to that in the Navaho society described by Kluckhohn: "In a society like the Navaho which is competitive and capitalistic, on the one hand, and still familistic on the other, any ideology which has the effect of slowing down economic mobility is decidedly adaptive. . . . The best hope for the preservation of the coherence of Navaho culture and the integrity of the Navaho way of life seems to rest in there being a gradual transition between the familistic type of social organization and a type more nearly resembling our own. A man cannot get rich very fast if he does his full duty by his extended family. Any pattern, such as witchcraft, which tends to discourage the rapid accumulation of wealth makes, therefore, for the survival of the society." Clyde Kluckhohn, *Navaho Witchcraft,* Cambridge, Massachusetts: Peabody Museum of American Archaeology and Ethnology, Harvard University, Volume 23, Number 2, 1944, p. 63.

18. That is, as "an existing group resolves itself into a number of new ones, as descent proceeds from father to son." Conrad Arensberg and Solon Kimball, *Family and Community in Ireland,* Cambridge, Massachusetts: Harvard University Press, 1940, p. 94.

19. This was illustrated, for example, during the illness of Aunt Malinda Brown, the widow of Tom "Splanter" Brown (son of Joshua Brown and brother of Preston, Julius, and Charlie). Aunt Malinda was living at the home of her granddaughter, Mrs. Edward D. (low-class) but kinsfolk of all classes came to visit or to "set up" with her.

20. Clyde Kluckhohn's approach to the task of understanding the cultural ethos was particularly helpful. He argued that a "factor implicit in a variety of diverse phenomena may be generalized as an underlying cultural principle," and that if "observed cultural behavior is to be correctly understood, the categories and presuppositions constituting the implicit culture must be worked out." The observer, he suggested, on the basis of consistencies in thought and action of the people in the society being studied, can determine that society's "set of systematically interrelated implicit themes." See, Clyde Kluckhohn, *Mirror for Man,* New York: Whittlesey House 1949, p. 33. Kluckhohn also pointed out that "the extent, and even the validity, of what is described as a configuration

depends upon the purpose at hand. . . . It may be that in most societies, regardless of whether one is justified in speaking of a single ethos, there are a relatively small number of 'dominant configurations' which have the right of way, as it were, and which tend to bring the more specific configurations under their sway." Clyde Kluckhohn, "Covert Culture and Administrative Problems," *American Anthropologist,* Volume 45, (April-June 1943,) p. 224.

It is obvious that analyses of this sort, and the resultant "themes" that are posited, can be directed toward various levels of abstraction; a number of themes, for example, may be subsumed under a broader premise (a premise of premises, or a pattern of patterns, so to speak). It is clear also that the nomenclature employed, i.e., the word labels assigned to the abstracted pattern, unless derived from a tightly formulated, systematic theory, will be to a certain extent arbitrary.

21. "Every culture," according to Linton, "always has several interests which are of primary importance and which together constitute an integrated system. To select even two or three of these as the focal points for the whole culture configuration probably involves a distortion of the actual condition, but such distortion is requisite to any comprehensible descriptive account." *Op. cit.,* p. 443.

22. "*Familism* is the term used to designate the type of social organization in which all the social relationships and institutions are permeated by and stamped with the characteristics of the family. Familism is the outstanding and fundamental trait in the Gestalt of such a society." P. A. Sorokin, C. C. Zimmerman, and C. J. Galpin, *A Systematic Source Book in Rural Sociology,* Minneapolis: University of Minnesota Press, 1930, Volume II, p. 41. Our discussion of the "familistic" traits of Beech Creek social life follows, in general, the nine indications of familism suggested by them, pp. 41–48.

23. For a more general discussion of the nature of the political institution in the mountain culture, and a more specific analysis of voting patterns in selected mountain counties, see Harry K. Schwarzweller and James S. Brown, "Education as a Cultural Bridge between Eastern Kentucky and the Great Society," *Rural Sociology,* 27 (December, 1962), pp. 363–365.

24. See James S. Brown, "Social Class, Intermarriage, and Church Membership ———," *op. cit.,* pp. 232–242.

25. Perry defines puritanism as "theocratic, congregational-presbyterian, Calvinistic, protestant, medieval Christianity." *Op. cit.,* p. 82.

26. *Ibid.,* p. 255.

27. *Ibid.,* p. 267.

28. *Ibid.,* p. 243.

29. *Ibid.,* p. 302.

30. *Ibid.,* p. 312.

31. See, for example, Harry M. Caudill, *Night Comes to the Cumberlands,* Boston: Little, Brown and Co., 1962.

32. *Op. cit.,* p. 443.

33. *Op. cit.,* p. 363.

34. *Ibid.,* p. 371.

35. But it must also be pointed out that at points these principles conflict,

for, as Myrdal has said, "valuations simply cannot be treated as if they existed on the same plane. . . . Some valuations have general and eternal validity; others have validity only for certain situations." *Op. cit.,* pp. 1027–1028.

## CHAPTER 4

1. For an earlier statement on the central thesis in this chapter, see James S. Brown, Harry K. Schwarzweller, and Joseph J. Mangalam, "Kentucky Mountain Migration and the Stem-family: An American Variation on a Theme by LePlay," *Rural Sociology,* 28, (March, 1963), pp. 48–69. A condensed version is included in Norman W. Bell and Ezra F. Vogel (Editors), *A Modern Introduction to the Family,* Glencoe: The Free Press, 1968.

2. See, for example, Pitirim A. Sorokin, Carle C. Zimmerman, and Charles J. Galpin, *A Systematic Source Book in Rural Sociology,* Minneapolis: The University of Minnesota Press, 1931, Vol. I, Ch. 4, pp. 186–259.

3. For example, in India thousands of Malayalees, caught by very high population density and limited employment opportunities, migrate from their homes in Kerala (Malabar Coast) to such urban areas as Bombay and New Delhi. They live in these cities in close proximity to one another, forming a cultural island within the local society. Their interaction with life in New Delhi, for example, is only segmental, being primarily in their occupational roles. The rest of the time they live a life of their own, their conduct being governed by the norms of the local world of their origin. They send money "home" for the support of their stem-families; they go "home" for marriage; and they are instrumental in bringing streams of Malayalees to New Delhi and in performing supportive functions for the newly arrived Malayalees, both as individuals and families. This is a pattern very similar to the pattern of migration from eastern Kentucky to Ohio.

4. For an account of how the land originally owned by Joshua Johnson (a fictitious name, of course) was divided and subdivided, see James S. Brown, *Social Organization of an Isolated Kentucky Mountain Neighborhood,* unpublished Ph.D. thesis, Harvard University, 1950, pp. 518–525.

5. In the course of field work for the initial study of Beech Creek, the inquiry was expanded to include those families residing along one of the branches of the creek and in two neighborhoods adjoining the Beech Creek basin neighborhood. Although detailed historical records are not available on the population growth of these localities, we know from historical accounts and stories supplied by a number of older residents that their settlement patterns and beginnings of out-migration paralleled that of the basin neighborhood. In the Laurel neighborhood, for example, the first settlers were members of the Andrews family, and this family group held exclusive ownership of the land in that locality until the late 1800's. After 1900, the beginnings of out-migration followed much the same pattern as that of the basin neighborhood. In the interest of accuracy, however, let it be noted that our descriptive account and historical data refer to the "main part of the Beech Creek basin neighborhood."

6. Between 1900 and 1909 twenty-two persons moved away from the basin neighborhood, the majority settling nearby, but three or four left the mountain region entirely. Between 1910 and 1919 forty-five persons left, and available records indicate that thirteen, ten men and three women, were young single people who had migrated out of the region.

7. One story has it that, during this early period when the trend of interregional migration was being set, a newly established paper factory in southern Ohio, in need of a large number of unskilled workers, systematically recruited men from the mountains. A railroad train was sent into the mountain counties and work recruiters for the factory contracted a labor force from around the Beech Creek area. These workers were transported by the train to Ohio and, as the story goes, they became the initial migrant "beach-heads" for scores of kinsfolk who followed them during subsequent years.

8. Of the one hundred sixty-four persons residing in and around the basin of the creek in 1920, only fifty-four were still there in 1942; fifteen had died and ninety-five had moved away. Between 1920 and 1929, sixty-eight persons left, and again a number of them, including two entire families, moved to southern Ohio and Indiana to work. Out-migration slowed down in the depression years from 1930 to 1939, and only five of the twenty-eight people who left went outside of the Mountains; the others moved to neighborhoods nearby. When the nation again armed for war and defense industries boomed, Beech Creek people left in even greater numbers than they had in the previous war period. From January 1, 1940 to July 1, 1942, sixty-six persons moved away from the creek basin, about half going to neighborhoods nearby and half leaving the mountain region entirely, mainly to enter the armed forces or to work in southern Ohio and Indiana.

9. At that time also there were twenty-nine persons in six households living on Fox Branch, which, along with the "original" basin area, comprises the present Beech Creek basin neighborhood. The total population, then, of the 1942 basin neighborhood was one hundred ninety-one persons in thirty-nine households. In addition, there were one hundred thirty-four persons in twenty-eight households in the Laurel neighborhood, and seventy-four persons in twelve households in the Flat Rock neighborhood. These three hundred ninety-nine persons became the "base population" for our 1961 follow-up survey (see Appendix A).

10. By 1961 the heavy out-migration during the preceding two decades was beginning to effect some drastic changes in the age structure of the resident population. In 1942, for example, 18 percent of the population was forty-five years of age or older and 46 percent was under fifteen years; the comparable figures for 1961 were 30 percent and 32 percent respectively. The population of the neighborhoods showed signs of aging.

11. For a more detailed discussion of migration trends in the region, see James S. Brown and George A. Hillery, "The Great Migration, 1940–1960," Chapter 4 in Thomas R. Ford (Editor), *The Southern Appalachian Region: A Survey,* Lexington, Kentucky: The University of Kentucky Press, 1962.

12. The data reported here are from tabulations made by the Department of Rural Sociology, Kentucky Agricultural Experiment Station, University of Kentucky. They are based upon primary data supplied by the United States Bureau of the Census through, for example, *Selected Area Reports, Current Population Reports,* and special tabulations.

13. What happened to the three hundred ninety-nine persons who were living in the Beech Creek locality in 1942? By July 1, 1961, forty-two had died, eighty still resided in the neighborhoods or had returned again after a temporary out-migration, and two hundred seventy-seven were living elsewhere. Thus, only 22.4 percent of the 1942 Beech Creek residents still living were residents of the neighborhoods in 1961. Of the two hundred seventy-seven Beech Creekers residing elsewhere in 1961, sixty-eight were in rural eastern Kentucky neighborhoods or towns, mainly nearby, four were in the military service, three were in prisons or asylums, and the remainder, two hundred two persons, were living in areas outside of eastern Kentucky. The latter included about one hundred forty-five persons in Ohio, twenty-five in Indiana, twenty-three in central and northern Kentucky, and ten widely scattered in other states.

Our figures here refer to the total population of persons who were residing in the Beech Creek area in 1942. For various reasons (see Appendix A) some of these persons were not interviewed in the 1961 follow-up survey. It is important to note, therefore, that data reported in the remainder of this and subsequent chapters are based upon information obtained from the survey population and that, henceforth, when we use the term "Beech Creekers" we are referring specifically to those persons who were included in that survey.

14. For a more detailed analysis of eastern Kentucky migration patterns, see Brown and Hillery, "The Great Migration: 1940-1960," *op. cit.* See also, George A. Hillery, James S. Brown and Gordon DeJong, "Migration Systems of the Southern Appalachians: Some Demographic Observations," *Rural Sociology,* 30, (March, 1965), pp. 33–48.

15. See, for example, Carter L. Goodrich *et al., Migration and Economic Opportunity,* Philadelphia: University of Pennsylvania Press, 1936; Donald J. Bogue, *The Population of the United States,* Glencoe: The Free Press, 1959, Ch. 15: "Internal Migration and Residential Mobility," pp. 375–418; K. M. George, *Association of Selected Economic Factors with Net Migration Rates in the Southern Appalachian Region, 1935–1957,* unpublished M.A. thesis, University of Kentucky, June, 1961.

16. Samuel A. Stouffer, "Intervening Opportunities: A Theory Relating to Mobility and Distance," *American Sociological Review,* 5, pp. 845–867.

17. For, as Lively and Taeuber point out, the "evaluation of relative opportunities is essentially a subjective matter." C. E. Lively and Conrad Taeuber, *Rural Migration in the United States,* Research Monograph 19, Works Progress Administration, U.S. Government Printing Office, Washington, D.C., 1939, p. 79.

18. On this point see also, for example, Donald J. Bogue and Margaret Jarman Hagood, *Differential Migration in the Corn and Cotton Belts: A Pilot Study of the Selectivity of Interstate Migration to Cities from Non-metropolitan Areas,* Scripps Foundation Studies in Population Distribution, No. 6, Miami University, Oxford, Ohio, 1953, especially pp. 28–30, 37, 99–100.

19. Schultz notes that the "post-war behavior of the economy clearly indicates that the *rate* of off-farm migration is highly sensitive to changes in unemployment that have characterized these post-war booms and recessions in business. . . . When 5, 6 or 7 percent of the labor force is unemployed, the adjustment process under consideration is brought to a halt; on the other hand, when unemployment declines to 3 or 4 percent off-farm migration becomes large." T. W. Schultz, "A Policy to Redistribute Losses from Economic Progress," University of Chicago

Office of Agricultural Economics, Research Paper No. 6008, October 31, 1960, pp. 13–14.

20.   Peter H. Rossi, "Why Families Move," in *The Language of Social Research,* edited by Paul F. Lazarsfeld and Morris Rosenberg, Glencoe: The Free Press, pp. 457–468.

21.   We would also regard individuals whose parents, in-laws, spouse, children, or other close kin are or have been residents of that area as having "roots" there.

22.   H. J. Habakkuk, "Family Structure and Economic Change in Nineteenth-Century Europe," Ch. 13 in Norman W. Bell and Ezra F. Vogel, *A Modern Introduction to the Family,* Glencoe: The Free Press, 1960, p. 167.

23.   *Ibid.,* p. 168.

24.   Conrad M. Arensberg and Solon T. Kimball, *Family and Community in Ireland,* Cambridge, Massachusetts: Harvard University Press, 1940, pp. 156–157.

25.   Sorokin *et al., op. cit.,* Vol. II, p. 41.

26.   The data reported in these tables vary slightly from data reported in Brown *et al.,* "Kentucky Mountain Migration . . . ," *op. cit.* In that article we were referring to a total enumeration of Beech Creekers, whereas here we are reporting on the *study population.* In any case, the patterns are essentially alike.

27.   One should recall that "family groups" consisted in the main of families of old parents and their adult children or of adult siblings and their grown children's families. The composition of these groups was determined, however, not merely by ascertaining kin relationships, but by considering also the groups of kin which had the closest social relationships. Thus, a conjugal family related by blood to a number of other families in the neighborhood was considered to belong to that family group with which it, as a family, had the strongest social bonds.

28.   Among the remaining members of the Andrews-Barnett family group: four had moved to neighborhoods near Beech Creek, two were in another part of Kentucky, two had migrated to City A in Ohio, one had located in X-town, and three were in other states.

29.   In order to utilize to full advantage all of the data available to us (and because of the small number of cases involved in this analysis) we are here referring to *all* Beech Creek migrants rather than simply to the study population. Our data here are accurate even though they may appear inconsistent in minor ways with data reported in previous tables.

30.   Carle C. Zimmerman and Merle E. Frampton, *Family and Society,* New York: D. Van Nostrand Company, 1935.

31.   *Ibid.,* p. 272.

32.   Frederic LePlay, *Les ouvriers européens,* 2nd Ed., 6 volumes, Paris: Tours A. Mame et fils, 1878; see also Frederic LePlay, *The Organization of Labor,* translated by G. Emerson, Philadelphia: Claxton, Remsen and Haffelfinger, 1872. For a discussion of LePlay's work, see Pitirim A. Sorokin, *Contemporary Sociological Theories,* New York and London: Harper and Brothers, 1928, Ch. 2, pp. 63–98.

33.   For LePlay's biography, see: Dorothy Herbertson, "The Life of Frederic

LePlay," Ledbury, Herfordshire, England: LePlay House Press, 1950, which is a reprint of Section 2, Vol. 38 (1946) of the *American Sociological Review*.

34. Sorokin, *Contemporary Sociological Theories, op. cit.,* p. 39, notes that LePlay realized "an isolated individual cannot constitute a social phenomenon." This is precisely why we contend that a great deal more could be learned about the process of migration if we focus our attention on the family as a basic social unit in that process.

35. *Op. cit.,* p. 98.

36. *Ibid.,* p. 47.

37. *Ibid.,* p. 286.

38. *Ibid.,* p. 286.

39. Bogue and Hagood, *op. cit.,* p. 37, note that: "This concept of the lonely migrant in the city, living in a large rooming house and slowly suffering personality deterioration because of isolation, could apply to only a very small part of the migrant population, and probably to a rather select part. If the data for the present study are at all typical of migration generally, the much more usual pattern is that the young migrant sets up his own household at an earlier age than non-migrants of his own age, both in the population at the place of origin and at the destination, that he lives with a relative, or that he is a lodger in a private home."

In support of this conclusion, see also Albert J. Reiss, Jr., "Rural-Urban and Status Differences in Interpersonal Contacts," *The American Journal of Sociology,* LXV (2) (Sept., 1959), pp. 182–195; and Lyle L. Shannon, "Effects of Occupational and Residential Adjustment of Rural Migrants," a paper read at the Conference on Labor Mobility and Population in Agriculture, November 8–10, 1960, Iowa State University, Ames, Iowa, p. 7.

40. Sharp and Axelrod, for instance, found that mutual aid among friends and relatives is widespread in Detroit and, though there is a difference in this phenomenon between natives and migrants, 66 percent of their migrant sample reported help given or received from friends or relatives. Harry Sharp and Morris Axelrod, "Mutual Aid Among Relatives in an Urban Population," in *Principles of Sociology,* Freedman *et al.,* New York: Henry Holt, 1956, pp. 433–439.

Smith, in his study of migrants in Indianapolis, concludes that "one of the primary functions performed by friends and relatives involves the dissemination of information about urban opportunities." Eldon D. Smith, "Migration and Adjustment Experiences of Rural Migrant Workers in Indianapolis," unpublished Ph.D. thesis, University of Wisconsin, 1953, p. 284.

This observation has been made also about Southern White migrants in Chicago. See William R. Simon, "The Southern White Migrant in the Metropolis," a paper read at the Social Science Research Institute, University of Chicago, May, 1961.

41. Adapted from J. J. Mangalam, *Human Migration,* Lexington: University of Kentucky Press, 1968.

42. Therefore, we would argue, if any Beech Creekers have migrated in this sense, then the "true" out-migrants are probably those who have moved to places outside eastern Kentucky.

43. These terms should not be confused with Linton's use of the terms "donor

and receiving societies" in reference to the process of cultural diffusion. We are referring to the system that sends out migrants and the system that receives or absorbs migrants as the "donor-recipient subsystems" whereas, following Linton's usage, one would generally think of the Beech Creek neighborhoods as the receiving society vis-a-vis the diffusion of cultural traits from the Great Society. See Ralph Linton, *The Study of Man*, New York: D. Appleton-Century Company, 1937, Chap. 19.

44. For the derivation of this conceptualization of adjustment, see Joseph J. Mangalam, "A Reconsideration of the Notion of Adjustment: An Exploration," paper read at the Southern Agricultural Workers Conference and published in the *Proceedings*, 1962.

45. James Sydney Slotkin, *From Field to Factory*, Glencoe, Illinois: The Free Press, 1960.

## CHAPTER 5

1. In this and subsequent chapters we rely upon data obtained from a 1961 follow-up survey of the Beech Creek people (see Appendix A for a more detailed explanation). Our *study population* includes two hundred seventy-one individuals, of which sixty-eight were (1961) residents in the Beech Creek neighborhoods, forty-two in nearby neighborhoods of eastern Kentucky, and one hundred sixty-one in areas outside of eastern Kentucky. Because 85 percent of the total base population and over 90 percent of the former Beech Creekers residing outside of eastern Kentucky were interviewed, the study population can be regarded as a fairly reliable representation of the base population, i.e., of persons who were resident in Beech Creek in 1942.

2. Of forty-one Beech Creekers who had never moved away from the Beech Creek locality, twenty-three had, nevertheless, changed their residence at one time or another. Residential movement within the neighborhoods was prompted in many respects by similar situational circumstances as movement from Beech Creek to other neighborhoods nearby. In short, Beech Creekers, even those who remained in the mountains, were a residentially restless population.

3. Nearly all the individuals in this study population were born and reared in Beech Creek or neighborhoods nearby. Only seven persons were born outside of eastern Kentucky, generally to Beech Creek families temporarily residing in Ohio. Nevertheless, by 1942, about 14 percent had lived for periods of six months or longer in areas outside of the mountain region, which, in almost all cases, was southern Ohio. Furthermore, over 21 percent of the Beech Creekers living within eastern Kentucky in 1961, as compared with only nine percent living outside eastern Kentucky, had experienced such a migration prior to 1942.

These simple facts tend to support our impressions that interregional migration was a traditional pattern for Beech Creek people, that some ties had already existed between persons in the area of origin and in the areas of destination, and that some knowledge about the recipient system (i.e., the urban industrial setting) and the cultural contact situation (i.e., the institutional expectations at the place of destination) was present in the donor system (i.e., the traditionalistic social organization of the Beech Creek neighborhoods) prior to the initiation of the 1942 study.

4. See Harry K. Schwarzweller, *Sociocultural Origins and Migration Patterns of Young Men from Eastern Kentucky,* Lexington, Kentucky: Kentucky Agricultural Experiment Station Bulletin 685, December, 1963, p. 22.

5. For a comprehensive discussion of this point, see J. J. Mangalam, *Human Migration,* Lexington, Kentucky: University of Kentucky Press, 1968.

6. The row categories in this table refer to the number of migrations from eastern Kentucky by individuals in the study population during the two decades; our temporal criterion here is one month or longer continuous residence outside the region. Three males who had been in the military service, yet had continued their legal residence in eastern Kentucky, had not moved away from the region for civilian reasons during the twenty years, and were still living in the area in 1961, are included under the category labeled "continuous residence." In the case of persons residing within the region in 1961, "two moves out" means they also had moved back to the mountains twice; the same category, of course, in the case of persons residing outside the region in 1961, means they had moved back to the mountains only once.

We call those persons who were living within the region "present non-migrants," and those who were living outside the region "present migrants." Under this division, we introduce the big move criterion.

The first column refers to persons who never resided for six months or longer outside the region during the period under consideration. The second column refers to persons who had made at least one such big move out of the region since 1942 but had returned; less than one-fourth of these people reported other migrations. The third column refers to those persons who made a big move out of the region, but then moved back to the mountains only to migrate out again at a later date; a third of them reported "three or more moves out." The fourth column refers to persons who never moved back to eastern Kentucky after once having made a big move.

7. Our information was derived from an examination of the specific case histories of individuals that were located in Table 5.1 (especially columns one and four) as "deviant cases."

8. In many respects, this pattern is similar to what the Germans call "auf die Wanderschaft."

9. It may be of interest to note that twenty-seven persons who had moved out of the region between 1942–61 were back, living in Beech Creek by 1961; all but one had resided in Ohio prior to returning, almost all (twenty-three) had lived outside eastern Kentucky for six months or longer, and almost all had returned to Beech Creek shortly after the end of World War II when jobs became scarce in Ohio.

10. A third of the initial migrations were in spring and a third in the fall. There was some recall problem, of course, in soliciting this information; of two hundred thirty migrants from the neighborhoods, eighteen could not remember the season; of one hundred ninety-four migrants from the region, six could not remember. In both sets of data, however, the pattern of response was similar.

11. Of those Beech Creekers who had moved to another community after their first big move out of eastern Kentucky (N = 97), over 60 percent had accumulated two or more years of residence in the community where they were living at the time of our survey.

12. At this point, to aid the reader who may be slightly confused and perhaps even overwhelmed by the various facts, here is a concise review: There are two hundred seventy-one persons in the study population. Of these, forty-one persons never moved away from Beech Creek and thirty-six persons moved away to nearby neighborhoods but never out of the region. Thus, one hundred ninety-four Beech Creekers made a big move, and of these, fifty persons moved first to nearby neighborhoods before moving out, while one hundred forty-four persons moved directly out of the region from Beech Creek. By 1961, sixty-eight persons in the study population were living in the original neighborhoods, and the twenty-seven persons who, therefore, had returned were all at one time or another migrants from the region.

13. In those cases (N = 97) where the individual's community of residence in 1961 was not the same as the area of destination at the time of the first big move (excluding migrants who returned to eastern Kentucky), over 44 percent said they moved there because it was "a better place to live," and over 46 percent said they moved there either "to get work," or to be with a spouse who needed to move elsewhere for employment reasons.

14. Based on responses to the question: "Who had the most influence in making this final decision?"

15. In many cases, however, as we shall demonstrate in the next section, migration from eastern Kentucky by a Beech Creek family was preceded by a "trial-and-error" work visit to the area of destination on the part of the principal breadwinner; two-thirds of the cases of moving "alone" were males.

16. When youngsters migrate they invariably accompany parents and are, therefore, a part of that migration unit and a subsequent member of that household in the area of destination. This, in fact, was the situation in 86 percent of the cases of Beech Creekers who were under sixteen years of age at the time of migration from the region. We would also assume that migrants who were very young when they moved would have great difficulty in recalling facts about the event and, hence, in supplying reliable information about it. For these reasons, the younger migrants were eliminated from many phases of our inquiry.

17. We must call attention to our delineation of an appropriate study population for this phase of the inquiry. As noted earlier, only 28.4 percent of the total Beech Creek study population had *not* made a "big move" out of the eastern Kentucky mountain region at any time between 1942 and 1961. These "permanent" residents of Appalachia, many of whom still resided in the Beech Creek neighborhoods in 1961, were excluded from the analysis.

Of the one hundred ninety-four persons who had experienced a migration, 34 percent (sixty-six cases) subsequently returned to the mountains. Many of them (50 percent), however, migrated out again during this period so that, by 1961, 83 percent (one hundred sixty-one cases) of the one hundred ninety-four "out-migrants" were residentially located in places outside eastern Kentucky. For our purposes, nevertheless, given the obvious difficulty of taking into account the temporal dimension of this phenomenon, i.e., the year when a migrant left, we shall concern ourselves with the total "big move" population, regardless of place of residence in 1961. This is a useful exploratory procedure, but one should bear in mind that we are treating a historical process as an "event" and, therefore, one must exercise caution in the interpretation of findings.

18. Of course, they themselves may have been head of that household, or, in the case of a female migrant, the spouse, or, depending upon the specific circumstances, one of the unmarried children.

19. Some migrants (15 percent) were drawn from incomplete nuclear or incomplete extended family situations; i.e., where the household head's spouse was absent. This was more common among females, for often the husband preceded his wife and family to the area of destination. Occasionally (10 percent), the migrant had been a member of a joint-family household; i.e., where two or more complete nuclear families resided together in the same household. This situation usually had represented a temporary resolution of a housing problem as, for example, where a newly married young couple were living with a parental family until they could acquire the means to set up their own household. In some instances (only 12 percent), the migrant had been involved in an extended family situation of one kind or another, i.e., where the household included, besides a complete nuclear family, one or more other persons who did not constitute a second nuclear family (nor were they members of the immediate family).

20. On this point, see Harry K. Schwarzweller, "Parental Family Ties and Social Integration of Rural to Urban Migrants," *Journal of Marriage and the Family,* 26 (November, 1964), pp. 410–416.

21. Individual cards, containing the appropriate information on each case as well as any information that might help in the interpretation of his or her pattern of migration, were sorted by hand. In effect, we sacrificed efficiency for the sake of validity (i.e., we wanted to be certain that any additional knowledge we had about each individual case was brought to bear in describing the patterns).

22. For a married man with children who migrated alone into a rooming house situation, in six out of seven cases he returned after about a year. If he migrated alone but joined kinsfolk, he returned in only one out of seven cases.

23. See J. J. Mangalam, *Human Migration,* Lexington, Kentucky: University of Kentucky Press, 1968. See also J. J. Mangalam and Harry K. Schwarzweller, "General Theory in the Study of Migration: Current Needs and Difficulties," *International Migration Review,* 3 (Fall, 1968), pp. 3–18.

# CHAPTER 6

1. The data reported here refer to one hundred thirty-eight migrant families. Information was supplied by either the male head or principal homemaker of a family.

2. We are using the word "ghetto" in its economic sense. Historically, of course, the term refers to an area of a city in which members of a minority group were compelled to live. In contemporary usage, as Downs explains, "The word retains this meaning of geographic constraint, but now refers to two different kinds of constraining forces. In its *racial* sense, a ghetto is an area to which members of an ethnic minority, particularly Negroes, are residentially restricted by social, economic, and physical pressures from the rest of society. In this meaning, a ghetto can contain wealthy and middle-income residents as well as poor ones. In its *economic* sense, a ghetto is an area in which poor people are compelled to live because they cannot afford better accommodations. In this meaning, a ghetto contains many poor people, regardless of race or color." Anthony Downs, "Alternative Futures for the American Ghetto," *Daedalus* 97 (Fall, 1968), pp. 1331–1378.

3. Of the thirty-nine persons who returned, 68 percent moved back to the Beech Creek neighborhoods. About a third of the returned migrants feel that in making this decision the influence of kinsfolk had been "very important."

4. For example, we asked the migrants whom they would turn to for help in the event of certain kinds of crises, such as: a serious illness in the immediate family, destruction of their home by fire, a member of the immediate family getting into serious trouble with the police, serious marital difficulties developing between the husband and wife, and having to find a job or wanting to change to some other kind of work. A Beech Creeker, we found, would rarely look for help from friends or neighbors in such situations. Community agencies and professional help are, of course, sought out for certain purposes. In the event of illness, one looks to a doctor, and in the event of fire, one looks to the fire department and then to insurance. But marital difficulties and finding a new job are generally interpreted as problems one must cope with himself. Yet family and kin play an important role throughout, especially in those kinds of crises such as serious illness and the aftermath of fire, where an individual knows he cannot cope with the problems solely on his own. There the family performs a supportive function, supplementing the functions performed by various community agencies.

5. Agricultural economists often talk about the "sponging effect" of low-income areas in absorbing surplus industrial manpower in periods of economic depression. One wonders about the morality of that thesis as well as, in the light of our findings, its feasibility as a practical solution to economic mismanagement.

6. The median size of the Beech Creek migrant household is 3.5 persons and the median number of children in a household who are less than fifteen years of age is approximately one (that is, slightly over half of the migrant family-households have either none or only one child). In 85.5 percent of the cases the household is a complete nuclear family unit. In most of the other cases (8.7 percent) it can be classed as an extended family unit. The latter, for example, might include a married daughter who lives with her parents while her husband is in the service.

7. In about two-thirds of the cases (of either the male heads or homemakers) there is at least one sibling living close-by within ten miles. And in about three-fourths of the cases there is at least one sibling living back in the mountains. Hence, the two ends of this migration system are bound together through kinship ties. Visiting contact within the sibling network, including those far apart as

well as close-by, averages about once a month or more often in nearly two-thirds of the cases. Hence, interactional bonds are relatively strong.

8. Of the families who had *not* visited in eastern Kentucky during the previous year, over two-thirds claimed to be planning a trip during the coming year. Hence, only about 6 percent of the Beech Creek migrant families seem to have severed all visiting obligations; most of these are the families of older people whose parents are deceased.

9. We found that on holidays and vacations 34 percent of the migrants usually undertake visits to the mountains, 11 percent usually visit family and friends nearby, 13 percent usually make sight-seeing-type trips, 11 percent go fishing, hunting, etc., and 31 percent stay around home.

10. To obtain this information we employed interviewing procedures from Charles C. Hughes, Marc-Adelhard Tremblay, Robert N. Rapport, and Alexander H. Leighton, *People of Cove and Woodlot*, New York: Basic Books, Inc., 1960.

11. We asked the migrants: "What people do you visit with most around here? (Not immediate or parental family.)" After these persons were identified (the migrant was requested to specify at least three), we proceeded to ask about their characteristics. We found that only 12.5 percent of the migrants could not specify three people, and only 3.8 percent could not name one. Of all the persons mentioned by male migrants, 63.3 percent were eastern Kentuckians. Of all those mentioned by female migrants, 38.4 percent were eastern Kentuckians.

12. Or, to put it another way, only 29 percent of the men but 47 percent of the women figured that they had *less* than three such close friends. (Since our questioning procedures were similar, the reader might be interested in comparing these findings with those from the Stirling County Study, Hughes, *et. al., op. cit.*)

13. For some descriptive information, see Earl D. C. Brewer, "Religion and the Churches," in *The Southern Appalachian Region: A Survey,* ed. Thomas R. Ford, Lexington: University of Kentucky Press, 1962; and W. D. Weatherford and Earl D. C. Brewer, *Life and Religion in Southern Appalachia,* New York: Friendship Press, 1962.

14. These statements are from a fundamentalism scale developed by Ralph E. Lamar, "Fundamentalism and Selected Social Factors in the Southern Appalachian Region," unpublished master's thesis, University of Kentucky, 1962. See also Thomas R. Ford, "Status, Residence and Fundamentalist Religious Beliefs in the Southern Appalachians," *Social Forces* 39 (1960), pp. 41–49.

15. We asked Beech Creek migrants whether they believe that "God is more pleased when people try to get ahead or when they are satisfied with what they have?" Only 26 percent of the males and 30 percent of the females feel that He is more pleased "when they try to get ahead." They reason that "God wants us to be our best" and that "you're supposed to use your talents." The majority of Beech Creekers, however, feel that God wants them to be satisfied with what they have. They, too, seem to base their reasoning upon Biblical authority; but in these cases we note an element of "fear of wrong-doing" which, if we interpret our data correctly, may be a remnant of Calvinism. In other words, regardless of the position taken, legitimation of the belief is derived from a literalistic interpretation of God's Word. Previous sociological research

suggests that this extreme fundamentalistic-type orientation may have important behavioral consequences. See, for example, Thomas R. Ford (1960), *ibid.*

16. For an additional note on the traditionalism of eastern Kentucky voting patterns, see Harry K. Schwarzweller and James S. Brown, "Education as a Cultural Bridge between Eastern Kentucky and the Great Society," *Rural Sociology* 27 (December, 1962), pp. 364–365.

17. However, of those migrants who had voted in eastern Kentucky prior to migrating, only about 15 percent have actually switched party affiliation. Therefore, this cannot account for the observed difference. Perhaps it can be explained by the fact that most of the "Democrat" families in Beech Creek have moved out over the years (political selectivity of rural migration!). Or perhaps many migrants who were young when they first migrated have abandoned family tradition and are voting "Democrat" (political socialization outside of the kin network!).

18. For an interesting African analogy to the Beech Creek case, see Josef Gugler, "Life in a Dual System," East African Institute of Social Research Conference Papers, January, 1965.

19. Only about 4 percent of the migrants do not especially like the community they are presently living in, and their dissatisfaction usually has to do with the general location and physical environment of that particular locality. If they like the community, and most do, it is because of the friends they have made and the pleasant neighbors, as well as the reasonably attractive physical surroundings and the adequacy of services to satisfy their needs. In almost all cases, of course, the evaluation is made vis-a-vis the community situation enjoyed by other members of their family group, whether they live in Ohio or in eastern Kentucky. But we cannot be certain what the individual's frame of reference was in referring to "this community"; we tried to talk about a locality larger than neighborhood, such as "this city" or "this part of the city," but even so a definitional vagueness remains.

20. The construction of a psychological anxiety scale and an anomia (despair) scale are discussed in a later chapter. If we focus on the extreme conditions as measured by these scales (with a score of 11 or more out of a possible 15 points being considered "highly anomic," and a score of 6 out of a possible 6 points being considered "high" on anxiety), we find that among the migrants: 54% of the males and 54% of the females are anomic; 4% of the males and 18% of the females manifest symptoms of anxiety. Among Beech Creekers in eastern Kentucky: 74% of the males and 70% of the females are anomic; 18% of the males and 32% of the females manifest symptoms of anxiety.

21. The jobs held by these male migrants prior to moving out of the mountains were as follows (N = 82): full-time farm work, thirty-five cases; farming and some occasional non-farm work, two; farming and some occasional work in the mines, four; full-time work in the coal mines, three; full-time non-farm work, fourteen; unemployed, unable to find work, one; unable or too young to work, seventeen; no information, six.

22. Of the eighty-two men, thirty-six had been in the military service but only five had attended special military schools which related to their present occupations.

23. Consider, for example, the following comparisons on sources of family income other than through employment:

% Beech Creek families reporting some income during 1960 from sources other than employment.

| Source of income | Migrant families (N = 133) | Families in eastern Kentucky (N = 64) |
|---|---|---|
| Social security: | 3.6% | 22.2% |
| Welfare: | 2.9 | 42.2 |
| Worker's benefits: | 18.8 | 3.2 |
| Veteran's benefits: | 15.9 | 26.6 |
| Other non-work sources: | 12.3 | 6.2 |

24. In 1959, the median family income for the United States was $5,600, while for the Southern Appalachian Region it was $3,882 and for Eastern Kentucky it was only $2,609. These facts were derived from U.S. Census data. See James S. Brown, "Population and Migration Changes in Appalachia," (mimeo) paper prepared for Rural Appalachia in Transition Conference, Morgantown, West Virginia, October 1967, pp. 42–45. For comparative data, see also Ralph J. Ramsey, *Forms and Scope of Poverty in Kentucky,* Lexington: University of Kentucky Research Development Series No. 10.

25. Our interviewing procedures were borrowed from Gerald Gurin, Joseph Veroff, and Sheila Feld, *Americans View Their Mental Health,* New York: Basic Books, 1960.

26. *Ibid.*

27. In general, the pattern of present sources of happiness of Beech Creekers in eastern Kentucky was very much like that of the migrants except that they were less inclined to mention job and work and more inclined to mention health.

## CHAPTER 7

1. We are indebted to M. J. Crowe for much of the information and many of the ideas drawn into this chapter, and we appreciate his permission to use these materials. See, Martin Jay Crowe, *The Occupational Adaptation of a Selected Group of Eastern Kentuckians in Southern Ohio,* unpublished Ph.D. dissertation, University of Kentucky, 1964.

2. There exists much confusion over the meanings and proper usages of terms such as adaptation, adjustment, and accommodation. For the exploratory purposes of this chapter we have defined "occupational adaptation" as a process by which an individual approaches, evaluates, and accepts a new occupational role. Our

definition was intended as a research guide, not as a conceptual clarification. See Crowe, *ibid.*, pp. 23–26, and Joseph J. Mangalam, "A Reconsideration of the Notion of Adjustment," *Proceedings,* Southern Agricultural Workers Conference, Jacksonville, Florida, 1962.

3. In order to supplement information collected earlier by survey, focused interviews of some length were conducted during the summer of 1962 with a selected group (N = 30) of male migrants from Beech Creek who were residing in or near City A in Ohio. Almost all of these men were married and had children. The median length of time they had lived outside eastern Kentucky was twelve years with a range of from five to twenty years. The median years of schooling they had completed was eight; their median annual income in 1961 was $5500. Two were unemployed at the time. Most of the others were employed in factories, at skilled levels ranging from "packer" to "finish-grinder" to "precision inspector." These men, in general, were fairly representative of the male migrant population from Beech Creek.

A series of interviews were also obtained during the spring of 1963 from a number of industrial relations personnel, foremen, and union representatives in the various factories where many of the Beech Creekers worked. As informants, they provided additional information about the characteristic and stereotyped "traits" of eastern Kentuckians within the industrial work situation.

4. James S. Slotkin, *From Field to Factory,* Glencoe, Illinois: The Free Press, 1960, pp. 99–100. Slotkin also describes the "permanently distressed" migrant as one who perceives the donor system as adequate in some respects but permanently inadequate in others. Hence, migration tends to be of a cyclical nature with the individual leaving and returning to the area of origin at specified times, year after year. This type of migrant did not exist in the Beech Creek case.

5. For example; operator of a potato peeling machine, general laborer, packer, can stacker, sawman, supply clerk, press helper, finish cleaner, staple machine operator, and assemblers of various kinds.

6. Eugene V. Schneider, *Industrial Sociology,* New York: McGraw-Hill, 1957, p. 305.

7. The best documented exception are members of the International Typographical Union. See Seymour M. Lipset, Martin Trow, and James Coleman, *Union Democracy,* New York: Anchor Books, Doubleday and Co., Inc., 1962.

8. See, for example, Robert Hoppock, *Job Satisfaction,* New York: Harper, 1935; Joseph Shister and L. G. Reynolds, *Job Horizons: A Study of Job Satisfaction and Labor Mobility,* New York: Harper, 1949; Nancy C. Morse and S. Weiss, "The Function and Meaning of Work and Job," *American Sociological Review,* 20 (April, 1955); Gladys L. Palmer, "Attitudes Toward Work in an Industrial Community," *American Journal of Sociology,* 63 (July, 1957). See also: J. C. Brown, *The Social Psychology of Industry,* Baltimore: English Pelican Edition, 1954, pp. 190–191, who points out that American research supports the generalization that: "Even under the existing conditions, which are far from satisfactory, most workers like their jobs. Every survey of workers' attitudes which has been carried out, no matter in what industry, indicates that this is so."

9. Drucker, for example, argues that "Satisfaction as such is a measureless

and meaningless word." See Peter Drucker, *The Practice of Management,* New York: Harper, 1954, p. 303.

10. This is *not* to say that behavioral deviancy is not associated with migration, nor that marital discord, crime, alcoholism, mental illness, and other signs of unmanaged tension are absent in migrant neighborhoods and "ghettos." On the contrary, there is much evidence to suggest that migration fosters the kinds of social conditions and situational circumstances from which deviant behaviors emerge. What we are saying is that where the family-kin network intervenes as a stabilizing instrumentality, as it did in the Beech Creek case, the individual migrant is more likely to remain anchored in a normative system which discourages deviancies. This is not a new idea: see, for example, Frederic Le Play, *Les ouvriers européens,* 2nd ed., 6 volumes, Paris: Tours A. Mame et fils, 1878.

## CHAPTER 8

1. A more detailed version of this chapter was published earlier. See Harry K. Schwarzweller and James S. Brown, "Social Class Origins, Rural-Urban Migration, and Economic Life Chances: A Case Study," *Rural Sociology,* 23 (March, 1967), pp. 5–19.

2. To determine whether there were differences in the migration patterns of persons from the three social class groupings, we focused our attention on one particular move—the Beech Creeker's initial "permanent" migration away from eastern Kentucky after 1942. Our subsequent analyses excluded those who did not move away from the mountains during the period 1942–61, as well as those whose social class position in Beech Creek was not determined in the original study. Hence, a total of one hundred seventy-one migrants is considered here.

3. We do not claim to have established a causal relationship between social class and time of migration. Our discussion of the observed concomitant variation is offered as a plausible explanation consistent with our knowledge of the Beech Creek case. Nevertheless, even in this case a number of other factors *may* account for differences in the timing of migration, e.g., differences in age, stage in family life cycle, and resources to actually carry out the migration.

4. For another study which focused on the differences in economic life chances between young male migrants and nonmigrants from eastern Kentucky, see Harry K. Schwarzweller, "Education, Migration, and Economic Life Chances of Male Entrants to the Labor Force from a Low-Income Rural Area," *Rural Sociology,* 29 (June, 1964).

5. Since our main concern was with the socioeconomic level or achievement of migrants in the urban, industrial opportunity structure, migrants who returned to eastern Kentucky were excluded from our analysis as were those for whom we had no information about social class position in the original Beech Creek neighborhoods. Hence, one hundred forty-four migrants are dealt with here.

6. We used the Cornell nine-item material level of living scale. See Robert A. Danley and Charles E. Ramsey, *Standardization and Application of a Level of Living Scale for Farm and Nonfarm Families,* Ithaca, N. Y.: Cornell University Agricultural Experiment Station Memoir 362 (July, 1959). The distributions on each of these items was reported earlier.

7. An important methodological correction was made in order to check the validity of our findings. We are dealing with a total migration universe and a small number of cases. Our methodology, then, becomes greatly complicated by various kinds of unique control problems, such as the choice of a proper (i.e., valid) "unit of analysis." For example, some Beech Creekers were married to other Beech Creekers prior to migration, a few married after 1942, and many married persons from "outside." The problem, then, is to reconcile a comparison between social class origin, a concept or attribute linked to the family, with socioeconomic status, a similarly linked "family attribute." We attempted to resolve such difficulties by the following procedure:

Our focus of analysis shifted to the Beech Creek migrant's family-household in the area of destination. We assumed, and the assumption was checked for validity insofar as possible, that only in rare instances did a Beech Creeker marry across class lines. Where the male head of a household was included in the study population, his social class origin is ascribed to that household. Where a homemaker had married outside the study population, her social class origin is ascribed to that household because we have no information about the social class origins of the male head; in most cases, however, the husband was an eastern Kentuckian, and the assumption of comparability, we would argue, is valid. In those cases where the husband was not an eastern Kentuckian, we assumed that social class differences in origin are not very great.

Using the Cornell level of living scale, as before, we found a very high correlation between the social class origins of Beech Creek migrant families and their socioeconomic status in the areas of destination. These findings are reported by Schwarzweller and Brown, "Social Class Origins ———," *op. cit.*

8. We used the North-Hatt Scale to classify migrant families on the basis of the household head's occupational prestige. See "Jobs and Occupations: A Popular Evaluation," in Reinhard Bendix and Seymour M. Lipset, *Class, Status and Power,* Glencoe, Ill.: The Free Press, 1953, pp. 411–426.

Our analyses yielded similar findings, though the relationships were not as marked as for level of living.

9. On this point see also Talcott Parsons, "An Analytical Approach to the Theory of Social Stratification," *American Journal of Sociology,* 45 (May, 1940), p. 850.

## CHAPTER 9

1. In formulating a perspective on this problem, there are a number of useful major works available to the student of migration. See, for example, William I. Thomas and Florian Znaniecki, *The Polish Peasant in Europe and America,* rev. ed., New York: Dover Publications and Kegan Paul, 1954; James S. Slotkin,

*From Field to Factory,* New York: The Free Press, 1960; Jerzy Zubrzycki, *Settlers of the Latrobe Valley,* Canberra: The Australian National University, 1964. Furthermore, especially in recent years, there have been numerous articles addressed to this phenomenon published in the various social science journals. See, for example, Eugene Litwak, "Geographic Mobility and Extended Family Cohesion," *American Sociological Review,* 25 (June, 1960), pp. 385–394; Marvin B. Susman and Lee Burchinal, "Kin Family Network: Unheralded Structure in Current Conceptualization of Family Functioning," *Marriage and Family Living,* 24 (August, 1962), pp. 231–240; Allan D. Coult and Robert W. Habenstein, "The Study of Extended Kinship in Urban Society," *Sociological Quarterly,* 3 (April, 1962), pp. 141–145; Harry K. Schwarzweller, "Parental Ties and Social Integration of Rural to Urban Migrants," *Journal of Marriage and the Family,* 26 (November, 1964), pp. 410–416; Felix M. Berado, "Kinship Interaction and Migrant Adaptation in an Aerospace-Related Community," *Journal of Marriage and the Family,* 28 (August, 1966), pp. 296–304.

2. We conceptualize adjustment as "A dynamic state in which the actors in a given meaningful interactional system are able to live in relation to other members of their significant membership group, satisfying their basic needs, fulfilling the responsibilities of their major role, and realizing the value ends of the system while maintaining the identity and integrity of the actors' individual selves." See Joseph J. Mangalam, "A Reconsideration of the Notion of Adjustment: An Exploration," paper read at the Southern Agricultural Workers Conference and published in the *Proceedings,* 1962.

3. In noting the relatively high degree of anxiety exhibited by migrant women, one is tempted into pursuing methodological doubts. It well may be that women, as a rule, are less hesitant about revealing psychosomatic symptoms, whereas men may sense a threat to their masculinity if they show signs of physical weakness. Such questions as these plague any survey analysis. In this case, however, we feel reasonably certain (based upon our field work experience with selected family groups) that the differences are valid and that symptoms of anxiety are far more prevalent among Beech Creek women than among the male segment of this migrant population.

4. Each observation reported in these summary tables (Tables 9.3 through 9.9) represents a relationship which exists between the independent and dependent variable (in a two-by-two table) under a specific condition. A + indicates a positive association and a − indicates a negative association.

As reported in Table 9.3, for example, a negative association was observed between frequency of visiting in eastern Kentucky and the feeling of residential stability within the host community in the case of male migrants but not in the case of female migrants. That there exists a moderately strong association between these two variables in the case of males is suggested by the strength (.46) of the coefficient of contingency. Employing the logic of multivariate analysis, we link the findings from these two "cases" (men and women) in the form of an empirical generalization. Since the original relationship between these variables (see Appendix C) is strengthened in the case of men but disappears in the case of women, we argue that some sociological attributes associated with sex (e.g., culturally derived role expectations, social situation in the area of destination, interactional needs) function as "conditions" affecting the relationship.

It must be noted, however, that in our analyses the "interactional effect" of the control variable is not taken into account; the strategy of analysis, with such few cases, is exploratory. The interpretation of findings, in the absence of clearly discernible "causality patterns," leans heavily towards our theoretical perspectives and the stem-branch family model.

5.  Jesse Stuart, *The Thread that Runs So True*, New York: Charles Scribner's Sons, 1949.

6.  See, for example, A. H. Roberts and M. Rokeach, "Anomie, Authoritarianism, and Prejudice," *American Journal of Sociology*, 62 (January, 1956), pp. 355–358; Ephraim H. Mizruchi, "Social Structure and Anomia in a Small City," *American Sociological Review*, 25 (October, 1960), pp. 645–654; Dorothy L. Meier and Wendell Bell, "Anomia and Differential Access to the Achievement of Life Goals," *American Sociological Review*, 24 (April, 1959), pp. 189–202.

7.  Harry K. Schwarzweller and James S. Brown, "Education as a Cultural Bridge Between Eastern Kentucky and the Great Society," *Rural Sociology*, 27 (December, 1962), pp. 357–373.

8.  Robert A. Danley and Charles E. Ramsey, *Standardization and Application of a Level-of-Living Scale for Farm and Nonfarm Families*, Ithaca, N.Y.: Cornell University Agricultural Experiment Station Memoir 362, July, 1959. Level of living was introduced into our analysis as a dichotomized variable. The "high" category includes those residing in households possessing at least six of the nine material items on the scale (41 percent of the migrants); scores were normally distributed.

9.  For a listing of recent studies defining "adjustment" in socioeconomic terms, see J. J. Mangalam, *Human Migration*, Lexington: University of Kentucky Press, 1968.

10.  Cleo Y. Boyd, *Detroit's Southern Whites and the Store Front Church*, Detroit Council of Churches, 1958; Earl H. Cunningham, *Religious Concerns of Southern Appalachian Migrants in a North Central City*, Ph.D. thesis, Boston University, 1962; Russel R. Dynes, "Rurality, Migration and Sectarianism," *Rural Sociology*, 21 (1956), pp. 25–28.

11.  Analysis focused upon differences in the adjustment patterns between these and migrants who are not affiliated with a formal religious group. We recognize, of course, that degree of involvement in church activity may be a more sensitive variable; parallel analyses, however, yielded parallel results and, therefore, are not reported here.

12.  See J. T. Drake, *The Aged in American Society*, New York: Ronald Press Co., 1958.

# APPENDIX A

1.  James S. Brown, *The Social Organization of an Isolated Kentucky Mountain Neighborhood*, unpublished Ph.D. thesis, Harvard University, 1950.

2.  J. J. Mangalam, *Human Migration: A Guide to Migration Literature in English During 1955–1962*, Lexington: University of Kentucky Press, 1968.

3.  Martin Jay Crowe, *The Occupational Adaptation of a Selected Group of*

*Eastern Kentuckians in Southern Ohio,* Unpublished Ph.D. dissertation, University of Kentucky, 1964.

4.   Robert Merton, M. Fiske and P. L. Kendall, *The Focused Interview,* Glencoe, Illinois: The Free Press, 1956.

## APPENDIX C

1.   This observation about the rural-to-urban migrant is also made by Donald J. Bogue and Margaret L. Hagood, *Differential Migration in the Corn and Cotton Belts: A Pilot Study of the Selectivity of Interstate Migration to Cities from Nonmetropolitan Areas,* Scripps Foundation Studies in Population Distribution, No. 6, Oxford, Ohio: Miami University, 1935, p. 37; Albert J. Reiss, Jr., "Rural-Urban and Status Differences in Interpersonal Contacts," *American Journal of Sociology,* 65 (September, 1959), pp. 182–195.

2.   This conception of extended family is like that suggested by Marvin B. Sussman and Lee Burchinal, "Parental Aid to Married Children: Implications for Family Functioning," *Marriage and Family Living,* 24 (November, 1962), p. 320. Let it be noted, however, that by introducing the criterion of geographical propinquity; i.e., area of destination, our definition departs somewhat from Sussman and Burchinal's conceptualization. That departure is deliberate, given the focus of inquiry and the nature of this particular migration system.

3.   Information for these indicators was obtained directly from the migrant in an interview situation. The migrant was asked to indicate all his and his spouse's living kin, where each of these persons lived, with whom they lived, and how often they visited. Cross-checking of information obtained and coding were done later, not in the field. Since the residence locations of all persons in the population were known by the researchers, interview data could be and were subjected to rigorous reliability checks.

4.   Throughout this appended chapter and Chapter 9, all reported relationships fall within the .90 level of probability on a Chi-square test of difference. One should not interpret these, in any strict sense, as tests of significance (this is a total population, not a sample). The statistical criterion is used as a convenient device to indicate the existence of concomitant variation among variables. The coefficient of contingency can be regarded as a crude estimate of degree of association and, in that sense, is perhaps more useful than a Chi-square value. Since the maximum value of C depends upon the number of cells in the contingency table, a correction factor is introduced so as to approximate more closely a correlation coefficient; see Thomas Carson McCormick, *Elementary Social Statistics,* New York: McGraw-Hill Book Company, 1941, p. 207.

5.   Both indicators were adapted from Charles C. Hughes, Marc-Adélard Tremblay, Robert N. Rapoport, and Alexander H. Leighton, *People of Cove and Woodlot,* New York: Basic Books, Inc., 1960.

6.   $\bar{C} = -.29$, $P > .05$ ($N = 161$, d.f. = 1)

7.   $\bar{C} = -.34$, $P > .01$ ($N = 161$, d.f. = 1)

8.   An earlier study of young male migrants from eastern Kentucky, for example, found that a somewhat nostalgic attachment to parents and extended family homestead did not hold back the transitional adjustment process to any measurable degree. See Harry K. Schwarzweller, *Family Ties, Migration, and Transitional Adjustment of Young Men from Eastern Kentucky,* Lexington: University of Kentucky Agricultural Experiment Station Bulletin 691 (May, 1964).

9.   Gerald Gurin, Joseph Veroff, and Sheila Feld, *Americans View Their Mental Health,* New York: Basic Books, 1960, pp. 22–24. See also Norman M. Bradburn and David Caplovitz, *Reports on Happiness,* Chicago: Aldine, 1965.

10.   *Ibid.,* pp. 28–30.

11.   Leo Srole, "Social Integration and Certain Corollaries: An Exploratory Study," *American Sociological Review,* 21 (December, 1956), pp. 709–716.

12.   *Ibid.,* pp. 175–187.

13.   This finding of a positive association between extent of worry and symptoms of psychological anxiety agrees with the observations reported by Gurin, *et al., op. cit.,* pp. 28–36, for a cross-section of the American population.

14.   Each observation reported in this summary table represents a relationship which exists between two variables (in a two-by-two contingency table). There are seven "interactional adjustment" and six "psychological adjustment" variables. A plus sign, then, indicates a positive association and a minus sign indicates a negative association. Where the coefficient of contingency is reported, the probability of association is at least 90 percent. The value of the coefficient indicates, in a crude way, the strength of that association (or, in other words, the magnitude of the differences observed within the contingency table).

# INDEX

Achievement orientation, 53–55,
 63–66, 161. *See also* Individualism; Puritanism; Social mobility
Adaptation to industrial work. *See*
 Work adaptation
Adjustment
 and economic success, 174
 and family homestead, 129
 and mutual aid, 128
 and parental ties, 112
 and social contacts, 134–135
 concepts of, 94–96, 209–210, 293n
 configurations of, 265–267
 interactional dimensions of, 177
  branch-family ties, 254–256
  stem-family ties, 257–259
  urban ties, 256–257
 patterns of
  by age, 197–201
  by church membership, 195–197
  by class, 172, 181–189
  by length of urban residence,
   201–205
  by level of living, 192–195
  by level of schooling, 189–192
  by sex, 178–181, 185
 psychological dimensions of, 178
  anomia, 263
  anxiety, 263–264
  community satisfaction, 140–142,
   260–261
  happiness, 145–149, 262
  nostalgia, 127, 139, 142, 146,
   152, 261–262
  worry, 149, 262–263
 *See also* Stem-family migration;
  Work adaptation
Anomia. *See* Adjustment, psychological dimensions
Anxiety. *See* Adjustment, psychological dimensions
Arensberg, Conrad, 32, 85, 272n

Beech Creek neighborhoods
 and neighboring, 20–22

Beech Creek neighborhoods
 (*continued*)
 climate, 5
 delineation of, 20–22, 271n
 division of labor in, 18–20, 152
 economy of
  contemporary, 228–230
  earlier, 5–7, 210–211
 geography, 4–5, 210
 mass migration out of, 75–79
 natural resources, 5, 68–69
 relative isolation of, 7–9, 270n
  breakdown of, 67–70, 214–215,
   227–228
 rhythm of life in, 11–18
 settlement patterns of, 3
 social changes in, 8–9, 76, 79–80,
  96, 163, 225–231
 *See also* Level of living; Social
  class; Visiting patterns
Bogue, Donald J., 81n, 279n
Branch-family network. *See* Stem-
 family migration
Brown, James S., 270n, 272n, 276n,
 277n, 278n, 279n, 289n, 291n

Calvinism. *See* Puritanism
Caudill, Harry M., 276n
Church participation, 133–138,
 195–197
 character of, 20, 25, 60, 62
 *See also* Religious beliefs; Puritanism
Community satisfaction. *See* Adjustment, psychological dimensions
Conjugal family
 defined, 272n
 husband-wife relationships, 28–33
 parent-child relationships, 32–33,
  130
 primacy of, 211–213
 *See also* Kinship structure; Marriage patterns; Socialization
  process
Crowe, Martin Jay, 289n